Selected Poems
of
Friedrich Hölderlin

Selected Poems
of
Friedrich Hölderlin

Translated by
Maxine Chernoff
and
Paul Hoover

OMNIDAWN PUBLISHING
RICHMOND, CALIFORNIA
2008

Cover photograph: Butte Montana 100 from "The Mining Project,"
© Copyright David Maisel 2008, www.davidmaisel.com

Book cover and interior design by Ken Keegan.

Offset printed in the United States on archival, acid-free recycled paper
by Thomson-Shore, Inc., Dexter, Michigan

green press
INITIATIVE

Omnidawn Publishing is committed to preserving ancient
forests and natural resources. We elected to print this title on
30% postconsumer recycled paper, processed chlorine-free. As
a result, for this printing, we have saved:

7 Trees (40' tall and 6-8" diameter)
2,553 Gallons of Wastewater
5 million BTUs of Total Energy
328 Pounds of Solid Waste
615 Pounds of Greenhouse Gases

Omnidawn Publishing made this paper choice because our
printer, Thomson-Shore, Inc., is a member of Green Press
Initiative, a nonprofit program dedicated to supporting authors,
publishers, and suppliers in their efforts to reduce their use of
fiber obtained from endangered forests.

For more information, visit www.greenpressinitiative.org

Environmental impact estimates were made using the Environmental Defense
Paper Calculator. For more information visit: www.edf.org/papercalculator

Library of Congress Catalog-in-Publication Data

Hölderlin, Friedrich, 1770-1843.
    [Poems. English. Selections]
    Selected poems of Friedrich Hölderlin /
        translated by Maxine Chernoff and Paul Hoover.
        p. cm.
    ISBN 978-1-890650-35-3 (pbk. : alk. paper)
    I. Chernoff, Maxine, 1952- II. Hoover, Paul, 1946- III. Title.
    PT2359.H2A22 2008
    831'.6--dc22

                                                2008031486

Published by Omnidawn Publishing, Richmond, California
www.omnidawn.com   (510) 237-5472   (800) 792-4957
        10 9 8 7 6 5 4 3 2 1

ISBN: 978-1-890650-35-3

Also by Maxine Chernoff

Poetry

The Turning (Apogee Press, 2008)

Among the Names (Apogee Press, 2005)

Evolution of the Bridge: New and Selected Prose Poems
(Salt Publications, 2003)

World: New and Selected Poems 1991-2001 (Salt Publications, 2001)

Leap Year Day: New and Selected Poems (ACP, 1991; Jensen-Daniels, 1999)

Japan (Avenue B Press, 1988)

New Faces of 1952 (Ithaca House, 1985)

Utopia TV Store (The Yellow Press, 1979)

A Vegetable Emergency (Beyond Baroque Foundation, 1976)

The Last Aurochs (Now Press, 1976)

Fiction

Some of Her Friends that Year: New and Selected Stories
(Coffee House Press, 2002)

A Boy in Winter (Crown Publishers, 1999)

American Heaven (Coffee House Press, 1996)

Signs of Devotion (Simon and Schuster, 1993)

Plain Grief (Summit, 1991)

Bop (Coffee House Press, 1985; Vintage Contemporary Fiction Series, 1986)

Also by Paul Hoover

Poetry

Edge and Fold (Apogee Press, 2006)

Poems in Spanish (Omnidawn, 2005)

Winter (Mirror) (Flood Editions, 2002)

Rehearsal in Black (Salt Publications, 2001)

Totem and Shadow: New & Selected Poems (Talisman House, 1999)

Viridian (University of Georgia Press, 1997)

The Novel: A Poem (New Directions, 1990)

Idea (The Figures, 1987)

Nervous Songs (L'Epervier Press, 1986)

Somebody Talks a Lot (The Yellow Press, 1983)

Letter to Einstein Beginning Dear Albert (The Yellow Press, 1979)

Fiction

Saigon, Illinois (Vintage Contemporaries, 1988)

Essays

Fables of Representation (University of Michigan Press, 2004)

Publications Edited

Black Dog, Black Night: Contemporary Vietnamese Poetry
(Milkweed Editions, 2008)

Postmodern American Poetry (W.W. Norton, 1994)

New American Writing, 1986 to present.

Acknowledgments

26 E (2006): "In the Forest" and "Sibyl."

Bombay Gin 32 (2006): "But When the Gods."

Chicago Review 51.4/52.1 (2006): "The Happy Life" and "The Stroll."

Cipher Journal (1/25/07): "Sung Beneath the Alps," "At the Source of the Danube," "Beginning at the Abyss," "The Time of Socrates," "The Tree," "To My Sister," and "To" (www.cipherjournal.com).

Circumference 2.2 (Autumn/Winter 2005): "Columbus."

The Experimental Form and Issues of Accessiblity (Woodland Editions / Five Fingers Press, 2005): "And to experience the lives…"

First Intensity 21 (2006): "Remembrance" and "Once I asked the muse…"

Free Verse: A Journal of Contemporary Poetry 13 (Winter 2007): "To the Fates," "Brevity," "To the Sun-God," "The Spirit of the Age," "My Possessions," "The Neckar," "Love," and "The Poet's Courage" (http://english.chass.ncsu.edu/freeverse/index.html).

Interim 26.1/2 (2008): "Bonaparte," "Palinode," "To the Germans" (long version), "The Course of Life," "Sung beneath the Alps," "Rememberance" "Home," "On Yellow Leaves," "What Is God?", "Once I asked the muse…," and "Tinian."

Interval(le)s 1 (2008): 'Evening Fantasy,' 'The Main,' 'It's true every day I follow . . . ,' 'Go Down, Lovely Sun,' and 'Rousseau.'

Jacket 27 (2005): "The Ister" and "The Titans" (www.jacket.com).

Mi Poesias: Revista Literaria 19.3 (2005): "Empedocles," "Her Recovery," and "Please" (www.mipoesias.com).

Poems for the Millennium, Vol. III: The University of California Book of Romantic and Post-Romantic Poetry, Ed. Pierre Joris and Jerome Rothenberg (Berkeley: University of California Press, 2008): "In the Forest."

Sentence 4 (2006): "In Lovely Blue."

Slope 23 (Spring/Summer 2006): "To the Fates," "Palingenesis," "If I listened now to their warnings...," "The Spirit of the Age," and "Bread and Wine" (http://slope.org/archive/issue23/23chernoffhoover.html).

Triquarterly 126 (2006): "The Night Songs": "Chiron," "Tears," "To Hope," "Vulcan," "Timidness," "Ganymede," "Half of Life," "The Ages of Life," and "The Shelter at Hardt."

Web Conjunctions (5/31/05): "Hyperion's Fate Song," "When I Was a Boy," "As When on Holiday," "The Course of Life," "The Blind Singer," "The Poet's Vocation," "Greece" (Third Version), "Tinian," and "Beginning at the Abyss" (www.conjunctions.com/webconj.htm).

Contents

Fragments of Hymns

Last Poems: 1807–1843

Introduction

Even though his poetry was not widely celebrated in his lifetime, and he suffered from mental illness for half of his life, Friedrich Hölderlin, 1770-1843, has come to be considered one of the great poets of European and world literature. Because of his complex syntax and themes, the proto-modernist fragmentation of his late works, and the influence of his thought, Hölderlin now outstrips Goethe and Schiller as the valued poet of his period. A profound influence on Rilke and Heidegger in his mystical concept of the Open *(das Offene)*, as well as on Transcendental Idealism and Hegel's philosophy (Hegel was his roommate and Schelling a classmate at a Lutheran seminary), he is the subject of numerous studies including those by Benjamin, Derrida, Blanchot, Adorno, and Lacoue-Labarthe. A Hellenist who addressed the gods and was the first to grieve their departure, he is a major figure of Romanticism and contributed, well in advance of Nietzsche and Heidegger, to the development of Existentialism.

Hölderlin's poetry production includes early and late odes; elegies and hymns; drafts of hymns; the so-called Last Poems *(Späteste Gedichte),* written 1807-1843; a work of questionable origin, the prose poem "In Lovely Blue"; and other fragments presented by Friedrich Beissner, editor of the definitive Stuttgart Edition of *Sämtliche Werke,* 1951, as *"Pläne und Bruchstücke"* (Plans and Fragments). He also wrote a two-volume novel, *Hyperion;* versions of Sophocles, "The Death of Oedipus" and "Antigone," derided by literary society as greatly eccentric and perhaps evidence of insanity; the verse play "Empedocles on Aetna," and eccentric translations of Pindar that attempt to recreate his Greek measures, as well as the strict word-for-word meaning. Hölderlin "praised Pindar's hymns as 'das *Summum* der Dichtkunst,' for they contained, he said, the essences of all three genres—the epic, and the dramatic, as well as the lyric" (Constantine 237). Abraham Cowley, who had also controversially translated Pindar, was of the opinion: "If a man should undertake to translate Pindar word for word, it would be thought that one Madman had translated another" (Constantine 237). It is for the hymns and drafts of hymns that Hölderlin is most recognized. This is due in part to Richard Sieburth's eye-opening *Hymns and Fragments of Friedrich Hölderlin* (Princeton, 1984), which focused exclusively on those works. Like odes and elegies, the hymn is an extended lyric poem of elevated tone and subject matter, perfectly suited for Hölderlin as a poet of heroic vision. Seeking to trace the gods and their departure, he identified with the rivers of Germany, the Rhine, Danube (also known as the Donau and Ister), Main, and Neckar; the landscape they so powerfully crossed including, especially, his native Swabia; Germany itself ("Germanien," "An die Deutschen," "Stuttgart"); and ancient Greece ("Griechenland," "Patmos," "Chiron," and "Ganymede"), which he idealized for its cultural genius. As can be seen in "Diotima" and "Bonaparte," the first two poems of this volume, Hölderlin also wrote short poems of great incisiveness, but their focus is also on the ultimate: "Poets are holy glass / In which life's wine, / The spirit of heroes, is kept" and "The beautiful sun of your days has gone down now / And in a colder night, the winds quarrel and rage." The early ode, "Empedocles," ends: "Deep as any hero I'd plunge, too, / If love didn't keep me here." Hölderlin's signal is always deep and strong; here it is prophetic of his own dissolution. The poet saw in the doomed philosopher what was possible in himself. In "The 'Sacred' Speech of Hölderlin," Blanchot comments, "The poet is the mediator; he connects the near to the far...essentially, poetry relates to existence in its totality; wherever poetry asserts itself, existence, considered as the All, also begins to assert itself" (114-115). The domestic in Hölderlin is also the far-reaching.

Hölderlin's essays and letters show him to be a powerful thinker and, quite likely, an influence on Schelling's *System of Transcendental Idealism* (1800) and Hegel's development of the dialectic. As the poet states in "Remarks on Oedipus":

For indeed, the tragic *transport* is actually empty and least restrained.

Thereby, in the rhythmic sequence of the representations wherein *transport* presents itself, there becomes necessary *what in the poetic meter is called caesura,* the pure word, the counter-rhythmic rupture; namely, in order to meet the onrushing change of representations at its highest point in such a manner that very soon there does not appear the change of representation but the representation itself (Pfau 101-102).

The concept of caesura as the "the pure word" is one of genius. Contemporary critical theories of parataxis are still asserting the value of rupture in the body of the poetic, and we consider the theme postmodern. The essay is thought to have been written in September, 1803, to accompany his eccentric translation of Sophocles' play. The poet would soon be incapacitated for this kind of intellectual effort by mental illness that would last the rest of his life. Yet some of his greatest poems were written from 1802, when he first showed signs of illness, to the time of his hospitalization in 1806. He entered into his mature work in 1796; thus, his valued writing was created in a period of only ten years.

Influenced by German Pietism, which granted spiritual freedom to the individual, Hölderlin's poetry emphasized "inwardness" *(Innigkeit).* But this inwardness, in its "pure spirit," overreaches, contributing to dissonance and the tragic note of discord: "Precisely because he expresses the deepest inwardness, the tragic poet denies altogether his individuality, his subjectivity, and thus also the object present to him; he conveys them into a foreign personality, into a foreign objectivity..." (Pfau 52). An active and transformative inwardness transcends the limitations of the ego, and proves necessary to objectivity.

Important to the understanding of Hölderlin's poetry is his concept of *der Wechsel der Töne,* or alternation of tones. It is difficult to quote Hölderlin on the matter without supplying the complete text of his essay, "On the Operations of the Poetic Spirit." The sentences in his essays, like those in his poems, often occupy most of the page. But, to summarize, poetry begins with an encounter between the actual and the individual poetic spirit, infinite in its purity and existing in freedom. After a complex transaction between the individual and the universal, material and spiritual, freedom and limit, a resolution is achieved in the work of art, which may be considered an "actualization of the infinite, the divine moment" (Pfau 71). Not all of the elements of the struggle are reconciled, and the process is far from purely subjective: "Since the poetic spirit cannot know the world in itself nor of itself, an external object is necessary" (Pfau 72). As the alternation of moods and emphases proceeds, the individual quickly drops away and the infinite and universal come into relation. The process of "beautiful progression and alternation" is a struggle ("dialectic" in Greek means controversy) that pulls the poet "on the way toward enactment." The result of the struggle is beauty, itself dynamic. In Hölderlin as in Heraclitus, all is change, interrelation, and transformation. As soon as we think we have settled on the meaning of his poetry and thought, the work escapes once more into *der Wechsel der Töne.*

Also of a dialectical and processual nature is Hölderlin's concept of *ein Entstehen durch ein Vergehen,* which Thomas Pfau translates as a "coming-to-be through a going-away" (172). In the essay, "Becoming in Dissolution," Hölderlin writes of "the struggle of death itself through the harmonic, comprehensible [and] living" (Pfau 97). Dissolution is not simply an element of the dialectic; new life, concepts, and practices are unable to emerge without it. Because Hölderlin's essay begins in reference to "the declining Fatherland," the violence implicit in the dialectic would have seemed inviting to German nationalists of the 1930s, eager for images of phoenix and apocalypse. But dissolution and union are continual and universal, in Hölderlin's view, at all levels of experience: "the *possible* which enters into *reality* as that *reality itself dissolves,* is operative and effects the sense of dissolution as well as the remembrance of that which

24

has been dissolved. Hence, the thoroughly original [nature] of any tragic language, the forever-creative...the genesis of the individual out of the infinite" (97). The incidents of memory emerge in shreds from a largely dissolved past, and must find a new context in the emerging present. With the new comes the death of the old, thus "dissolution is necessary and holds its peculiar character between being and non-being. In the state between being and non-being, however, the possible becomes real everywhere, and the real becomes ideal, and in the free imitation of art this is a frightful but divine dream" (97). The process does not compel us psychologically toward death and violence; instead, it represents growth, creativity, and even love.

In the Godard film, *Contempt* (1963), Fritz Lang, playing himself, quotes a notable Hölderlin line, which we translate, "As long as God's absence comes to his aid," to a crass American film producer played by Jack Palance. It is Lang's way of displaying the cultural rift between Europe and the United States. Here is the phrase in its original context, Hölderlin's "The Poet's Vocation":

> But if he must, the man remains fearless.
>> Alone before god, simplicity keeps him safe,
>>> He needs no weapons and no cunning,
>>>> As long as God's absence comes to his aid.

God's absence contributes to man's sense of freedom. God's all-consuming presence would not allow for the indeterminate character, or negative capability, that allows poetry to thrive. In his essay, "The Caesura of the Speculative," Lacoue-Labarthe seizes on the positive value of a "necessary infidelity" of both god and man in Hölderlin's poetry, as it relates to the poet's definition of the tragic in the essay, "Remarks on Oedipus":

> The presentation of the tragic rests principally upon this: that the monstrous, the face that God and man couple, and the fact

that without limit the power of nature and the innermost of man become one in fury, is conceived in that the limitless becoming-one is purified through limitless separation (Lacoue-Labarthe 231-232).

Hölderlin's play, "The Death of Empedocles," comes to mind. By casting himself into the fires of Aetna, the philosopher merges with the mystery of the One, from which there can no longer be any turning away.

Hölderlin remarks further:

In the scenes the frightfully festive forms, the drama like an auto-da-fe, as language for a world where under pest and confusion of senses and under universally inspired prophecy in idle time, with the god and man expressing themselves in the all-forgetting form of infidelity—for divine infidelity is best to retain—so that the course of the world will not show any rupture and the memory of the heavenly ones will not expire.

At such moments man forgets himself and the god and turns around like a traitor, naturally in saintly manner.—In the utmost form of suffering, namely, there exists nothing but the conditions of time and space.

Inside it, man forgets himself because he consists entirely for the moment, the god because he is nothing but time; and either one is unfaithful, time, because it is reversed categorically at such a moment, no longer fitting beginning and end; man, because at this moment of categorical reversal he has to follow and thus can no longer resemble the beginning in what follows.

Thus Haemon stands in "Antigone." Thus Oedipus himself in the tragedy of "Oedipus" (Pfau 107-108).

If man's transgression is finitude (Lacoue-Labarthe 244), God's is infinity. Only in metaphysical acts such as mysticism and poetry do they turn to face each other.

It is easy to make Hölderlin into a windswept romantic, or young Werther, a victim of his tragic love affair with Susette Gontard, a genial madman gathering flowers by the garden path, or an intellectual narcissist and passionate lover. To some degree, he played all of these roles. But it is difficult for anyone who has read his mature poems to portray him as a poet of German nationalism and will to power, as the Nazi Party strived to do, thus enacting Hölderlin's final tragedy. His homeland was the Duchy of Württemberg, one of many independent states. His dialect of German was that of provincial Swabia. But there is also a yearning for home, *die Heimat,* as native place. He found that place in an imaginary ancient Greece, toward which he propelled himself on a fateful walking tour of Bourdeaux. But he was unable to resolve the dialectic of Greece and the Germany in which he had become increasingly foreign, through personal losses in love and his ambitions as a poet. On his return from France, he was transformed, substantially for the worse.

Johann Christian Friedrich Hölderlin was born on March 20, 1770, in the city of Lauffen, in the Swabian region of southwest Germany near Tübingen and Stuttgart. The family home was located on the Neckar River and not far from the Danube and Rhine rivers of which he was to write some of his most powerful poems. When he was two years old, his father died, and when he was four, his mother married Johann Cristoph Gok, the burgomaster of Nürtingen. In 1779, his stepfather died. His mother never remarried. At the age of 14, he entered the Lower Monastery School at Denkendorf, and two years later the Higher Monastery School in Maulbronn, where he began to doubt his mother's plan for his career in the Lutheran ministry. He was writing poetry under the influence of Klopstock and Schiller. In 1788, he entered the Lutheran Seminary, or Stift, in Tübingen, where he developed lasting relationships with fellow students Schelling and Hegel. His first publication as a poet comes in

1791, in Stäudlin's *Musenalmanach;* the publisher also introduces the poet to his hero Schiller. In 1792, he begins work on his poetic novel *Hyperion,* which on Schiller's recommendation was published by Cotta in two volumes, 1797 and 1799.

At the age of 24, on Schiller's recommendation, Hölderlin accepts a post in the home of Charlotte Von Kalb to tutor her son. Because he is too strict with the boy, especially with regard to his "self-abuse," Hölderlin is dismissed with three months of severance pay. During this period, he lives in the intellectual center of Jena, where he attends the philosophical lectures of Fichte, contributes to Schiller's journal *Die Horen,* and befriends Isaak von Sinclair, who advocated radical sympathy with the French Revolution. At Schiller's house, he is introduced to Goethe, who was at that moment examining some poems of Hölderlin. Mishearing the name, Hölderlin unfortunately snubs the great writer. In June, 1795, he abruptly leaves Jena in a state of depression, a sign of more serious trouble to come.

Convinced of his vocation as a writer and certain that he will not enter the ministry, in 1796 Hölderlin accepts the post of tutor in the home of Gontard, a wealthy Frankfurt banker. He soon falls in love with Susette, Gontard's wife, who becomes the Diotima of Hölderlin's poems and novel. From July to September of this year, he flees with Susette and her children to escape Napoleon's invasion of the region. Susette's husband remains in Frankfurt to protect his business interests.

When the first volume of *Hyperion* appears, Hölderlin sends a copy to Schiller along with two poems, "The Aether" and "The Wanderer." Schiller shares them with Goethe, who recommends their publication but offers a damaging assessment:

> The poet has a cheerful view of nature with which, however, he seems to be familiar through second-hand accounts only.... I would like to say that there are good ingredients for a poet in both poems which alone do not make up a poet. Perhaps he

would do best were he to select a very simple idyllic factum and represent it; then it could be seen how he fares with the human gallery, which in the end is what it all comes to (Thompson 50).

Schiller responds, "Frankly I found much of my own style in these poems and it is not the first time the author has reminded me of myself. He possesses an intense subjectivity to which he unites a certain philosophical spirit and pensiveness" (Thompson 50).

In September, 1798, an encounter between Gontard and Hölderlin causes the poet to resign his post and leave the house; to her later regret, Susette does not intervene. For the next two years, the two carry on a secret correspondence and carefully planned liaisons, with Hegel and Susette's maid sometimes acting as intermediaries. Their meetings first take place at the musical theater, but Susette is worried to be seen at an event so beneath her level of taste. The couple arranges that, at a time when the children are occupied with the governess elsewhere in the house and Susette is alone in her upstairs study, the poet will rush through the garden and straight up the stairs for an hour's visit. Fearful of discovery, Susette begins dropping notes from her window for the poet to recover. Believing that a neighbor has observed this practice, she requests that Hölderlin merely appear on a sidewalk within viewing distance of the property. The couple's last meeting is in May, 1800, at the same time that the poet is writing some of his greatest poems including "Bread and Wine," "The Rhine," "Patmos," "Remembrance," "The Ister," and the Night Songs ("Half of Life," "Chiron," "Ganymede," "Tears," "To Hope," "The Shelter at Hardt," "Vulcan," "Timidness," and "The Ages of Life"). In July, 1802, his mental health already threatened, Hölderlin receives a letter from Isaak von Sinclair informing him of Susette's death from German measles. He recovers under a doctor's care and continues work on his hymns, but ultimately he continues a downward spiral that includes a break-up with Sinclair amid accusations that he had engaged with him in a political conspiracy. Judged too mentally ill to stand trial, in 1806 he is placed in the Autenrieth Clinic, notorious for its mask, used to prevent patients from screaming. Treatments last for months and prove unsuccessful. Luckily, Ernst Zimmer, a successful cabinet-maker who admired *Hyperion,* takes Hölderlin into his care. Given three years to live by doctors, he thrives in the Zimmer household, taking daily walks, greeting occasional guests such as Clemens Brentano, Eduard Mörike, and Wilhelm Waiblinger, whose novel *Phaethon* (1823), based on Hölderlin's life, contains a passage of Hölderlin's prose, presented here as "In Lovely Blue." When he is not playing the flute and piano for hours at a time, Hölderlin is restless and on his feet most of the day. He never recovers from his mental illness. His last poems, written in a comparatively naïve style on the subject largely of the seasons, are frequently signed "Scardanelli" and given fictitious dates such as "March 24, 1671" and "March 9, 1940." When he is presented with a copy of his *Selected Poems* in 1826, he says he remembers having written some of them but fiercely denies that their author is named Hölderlin. Having outlived Zimmer, to whom he wrote several poems, and now cared for by Zimmer's daughter, he dies on June 7, 1843.

Thus half of the great poet's life is spent in mental illness and seclusion. It is a life of "shipwreck," as he describes in a letter. He writes in "To the Germans":

> The hall   has long
> Been silent, poor visionary! yearning dims your eye,
> And nameless you slumber,
> With no one to weep or remember.

To many, his fate will seem parallel to that of Empedocles. Possessing the spiritual hero's lack of moderation, he grows strongest at the moment he dissolves in fire. Such an assessment also applies to Hölderlin's poetry. While his production in the period 1796-1803 is undeniably powerful, it is with the fragments, 1804-1807, that Hölderlin takes on his full stature.

Especially important in presaging modern and postmodern discontinuity are works like "In the Forest," "Beginning at the Abyss," and "Columbus." Clinically, Hölderlin was probably schizophrenic. His persistent images of wounding, blindness, and homelessness may well have been a presentiment of his own fate. As a wanderer upon the land in "My Possessions," he seeks a home that may not be granted:

> For like the plant unable to root in its own ground,
> The soul of a mortal will quickly die out,
> Who must roam in daylight, a poor man
> Wandering the holy earth.

He addresses his song as "my friendly asylum," which must comfort him in his innocence, while "powerful, almighty Time, / So changeable, roars far away." The modernist selects this freedom for aesthetic purposes. After Mallarmé and Gertrude Stein, a post-symbolist style of the flood stage is ready and waiting, but it is never necessary. Hölderlin was caught in something much more terrible. As he writes in "Rousseau": "In the first sign he sees the final meaning."

Even when he was deemed to be insane, Hölderlin kept his balance as a maker. In "And to experience the lives…" for instance:

> Their lives
> As fresh as pearls, boys play near the shapes
> Of their teachers, or of corpses, or the soft
> Cries of swallows
> As they circle
> The crowns of towers.

Such dark beauty is entirely accurate, as is the extraordinarily precise dream-like observation, "Hunters' gunshots / Hiss toward the sea." We also find proto-surrealist imagery in his early poems, such as "Brevity":

> The earth is cold, and the bird of night
> Flies down, so close you cover your eyes.

The tempering aspects of imagination, adjustments of tone and measuring of the lyric are very much evident. In an essay on "As when on holiday…," Heidegger comments: "[In] the shaking of Chaos, which offers no support, the terror of the immediate, which frustrates every intrusion, the holy is transformed, through the quietness of the protected poet, into the mildness of the mediated and mediating word" (1981, 92). Language is temperate by its nature and begins to harness and make productive the energies of the inchoate. In this context, it's important to remember the significance of the poet's frequently used word "holy," which in Old English meant "free from injury, whole, hale," therefore in a meaningful sense "wholly." The holy is mystically the All, a unity so powerful it's difficult to comprehend. To go to the source is to enter the fountainhead of being. The English word "quell" means to well out like water or to kill, slaughter, or suppress. Concepts like Chaos, *Quelle,* and the All lie beyond reason and explanation. But for Hölderlin, they were entirely generative.

Hölderlin was Promethean in longing and his life-long search for connection with the gods. But this intimation of the gods' presence, acutely sensed in the surge of rivers, in mountains and thunderstorms, is equally attended by a sense of the gods' departure. This rift is central to the *ubi sunt* theme of his lyric, "Half of Life," with its wintry clatter of weathervanes.

In D. E. Sattler's great compilation of Hölderlin's fragments, "In the Forest," man is bereft even of the comforts of meaning:

He remains nowhere.
No sign
Binds.
Not ever

A vessel to contain him.

When no sign binds, meaning comes in flood:

> and Innocent interrupted the lecture
> and named it the Nur-
> sery of French Bishops
> Aloisia Sigea *differentia vitae*
> *urbanae et rusticae* Thermidon
> a river in Cappadoccia Val-
> telino Schönberg Scotus Schönberg Tenerife

The poet's syntax is here much deformed, but the lines of "In the Forest" immediately to follow are among his most lyrical:

> When the vineyard is in flames
> And looks black as coal
> Around the time
> In Autumn, because
> The reeds of life breathe fire
> In shadows of the vines. But
> How pretty when the soul unfolds
> And this brief life.

The long poem pulses with artistic counterpoint, with textural and tonal adjustment, for, in all of Hölderlin's work, the poetic persona is urgently in demand of meaning. When no sign binds, meaning seems impossible. At the same time, language immediately restores distinctness and precision. It is not a world empty of meaning that speaks in Hölderlin but rather the precariousness of consciousness. In "Sung beneath the Alps," the poet's dilemma is presented in dramatic terms:

> To be alone with the gods, and when
> The light passes over, and wind and flood, and
> When time hurries to its place, you have a steady
> Eye for them,
>
> Nothing is holier that I know and want,
> As long as the flood doesn't take me, like
> The willows, well cared for, sleeping as I must
> On the waves;
>
> He who holds divine things in his heart
> Will gladly stay home, however, and I'll be free,
> As long as needed, to translate and sing
> In the tongues of heaven.

Sleeping on the waves is a perfect emblem for the dangers of the visionary mode. The poet risks drowning in his own consciousness. Perhaps the gods can save him, but, as "Patmos" reminds us, "The god / Is near and difficult to grasp." We can have powerful intimations of the gods, but we can never face them directly. Their glare would blind us. So, like Perseus viewing Medusa in the mirror of his shield, we use the medium of language. Heidegger puts it this way: "The poet himself stands between the former—the gods—and the latter—the people. He is the one who has been cast out—out into that *between*, between gods and men" (1981, 64).

From one period of production to another, from the odes to hexameters, from the hymns to fragments of hymns, we feel the poet's pitiable heroism:

The poets' faces are also sad,
They seem to be alone, but they're always
Having a premonition, as Nature does when she rests.

("As when on holiday…")

Blanchot writes that in Hölderlin nature is without speech; it is the poet who names, including nature itself. Nature rests in a silence of the pure word. The poet is at his finest when his words are closest to this silence:

> This, it seems, is fundamental: that the poet must exist as a presentiment of himself, as the future of his existence. He does not exist, but he has had to be already what he will be later, in a "not yet" that constitutes the essential part of his grief, his misery, and also his great wealth (117).

The poet waits without rest for a premonition, for he "exists only if he foresees the time of the poem; he is second to the poem" (118).

In the Last Poems, a new temperament emerges. Because the poet is beyond defeat, he no longer feels its inevitability. The mysteries of god, nature, and consciousness are now viewed with sweetness, directness, and simplicity. He abandons Prometheanism, his characteristically tortured syntax, and sentences of half a page:

> How quiet it is by the gray wall,
> Where a tree hangs over, laden with ripeness,
> With black, dewy fruit, leaves full of sadness,
> But the fruit is plentiful, the tree heavy and full.

There, in the church, it's dark and quiet,
And on this night the altar is also bare,
Though pretty things still lie within it;
But in the summer, crickets sing in the field.

When someone hears the minister talking there,
Surrounded by a group of friends who've
Come to be with the dead one, how rare
This life, what a spirit; piety never ends.

("The Churchyard")

Hölderlin adopts a new manner but not a new vision. He remains in touch with the "primal image-source," and retains, though less insistently, his dialectic point of view. The late anomalous prose poem, "In Lovely Blue," however, is more in line with the associational sinuousness of modernism. Its brilliance of observation and mysticism by way of analogy and paradox ("Man's image has eyes as the moon has light") are reminiscent of Hölderlin's essays.

As poet-translators, Maxine Chernoff and I have sought the poetic in Hölderlin's often difficult poems, rather than attempted to replicate in English his German measures, some of which are themselves patterned after ancient Greek alcaics ("Mein Eigentum," "Der Blinde Sänger," "Abendphantasie," and "Der Gefesselte Strom," among others). We have wanted to elucidate while retaining a sense of the poet's complexity of syntax and theme. The drama of Hölderlin's consciousness, the beauty of his lyrics, and the largeness of his vision drew us closer to him with each working day. Like Beissner, we present the poems according to their formal structure, which parallels, for the most part, the historical periods of their production.

We are grateful to have had the translations of Michael Hamburger and Richard Sieburth to judge against our own progress. We would also like to acknowledge the brilliant work of D. E. Sattler, who has reconstructed certain works using variant texts and the plans and fragments; they include "Die Nymphe," "Der Adler," "Kolumb," "Griechenland," and the magnificent "Im Walde." Thanks to Andrew Joron for his expertise in proofreading the text. Our deep gratitude to Michael Hulse for his careful reading and lucid suggestions, as well as to our publishers, Rusty Morrison and Ken Keegan, for their tireless work and friendship.

—Paul Hoover

Sources

Blanchot, Maurice. "The 'Sacred' Speech of Hölderlin." *The Work of Fire,* translated by Charlotte Mandel. (Paris: Editions Gallimard, 1949; reprinted by Stanford University Press, 1995).

Constantine, David. *Hölderlin* (Oxford: Clarendon Press, 1988).

Heidegger, Martin. *Elucidations of Hölderlin's Poetry,* translated by Keith Hoeller (New York: Humanity Books, 2000). First published as *Erläuterungen zu Holderlins Dichtung* (Frankfurt am Main: Vittorio Klostermann, 1981).

Heidegger, Martin. "What Are Poets For?" *Poetry, Language, Thought,* translated by Albert Hofstadter (New York: Perennial Classics, 2001). First published: 1971.

Keats, John. "Letter 45. To George and Tom Keats. 21, 27 [?] December 1817." *Criticism: Major Statements,* Third Edition, ed. Charles Kaplan & William Anderson (New York: St. Martin's Press, 1991).

Lacoue-Labarthe, Philippe. *Typography: Mimesis, Philosophy, Politics.* Edited by Christopher Fynsk; introduction by Jacques Derrida. (Stanford: Stanford University Press, 1998).

Pfau, Thomas, Editor and Translator. *Friedrich Hölderlin: Essays and Letters on Theory* (Albany: State University of New York Press, 1988).

Thompson, Scott J. Unpublished manuscript of Hölderlin's letters.

Selected Poems
of
Friedrich Hölderlin

Early Odes

An Diotima

Schönes Leben! du lebst, wie die zarten Blüthen im Winter,
    In der gealterten Welt blühst du verschlossen, allein.
Liebend strebst du hinaus, dich zu sonnen am Lichte des Frühlings,
    Zu erwarmen an ihr suchst du die Jugend der Welt.
Deine Sonne, die schönere Zeit, ist untergegangen
    Und in frostiger Nacht zanken Orkane sich nun.

To Diotima

Beautiful creature, you live like a pale flower in winter.
    Locked up and alone, you blossom in an aged world.
As if in love, you stretch for warmth toward
    The light of spring. You want a younger world.
The beautiful sun of your days has gone down now
    And in a colder night, the winds quarrel and rage.

Buonaparte

Heilige Gefäße sind die Dichter,
    Worinn des Lebens Wein, der Geist
      Der Helden sich aufbewahrt,

Aber der Geist dieses Jünglings
    Der schnelle, müßt' er es nicht zersprengen
      Wo es ihn fassen wollte, das Gefäß?

Der Dichter laß ihn unberührt wie den Geist der Natur,
    An solchem Stoffe wird zum Knaben der Meister.

Er kann im Gedichte nicht leben und bleiben,
    Er lebt und bleibt in der Welt.

Bonaparte

Poets are holy glass
   In which life's wine,
      The spirit of heroes, is kept.

But the spirit of the young
   And eager overflows any glass
      That seeks to contain it.

Poets should leave the young as untouched as nature.
   Such stuff makes crafty men into awkward boys.

One can't live for long in a poem.
   One lives and endures in the world.

Empedokles

Das Leben suchst du, suchst, und es quillt und glänzt
   Ein göttlich Feuer tief aus der Erde dir,
      Und du in schauderndem Verlangen
         Wirfst dich hinab, in des Aetna Flammen.

So schmelzt' im Weine Perlen der Übermuth
   Der Königin; und mochte sie doch! hättst du
      Nur deinen Reichtum nicht, o Dichter
         Hin in den gährenden Kelch geopfert!

Doch heilig bist du mir, wie der Erde Macht,
   Die dich hinwegnahm, kühner Getödteter!
      Und folgen möcht' ich in die Tiefe,
         Hielte die Liebe mich nicht, dem Helden.

Empedocles

You search and search for life, and it rises gleaming,
   A god's fire from deep in the earth.
     Shuddering with desire,
       You plunge into Aetna's flames.

So the queen in her excitement dissolved
   Rare pearls in wine, and why not! And haven't
     You, poet, offered your own wealth
       To a cup of sparkling wine?

Yet you are as holy to me as the power of earth
   That lured you to the boldest of deaths.
     Deep as any hero I'd plunge, too,
       If love didn't keep me here.

An die Parzen

Nur Einen Sommer gönnt, ihr Gewaltigen!
   Und einen Herbst zu reifem Gesange mir,
      Daß williger mein Herz, vom süßen
         Spiele gesättiget, dann mir sterbe.

Die Seele, der im Leben ihr göttlich Recht
   Nicht ward, sie ruht auch drunten im Orkus nicht;
      Doch ist mir einst das Heil'ge, das am
         Herzen mir liegt, das Gedicht gelungen,

Willkommen dann, o Stille der Schattenwelt!
   Zufrieden bin ich, wenn auch mein Saitenspiel
      Mich nicht hinab geleitet; Einmal
         Lebt ich, wie Götter, und mehr bedarfs nicht.

To the Fates

Give me just one summer, stark sisters,
    One more autumn to ripen my song.
        Then I'll gladly die, my heart filled
            With that sweet music.

The soul, which never had its godly rights
    In life, won't find peace in Orkus either.
        When just once the sacred lies
            In my heart, the poem is perfected.

Then I will welcome the world
    Of silence and shadows and happily leave
        My song behind; once I lived
            Like the gods, no more is required.

Diotima

Du schweigst und duldest, und sie versteh'n dich nicht,
  Du heilig Leben! welkest hinweg und schweigst,
    Denn ach, vergebens bei Barbaren
      Suchst du die Deinen im Sonnenlichte,

Die zärtlichgroßen Seelen, die nimmer sind!
  Doch eilt die Zeit. Noch siehet mein sterblich Lied
    Den Tag, der, Diotima! nächst den
      Göttern mit Helden dich nennt, und dir gleicht.

Diotima

They don't understand you, transcendent being, and you
    Suffer in silence! In silence, you fade away,
        For, among such barbarians, how futilely
            Under sunlight you seek your own kind,

Those great and tender souls that exist no more!
    Still, time passes quickly. My mortal song
        Will yet see the day, Diotima, when the heroes
            Take you for their model, name you among the gods.

An ihren Genius

Send' ihr Blumen und Frücht' aus nieversiegender Fülle,
    Send' ihr, freundlicher Geist, ewige Jungend herab!
Hüll' in deine Wonnen sie ein und laß sie die Zeit nicht
    Sehn, wo einsam und fremd sie, die Athenerin, lebt,
Bis sie im Lande der Seeligen einst die fröhlichen Schwestern,
    Die zu Phidias Zeit herrschten und liebten, umfängt.

To Her Genius

Send her flowers and fruit from a never-ending plenty,
    Send her, friendly spirit, eternal youth from above!
Wrap her up in your delight and don't let her see a time
    When, she, the true Athenian, lives lonely and estranged,
Until in the land of the blessed she embraces the happy sisters
    Who ruled and loved in the time of Phidias.

Abbitte

Heilig Wesen! gestört hab' ich die goldene
   Götterruhe dir oft, und der geheimeren,
     Tiefern Schmerzen des Lebens
       Hast du manche gelernt von mir.

O vergiß es, vergieb! gleich dem Gewölke dort
   Vor dem friedlichen Mond, geh' ich dahin, und du
     Ruhst und glänzest in deiner
       Schöne wieder, du süßes Licht!

Forgive Me

Heavenly creature! I have often disturbed
   Your golden, godlike calm, and you have
      Learned much from me of the deeper,
         More private, pains of life.

Forget and forgive! Like clouds on high
   That cover the peaceful moon, I drift away,
      And you remain as before, sweet light,
         Glowing in your beauty!

Ehmals und Jezt

In jüngern Tagen war ich des Morgens froh,
  Des Abends weint' ich; jezt, da ich älter bin,
    Beginn ich zweifelnd meinen Tag, doch
      Heilig und heiter ist mir sein Ende.

Then and Now

When I was young, I was happy every morning,
    Only to weep at night; now that I am older,
        I begin each day in doubt, even though,
            Serene and holy, its end is peaceful enough.

Die Kürze

»Warum bist du so kurz? liebst du, wie vormals, denn
  »Nun nicht mehr den Gesang? fandst du, als Jüngling, doch,
    »In den Tagen der Hoffnung,
      »Wenn du sangest, das Ende nie!

Wie mein Glük, ist mein Lied.—Willst du im Abendroth
  Froh dich baden? hinweg ists! und die Erd' ist kalt,
    Und der Vogel der Nacht schwirrt
      Unbequem vor das Auge dir.

Brevity

"Why are you so brief? Don't you love
　　Your songs as once you did? When in your youthful
　　　　Days of hope, you wanted your singing
　　　　　　Never to come to an end?"

My joy is like my song.—Wouldn't you happily bathe
　　In the red glow of evening? Now it's gone away!
　　　　The earth is cold, and the bird of night
　　　　　　Flies down, so close you cover your eyes.

Menschenbeifall

Ist nicht heilig mein Herz, schöneren Lebens voll,
    Seit ich liebe? warum achtetet ihr mich mehr,
        Da ich stolzer und wilder,
            Wortereicher und leerer war?

Ach! der Menge gefällt, was auf den Marktplaz taugt,
    Und es ehret der Knecht nur den Gewaltsamen;
        An das Göttliche glauben
            Die allein, die es selber sind.

Human Applause

Because I love, isn't my heart holy,
    Full of lovelier life? Why did you value me more
        When I was prouder and wilder,
            Filled with richer words, and more empty?

The crowd likes what sells in the market-place,
    And the slave respects only boorishness and violence;
        Only he who is godlike
            Can truly believe in the godly.

Die Heimath

Froh kehrt der Schiffer heim an den stillen Strom
  Von fernen Inseln, wo er geerndtet hat;
    Wohl möcht' auch ich zur Heimath wieder;
      Aber was hab' ich, wie Laid, geerndtet?—

Ihr holden Ufer, die ihr mich auferzogt,
  Stillt ihr der Liebe Laiden? ach! gebt ihr mir,
    Ihr Wälder meiner Kindheit, wann ich
      Komme, die Ruhe noch Einmal wieder?

Home

From distant islands, the sailor turns happily
   Toward the quiet stream of home, once his harvest is done;
      I too would gladly turn home again now,
         But what have I gathered but pain?—

You soft river-banks that raised me,
   Can you quiet love's sorrow, give me back,
      You forests of my childhood, when
         I come, peace anew once more?

An die Deutschen

Spottet ja nicht des Kinds, wenn es mit Peitsch' und Sporn
Auf dem Rosse von Holz muthig und groß sich dünkt,
Denn, ihr Deutschen, auch ihr seyd
Thatenarm und gedankenvoll.

Oder kömmt, wie der Stral aus dem Gewölke kömmt,
Aus Gedanken die That? Leben die Bücher bald?
O ihr Lieben, so nimmt mich,
Daß ich büße die Lästerung.

To the Germans

Don't make fun of the child, when with his whip and spurs,
    He thinks himself big and brave, upon his rocking-horse,
        For you Germans are also
            Poor in deeds and full of thoughts!

Or come leaping out, like lightning from clouds,
    As deeds do from thoughts. Can books come to life?
        O, you loved ones! Lay your hands on me,
            Make me pay for my blasphemous words.

Dem Sonnengott

Wo bist du? trunken dämmert die Seele mir
   Von aller deiner Wonne; denn eben ists,
      Daß ich gesehn, wie, müde seiner
         Fahrt, der entzükende Götterjüngling

Die jungen Loken badet' im Goldgewölk';
   Und jezt noch blikt mein Auge von selbst nach ihm;
      Doch fern ist er zu frommen Völkern,
         Die ihn noch ehren, hinweggegangen.

Dich lieb' ich, Erde! trauerst du doch mit mir!
   Und unsre Trauer wandelt, wie Kinderschmerz,
      In Schlummer sich, und wie die Winde
         Flattern und flüstern im Saitenspiele,

Bis ihm des Meisters Finger den schönern Ton
   Entlokt, so spielen Nebel und Träum' um uns,
      Bis der Geliebte wiederkömt und
         Leben und Geist sich in uns entzündet.

To the Sun-God

Where are you? Drunk, my soul grows dim
    From all your delight; for only now
        I watched how, exhausted by his travels,
            The enchanting young god

Bathed his hair in golden clouds,
    And now my eyes fill with the sight of him;
        Though already he's far from here, well along his way
            To the pious folk who revere him.

I love you, Earth, who joins me in mourning him,
    And our sadness turns to sleep like the grief
        Of children, and, as the winds flutter
            And whisper in the strings of the lyre

Until the master's fingers unlock a purer sound,
    Fog and dreams play all around us
        Until the loved one returns,
            Igniting in us love and spirit.

Sokrates und Alcibiades

»Warum huldigest du, heiliger Sokrates,
    »Diesem Jünglinge stets? kennest du Größers nicht?
        »Warum siehet mit Liebe,
            »Wie auf Götter, dein Aug' auf ihn?

Wer das Tiefste gedacht, liebt das Lebendigste,
    Hohe Jugend versteht, wer in die Welt geblikt
        Und es neigen die Weisen
            Oft am Ende zu Schönem sich.

Socrates and Alcibiades

"Why, holy Socrates, do you constantly
    Embrace this man? Don't you have greater concerns?
        Why do you gaze on him
            With such love, as on a god?"

He who thinks deepest loves the liveliest things.
    He who truly sees has the wisdom
        To rely on the majesty of youth
            And in the end bows to the beautiful.

Later Odes

Hyperions Schiksaalslied

Ihr wandelt droben im Licht
   Auf weichem Boden, seelige Genien!
     Glänzende Götterlüfte
      Rühren euch leicht,
        Wie die Finger der Künstlerin
        Heilige Saiten.

Schiksaallos, wie der schlafende
   Säugling, athmen die Himmlischen;
     Keusch bewahrt
      In bescheidener Knospe,
       Blühet ewig
        Ihnen der Geist,
         Und die seeligen Augen
         Bliken in stiller
          Ewiger Klarheit.

Doch uns ist gegeben,
   Auf keiner Stätte zu ruhn,
     Es schwinden, es fallen
      Die leidenden Menschen
       Blindlings von einer
        Stunde zur andern,
         Wie Wasser von Klippe
         Zu Klippe geworfen,
          Jahr lang ins Ungewisse hinab.

Hyperion's Fate Song

You walk above in the light,
  Soulful genius, on a yielding floor!
    God's shining breezes
      Gently touch you
        As the fingers of a musician
          On otherworldly strings.

Fateless, like a nursing infant asleep,
  The gods draw breath;
    Chastely preserved
      In modest buds,
        Their minds are always
          In flower,
            And their soulful eyes
              Gaze calmly and eternally
                In silent clarity.

But it's our fate
  To have no place to rest,
    As suffering mortals
      Blindly fall and vanish
        From one hour
          To the next,
            Like water falling
              From cliff to cliff, downward
                For years to uncertainty.

Da ich ein Knabe war…

Da ich ein Knabe war,
   Rettet' ein Gott mich oft
      Vom Geschrei und der Ruthe der Menschen,
        Da spielt' ich sicher und gut
          Mit den Blumen des Hains,
            Und die Lüftchen des Himmels
             Spielten mit mir.

Und wie du das Herz
Der Pflanzen erfreust,
Wenn sie entgegen dir
Die zarten Arme streken,

So hast du mein Herz erfreut
Vater Helios! und, wie Endymion,
War ich dein Liebling,
Heilige Luna!

Oh all ihr treuen
Freundlichen Götter!
Daß ihr wüßtet,
Wie euch meine Seele geliebt!

Zwar damals rieff ich noch nicht
Euch mit Nahmen, auch ihr
Nanntet mich nie, wie die Menschen sich nennen
Als kennten sie sich.

When I was a boy...

When I was a boy
    Often a god would save me
        From the shouts and blows of men;
    I played safely and well
          With the flowers of the fields
        And the winds of heaven
        Played with me.

And you make happy
The hearts of plants
When they extend to you
Their delicate arms,

So you make my heart happy,
Father Sun, and like Endymion
I was your favorite,
Holy Moon!

Oh, you true
And neighborly gods!
If only you knew
How my soul loved you then!

True, at that time, I didn't
Know your names, and you
Never bothered to name me, like men
Pretending to know one another.

Doch kannt' ich euch besser,
Als ich je die Menschen gekannt,
Ich verstand die Stille des Aethers
Der Menschen Worte verstand ich nie.

Mich erzog der Wohllaut
Des säuselnden Hains
Und lieben lernt' ich
Unter den Blumen.

Im Arme der Götter wuchs ich groß.

Yet I knew you better
Than I've ever known anyone,
I understood the silence of the Upper Air,
But I've never understood the words of men.

I was raised by the sounds
Of the rustling grove
And learned to love
Among the flowers.

I grew up in the arms of the gods.

Hört' ich die Warnenden izt...

Hört' ich die Warnenden izt, sie lächelten meiner und dächten,
    Früher anheim uns fiel, weil er uns scheute, der Thor.
Und sie achtetens keinen Gewinn,

Singt, o singet mir nur, unglükweissagend, ihr Furchtbarn
    Schiksaalsgötter das Lied immer und immer ums Ohr
Euer bin ich zulezt, ich weiß es, doch will zuvor ich
    Mir gehören und mir Leben erbeuten und Ruhm.

If I listened now to their warnings…

If I listened now to their warnings, they'd smile at me and think,
    Because he shunned us, the sooner he fell to us, the fool.
Yet they'd count it no victory,

Sing, o sing then, your song of my doom, you terrible
    Gods of fate, repeat it in my ear again and again.
At long last I'll be yours, I know, but before that happens
    I'll belong only to myself and seize both life and fame.

Der Zeitgeist

Zu lang schon waltest über dem Haupte mir
  Du in der dunkeln Wolke, du Gott der Zeit!
    Zu wild, zu bang ist's ringsum, und es
      Trümmert und wankt ja, wohin ich blike.

Ach! wie ein Knabe, seh' ich zu Boden oft,
  Such' in der Höhle Rettung von dir, und möcht'
    Ich Blöder, eine Stelle finden,
      Alleserschütt'rer! wo du nicht wärest.

Lass' endlich, Vater! offenen Aug's mich dir
  Begegnen! hast denn du nicht zuerst den Geist
    Mit deinem Stral aus mir gewekt? mich
      Herrlich an's Leben gebracht, o Vater!—

Wohl keimt aus jungen Reben uns heil'ge Kraft;
  In milder Luft begegnet den Sterblichen,
    Und wenn sie still im Haine wandeln,
      Heiternd ein Gott; doch allmächt'ger wekst du

Die reine Seele Jünglingen auf, und lehrst
  Die Alten weise Künste; der Schlimme nur
    Wird schlimmer, daß er bälder ende,
      Wenn du, Erschütterer! ihn ergreiffest.

The Spirit of the Age

For too long you have ruled above my head,
    You in the dark cloud, you God of Time!
        Too wild and fearful around me,
            Whatever I look at shatters and wavers.

Like a boy, I looked down at the ground,
    Sought refuge from you in caverns, and, weakling
        That I am, must find a place where you,
            Breaker of all things, might not be.

Finally, Father, let me meet you
    With open eyes! Wasn't it you who first
        Flashed awake the spirit within me, you
            Who so splendidly brought me to life, o Father!—

It's true, a sacred force gathers in young vines;
    In mild air or when they wander calmly
        Through the grove, men meet a serene God;
            Yet, all-powerful, you awaken

The pure souls of youth and teach
    The old, wise arts; only the bad man
        Grows worse, sooner to meet his end,
            When you, earth shaker, will seize him!

Abendphantasie

Vor seiner Hütte ruhig im Schatten sizt
   Der Pflüger, dem Genügsamen raucht sein Heerd.
      Gastfreundlich tönt dem Wanderer im
         Friedlichen Dorfe die Abendgloke.

Wohl kehren izt die Schiffer zum Hafen auch,
   In fernen Städten, fröhlich verrauscht des Markts
      Geschäfft'ger Lärm; in stiller Laube
         Glänzt das gesellige Mahl den Freunden.

Wohin denn ich? Es leben die Sterblichen
   Von Lohn und Arbeit; wechselnd in Müh' und Ruh'
      Ist alles freudig; warum schläft denn
         Nimmer nur mir in der Brust der Stachel?

Am Abendhimmel blühet ein Frühling auf;
   Unzählig blühn die Rosen und ruhig scheint
      Die goldne Welt; o dorthin nimmt mich
         Purpurne Wolken! und möge droben

In Licht und Luft zerrinnen mir Lieb' und Laid!—
   Doch, wie verscheucht von thöriger Bitte, flieht
      Der Zauber; dunkel wirds und einsam
         Unter dem Himmel, wie immer, bin ich—

Komm du nun, sanfter Schlummer! zu viel begehrt
   Das Herz; doch endlich, Jugend! verglühst du ja,
      Du ruhelose, träumerische!
         Friedlich und heiter ist dann das Alter.

Evening Fantasy

Outside of his hut, the ploughman sits
   In the shade, his hearth comfortably smoking.
      The evening bells graciously welcome
         A wanderer into the peaceful village.

Now, too, the sailors make for the harbor
   In distant towns, the happy sounds of the markets
      Subside; and a pleasant meal awaits friends
         In the quietest part of the arbor.

But where shall I go? Doesn't a mortal live
   By work and reward; it's a joy to mingle
      Rest and toil; why then must I never find
         Relief from the thorn in my breast?

Spring blossoms up in the evening sky;
   Countless roses bloom, and the golden world
      Shines peacefully; o take me there,
         Purple clouds! Up there at last,

Into the light and air, my love and sorrow will melt!—
   As if my foolish request had been answered,
      The spell breaks; it becomes dark and lonely,
         And, as always, I stand alone under the heavens—

Come now, soft slumber! The heart demands too much;
   Endless youth, please cease your glowing,
      You restless ones in dreams!
         In my old age, leave me peaceful and serene.

Der Main

Wohl manches Land der lebenden Erde möcht'
  Ich sehn, und öfters über die Berg' enteilt
    Das Herz mir, und die Wünsche wandern
      Über das Meer, zu den Ufern, die mir

Vor andern, so ich kenne, gepriesen sind;
  Doch lieb ist in der Ferne nicht Eines mir,
    Wie jenes, wo die Göttersöhne
      Schlafen, das trauernde Land der Griechen.

Ach! einmal dort an Suniums Küste möcht'
  Ich landen, deine Säulen, Olympion!
    Erfragen, dort, noch eh der Nordsturm
      Hin in den Schutt der Athenertempel

Und ihrer Götterbilder auch dich begräbt;
  Denn lang schon einsam stehst du, o Stolz der Welt,
    Die nicht mehr ist!—und o ihr schönen
      Inseln Ioniens, wo die Lüfte

Vom Meere kühl an warme Gestade wehn,
  Wenn unter kräft'ger Sonne die Traube reift,
    Ach! wo ein goldner Herbst dem armen
      Volk in Gesänge die Seufzer wandelt,

Wenn die Betrübten izt ihr Limonenwald
  Und ihr Granatbaum, purpurner Äpfel voll
    Und süßer Wein und Pauk' und Zithar
      Zum labyrintischen Tanze ladet—

The Main

True, on this living earth there are many lands
    I'd like to see, and my heart runs away from me
        Often over the mountains, and my wishes wander
            Over the sea and to the shore, which more

Than the others, I know, has been much praised;
    But in the distance there is no other I could
        Love more than the one where the sons of the gods
            Are sleeping, melancholy land of the Greeks.

Ah! Just once I'd like to land on Sunium's coast
    And inquire about your columns,
        Olympion! There, before the North Wind
            Buries you, too, in the rubble

Of the Athenian temple and their images of God;
    For a long time you have stood empty, pride
        Of the gone world!—and o your beautiful
            Ionian islands, where breezes

From the sea spread coolness on warm shores,
    When the grapes ripen under the sun's strength,
        Where a golden autumn turns
            The sighing of the poor into songs,

When, overladen, their lemon grove
    And pomegranate are full of purple fruit
        And sweet wine, and kettledrum and zither
            Draw them to the labyrinth-dances—

Zu euch vieleicht, ihr Inseln! geräth noch einst
   Ein heimathloser Sänger; denn wandern muß
     Von Fremden er zu Fremden, und die
       Erde, die freie, sie muß ja leider!

Statt Vaterlands ihm dienen, so lang er lebt,
   Und wenn er stirbt—doch nimmer vergeß ich dich,
     So fern ich wandre, schöner Main! und
       Deine Gestade, die vielbeglükten.

Gastfreundlich nahmst du Stolzer! bei dir mich auf
   Und heitertest das Auge dem Fremdlinge,
     Und still hingleitende Gesänge
       Lehrtest du mich und geräuschlos Leben.

O ruhig mit den Sternen, du Glüklicher!
   Wallst du von deinem Morgen zum Abend fort,
     Dem Bruder zu, dem Rhein; und dann mit
       Ihm in den Ocean freudig nieder!

On you perhaps, islands, a homeless singer
   Might someday still prosper; for he has wandered
      From stranger to stranger, and the earth,
         The unbounded, it's sad to say, must serve

Instead of a fatherland his whole life long,
   And when he dies—but never will I forget you,
      As far as I wander, lovely Main! And
         The blessings of your shores.

Hospitably, yet proud, you took me in
   And brightened the stranger's eye,
      And taught me quiet, rhyming songs
         And how to live a quiet life.

O peacefully as the stars, you happy one!
   You move from morning to evening,
      Toward your brother, the Rhine, and then
         With him joyfully down to the ocean.

Mein Eigentum

In seiner Fülle ruhet der Herbsttag nun,
　　Geläutert ist die Traub und der Hain ist roth
　　　Vom Obst, wenn schon der holden Blüthen
　　　　Manche der Erde zum Danke fielen.

Und rings im Felde, wo ich den Pfad hinaus
　　Den stillen wandle, ist den Zufriedenen
　　　Ihr Gut gereift und viel der frohen
　　　　Mühe gewähret der Reichtum ihnen.

Vom Himmel bliket zu den Geschäfftigen
　　Durch ihre Bäume milde das Licht herab,
　　　Die Freude theilend, denn es wuchs durch
　　　　Hände der Menschen allein die Frucht nicht.

Und leuchtest du, o Goldnes, auch mir, und wehst
　　Auch du mir wieder, Lüftchen, als seegnetest
　　　Du eine Freude mir, wie einst, und
　　　　Irrst, wie um Glükliche, mir am Busen?

Einst war ichs, doch wie Rosen, vergänglich war
　　Das fromme Leben, ach! und es mahnen noch,
　　　Die blühend mir geblieben sind, die
　　　　Holden Gestirne zu oft mich dessen.

Beglükt, wer, ruhig liebend ein frommes Weib,
　　Am eignen Heerd in rühmlicher Heimath lebt,
　　　Es leuchtet über vestem Boden
　　　　Schöner dem sicheren Mann sein Himmel.

My Possessions

Now the autumn day rests in its fullness,
   The grape is pure and the orchard red
      With fruit, but many lovely blossoms,
         In thanks, fell to the earth long ago.

And around the field, where I cross the path
   In silent thought, are the satisfied men whose crops
      Have ripened, and their months of work
         Have won them much wealth.

From heaven to those busy ones, a mild light
   Filters down through their trees,
      To share their pleasure, for human hands
         Alone don't make the fruit grow.

O goldenness, will you also shine on me,
   Also, little breeze, will you blow some
      Happiness my way, as once before,
         Lose your way and bring joy to my heart?

In my happy life, I too was once
   Ephemeral as a rose, ah! but too often now
      The lovely stars that remain to flower
         For me serve as a warning.

Blessed is a man who, loving a faithful wife,
   Can live beside his hearth in a worthy country;
      The more certain a man of his heaven,
         The more brightly he walks on the ground.

Denn, wie die Pflanze, wurzelt auf eignem Grund
Sie nicht, verglüht die Seele des Sterblichen,
Der mit dem Tageslichte nur, ein
Armer, auf heiliger Erde wandelt.

Zu mächtig ach! ihr himmlischen Höhen zieht
Ihr mich empor, bei Stürmen, am heitern Tag
Fühl ich verzehrend euch im Busen
Wechseln, ihr wandelnden Götterkräfte.

Doch heute laß mich stille den trauten Pfad
Zum Haine gehn, dem golden die Wipfel schmükt
Sein sterbend Laub, und kränzt auch mir die
Stirne, ihr holden Erinnerungen!

Und daß mir auch zu retten mein sterblich Herz,
Wie andern eine bleibende Stätte sei,
Und heimathlos die Seele mir nicht
Über das Leben hinweg sich sehne,

Sei du, Gesang, mein freundlich Asyl! sei du
Beglükender! mit sorgender Liebe mir
Gepflegt, der Garten, wo ich, wandelnd
Unter den Blüthen, den immerjungen,

In sichrer Einfalt wohne, wenn draußen mir
Mit ihren Wellen allen die mächtge Zeit
Die Wandelbare fern rauscht und die
Stillere Sonne mein Wirken fördert.

For like the plant unable to root in its own ground,
   The soul of a mortal will quickly die out,
      Who must roam in daylight, a poor man
         Wandering the holy earth.

Too strongly, ah! You pull me toward the heights
   Of heaven, storms that rage on a bright day,
      I feel them ripping my very heart, you changing ones,
         And they destroy me with their godly power.

Today, however, in silence, let me walk the usual path
   To the grove where the golden tree-tops are
      Decorated with dying leaves, and also touch
         My brow with loving memories,

So that my mortal heart can be saved,
   And, as others find a resting place or home,
      And so that my soul will never be homeless
         And not over-reach life in its longing.

Stay, you song, my friendly asylum! and you,
   Giver of joy, tend to me with loving care,
      In the garden, where I wander among
         Eternally youthful blossoms,

I live in a kind of innocence, while outside me,
   With its waves, powerful, almighty Time,
      So changeable, roars far away,
         And the quiet sun benefits my labors.

Ihr seegnet gütig über den Sterblichen
   Ihr Himmelskräfte! jedem sein Eigentum,
      O seegnet meines auch und daß zu
         Frühe die Parze den Traum nicht ende.

Above us mortals, you bless our possessions,
  Heavenly powers, each to his own degree,
    O bless mine also, so that fate won't put
      Too early an end to my dreaming.

Palinodie

Was dämmert um mich, Erde! dein freundlich Grün?
   Was wehst du wieder, Lüftchen, wie einst, mich an?
      In allen Wipfeln rauschts,

Was wekt ihr mir die Seele? was regt ihr mir
   Vergangnes auf, ihr Guten! o schonet mein
      Und laßt sie ruhn, die Asche meiner
         Freuden, ihr spottetet nur! o wandelt,

Ihr schiksaallosen Götter, vorbei und blüht
   In eurer Jugend über den Alternden
      Und wollt ihr zu den Sterblichen euch
         Gerne gesellen, so blühn der Jungfraun

Euch viel, der jungen Helden, und schöner spielt
   Der Morgen um die Wange der Glüklichen
      Denn um ein trübes Aug' und lieblich
         Tönen die Sänge der Mühelosen.

Ach! vormals rauschte leicht des Gesanges Quell
   Auch mir vom Busen, da noch die Freude mir
      Die himmlische vom Auge glänzte

Versöhnung o Versöhnung, ihr gütigen
   Ihr immergleichen Götter und haltet ein
      Weil ihr die reinen Quellen liebt

Palinode

What shines around me, Earth, your pleasant greenness?
　　Why do you breathe on me once again, little wind?
　　　　There's a rustling in all the tree-tops,

Why do you awaken my soul, you good ones,
　　And stir up the past in me? Better yet,
　　　　Let the ashes of my joys rest in peace,
　　　　　　You're only teasing me! Go away,

You fateless gods, pass on by and blossom
　　On high, in your youth, over this old man,
　　　　And if you want the company of mortals,
　　　　　　Young women also blossom

For you, as well as young heroes, and morning plays
　　More beautifully on the cheeks of good fortune
　　　　Than on a gloomy eye, and the songs
　　　　　　Of the carefree sound pleasant on the ear.

Ah! The source of song once flowed lightly
　　From my breast, when the pure joy
　　　　Of the gods still shone from my eyes

A little mercy, please, relent for once,
　　You unchanging gods, hold back a little, if only
　　　　Because you love the purest of sources

Wohl geh' ich täglich…

Wohl geh' ich täglich andere Pfade, bald
   Ins grüne Laub im Walde, zur Quelle bald,
     Zum Felsen, wo die Rosen blühen,
       Blike vom Hügel ins Land, doch nirgend

Du Holde, nirgend find ich im Lichte dich
   Und in die Lüfte schwinden die Worte mir
     Die frommen, die bei dir ich ehmals

Ja, ferne bist du, seeliges Angesicht!
   Und deines Lebens Wohllaut verhallt von mir
     Nicht mehr belauscht, und ach! wo seid ihr
       Zaubergesänge, die einst das Herz mir

Besänftiget mit Ruhe der Himmlischen?
   Wie lang ist's! o wie lange! der Jüngling ist
     Gealtert, selbst die Erde, die mir
       Damals gelächelt, ist anders worden.

Leb immer wohl! es scheidet und kehrt zu dir
   Die Seele jeden Tag, und es weint um dich
     Das Auge, daß es helle wieder
       Dort wo du säumest, hinüberblike.

It's true every day I follow...

It's true every day I follow a different path, now
    In green leaves of the forest, now to the spring,
        To the rocks where roses bloom,
            From the hilltop overlooking the land, yet nowhere,

Darling, can I find you in the light
    And in the air all my words disappear,
        So gentle and good, when with you I once...

Yes, you are far from me, saintly face!
    And now your life's harmony is lost
        To me, never to be heard, and o! where are you,
            Magic songs, that once soothed

My heart with the peace of heaven?
    How long it has been, how long! The young man
        Has grown old; even the earth that once
            Smiled upon me has completely changed.

Farewell forever! Every day the soul departs
    From you and returns, and the eye
        Cries for you, so that it may gaze more clearly
            Into the distance, where you stand hesitating.

Geh unter, schöne Sonne…

Geh unter, schöne Sonne, sie achteten
    Nur wenig dein, sie kannten dich, Heilge, nicht,
        Denn mühelos und stille bist du
            Über den mühsamen aufgegangen.

Mir gehst du freundlich unter und auf, o Licht!
    Und wohl erkennt mein Auge dich, herrliches!
        Denn göttlich stille ehren lernt' ich
            Da Diotima den Sinn mir heilte.

O du des Himmels Botin! wie lauscht ich dir!
    Dir, Diotima! Liebe! wie sah von dir
        Zum goldnen Tage dieses Auge
            Glänzend und dankend empor. Da rauschten

Lebendiger die Quellen, es athmeten
    Der dunkeln Erde Blüthen mich liebend an,
        Und lächelnd über Silberwolken
            Neigte sich seegnend herab der Aether.

Go down, lovely sun…

Go down, lovely sun, for how little
    They thought of you, nor knew your worth, holy one,
        For without effort you rose and traveled
            Quietly over those who struggle.

To me, light, you rise and set like a friend!
    And my eyes recognize you, Master!
        For I learned a godly and noble silence
            When Diotima healed my senses.

Heavenly messenger, how I listened to you!
    You, Diotima, love! How I looked up
        With glistening and thankful eyes
            At the golden day you showed me.

Once more the streams rushed to life
    And on me earth's dark blossoms
        Breathed their scent and over the silver clouds
            The Upper Air bowed down to bless me.

An die Deutschen

Spottet nimmer des Kinds, wenn noch das albernne
   Auf dem Rosse von Holz herrlich und viel sich dünkt,
     O ihr Guten! auch wir sind
       Thatenarm und gedankenvoll!

Aber kommt, wie der Stral aus dem Gewölke kommt,
   Aus Gedanken vieleicht, geistig und reif die That?
     Folgt die Frucht, wie des Haines
       Dunklem Blatte, der stillen Schrift?

Und das Schweigen im Volk, ist es die Feier schon
   Vor dem Feste? die Furcht, welche den Gott ansagt?
     O dann nimmt mich, ihr Lieben!
       Daß ich büße die Lästerung.

Schon zu lange, zu lang irr ich, dem Laien gleich,
   In des bildenden Geists werdender Werkstatt hier,
     Nur was blühet, erkenn ich,
       Was er sinnet, erkenn ich nicht.

Und zu ahnen ist süß, aber ein Leiden auch,
   Und schon Jahre genug leb' ich in sterblicher
     Unverständiger Liebe
       Zweifelnd, immer bewegt vor ihm,

Der das stetige Werk immer aus liebender
   Seele näher mir bringt, lächelnd dem Sterblichen
     Wo ich zage, des Lebens
       Reine Tiefe zu Reife bringt.

To the Germans

Never make fun of the child, when the silly one
　　Feels proud and masterful upon his rocking-horse,
　　　　My friends, we are also
　　　　　　Poor in deeds and full of high thoughts!

Or perhaps deeds come leaping out from the mind,
　　Fully formed and ripe, like lightning from clouds?
　　　　Does the fruit grow, like the orchard's
　　　　　　Dark leaves, from quiet books?

And the silence of the crowd, is it the celebration
　　Before its cause? The feeling of awe before
　　　　God brings his word? Then take me, my dear ones,
　　　　　　Make me repent my blasphemy.

For too long, I've gone astray like a novice
　　In the workshop where spirits are formed.
　　　　I can only know what I see growing,
　　　　　　What he's thinking, I have no idea.

It's sweet to surmise but also painful,
　　And I've already spent enough years doubting
　　　　In misapprehending love, as mortals do,
　　　　　　Always moved by him whose constant work

Brings me closer to his loving soul,
　　Smiling down at us mortals,
　　　　Where I hesitate, bringing life's
　　　　　　Pure depth to its ripeness.

Schöpferischer, o wann, Genius unsers Volks,
    Wann erscheinest du ganz, Seele des Vaterlands,
        Daß ich tiefer mich beuge,
            Daß die leiseste Saite selbst

Mir verstumme vor dir, daß ich beschämt
    Eine Blume der Nacht, himmlischer Tag, vor dir
        Enden möge mit Freuden,
            Wenn sie alle, mit denen ich

Vormals trauerte, wenn unsere Städte nun
    Hell und offen und wach, reineren Feuers voll
        Und die Berge des deutschen
            Landes Berge der Musen sind,

Wie die herrlichen einst, Pindos und Helikon,
    Und Parnassos, und rings unter des Vaterlands
        Goldnem Himmel die freie,
            Klare, geistige Freude glänzt.

Wohl ist enge begrenzt unsere Lebenszeit,
    Unserer Jahre Zahl sehen und zählen wir,
        Doch die Jahre der Völker,
            Sah ein sterbliches Auge sie?

Wenn die Seele dir auch über die eigne Zeit
    Sich die sehnende schwingt, trauernd verweilest du
        Dann am kalten Gestade
            Bei den Deinen und kennst sie nie,

When, Creator, genius of the people,
    When will you fully appear, soul of our country,
        That I might bow more deeply,
           That my faintest strings

Grow silent, that, ashamed
    As a flower of night, I'll bow down to you,
        Heavenly day. In joy, I'd close myself
           Up from you, when everyone with whom

I've once mourned, when our towns now brighten
    And open and awaken, full of a purer fire,
        And the mountains of Germany
           Are the mountains of the muses,

Like those masterful men of old, Pindos and Helicon
    And Parnassus, and all around,
        Under the country's golden sky,
           Free and clear, spiritual joy gleams.

True, our lifetimes are narrowly
    Circumscribed. See how the tally grows.
        But are the years of the people
           All that a mortal eye sees?

When the soul soars with yearning
    Beyond its time, you wait there sadly
        On the cold shoreline,
           Among your own kind a stranger,

Und die Künftigen auch, sie, die Verheißenen
   Wo, wo siehest du sie, daß du an Freundeshand
     Einmal wieder erwarmest,
       Einer Seele vernehmlich seist?

Klanglos,   ists in der Halle längst,
   Armer Seher! bei dir, sehnend verlischt dein Aug
     Und du schlummerst hinunter
       Ohne Namen und unbeweint.

And the future generations also, those promised to us,
    Where, where are they? To be warmed
        Again by a friendly hand,
           To be perceived by a living soul?

The hall   has long
    Been silent, poor visionary! yearning dims your eye,
        And nameless you slumber,
           With no one to weep or remember.

Rousseau

Wie eng begränzt ist unsere Tageszeit.
    Du warst und sahst und stauntest, schon Abend ists,
        Nun schlafe, wo unendlich ferne
            Ziehen vorüber der Völker Jahre.

Und mancher siehet über die eigne Zeit
    Ihm zeigt ein Gott ins Freie, doch sehnend stehst
        Am Ufer du, ein Ärgerniß den
            Deinen, ein Schatten, und liebst sie nimmer,

Und jene, die du nennst, die Verheißenen,
    Wo sind die Neuen, daß du an Freundeshand
        Erwarmst, wo nahn sie, daß du einmal
            Einsame Rede, vernehmlich seiest?

Klanglos ists, armer Mann, in der Halle dir,
    Und gleich den Unbegrabenen, irrest du
        Unstät und suchest Ruh und niemand
            Weiß den beschiedenen Weg zu weisen.

Sei denn zufrieden!   der Baum entwächst
    Dem heimatlichen Boden, aber es sinken ihm
        Die liebenden, die jugendlichen
            Arme, und trauernd neigt er sein Haupt.

Des Lebens Überfluß, das Unendliche,
    Das um ihn   und dämmert, er faßt es nie.
        Doch lebts in ihm und gegenwärtig,
            Wärmend und wirkend, die Frucht entquillt ihm.

Rousseau

How narrow and confined is our daytime here.
    You were and saw and were amazed, and soon it was evening;
        Now sleep, where the years
            Of the people drag endlessly by.

And some see beyond their own time;
    In the open air, a god points their way, but, in yearning,
        You stand at the water's edge, an outcast
            From your people, and no longer love them.

And each that you name of the new generation,
    Those promised to us, who with a friendly hand
        Might warm you, drawing near you once,
            Could you comprehend their lonesome words?

In the hall only silence responds, poor man,
    And like the unburied, you roam around,
        Restlessly seeking rest, and no one knows
            How to show you the right direction.

So be content!   the tree outgrows
    His native ground, but his arms like branches
        Will slip from around the lovely and youthful
            And sadly he'll bow his head.

Life's overflow is the infinite,
    Which glimmers   around him, he'll never catch it.
        Yet it lives in him, and, present, warming,
            And fertile, the fruit contains its surfeit.

Du hast gelebt!   auch dir, auch dir
   Erfreuet die ferne Sonne dein Haupt,
     Und die Stralen aus der schönern Zeit. Es
     Haben die Boten dein Herz gefunden.

Vernommen hast du sie, verstanden die Sprache der Fremdlinge,
   Gedeutet ihre Seele! Dem Sehnenden war
     Der Wink genug, und Winke sind
     Von alters her die Sprache der Götter.

Und wunderbar, als hätte von Anbeginn
   Des Menschen Geist das Werden und Wirken all,
     Des Lebens Weise schon erfahren

Kennt er im ersten Zeichen Vollendetes schon,
   Und fliegt, der kühne Geist, wie Adler den
     Gewittern, weissagend seinen
     Kommenden Göttern voraus,

You've lived!   yours too, yours too
   Is made happy by the light of a distant sun,
      The radiance of a better age. The messengers
         Who sought your heart have found it.

You've heard and understood the language of strangers,
   Interpreted their souls! For those who yearn,
      A sign is enough, and ever since the ancients,
         Signs are the words of the gods.

And wonderful, as in the very beginning,
   The mind of man has come to know
      Life's movement in genesis and fulfillment.

In the first sign he sees the final meaning,
   And flies, this bold spirit, as eagles do
      Ahead of thunderstorms, to warn
         Of the gods' approach,

Die Götter

Du stiller Aether! Immer bewahrst du schön
   Die Seele mir in Schmerz, und es adelt sich
      Zur Tapferkeit vor deinen Stralen,
         Helios! oft die empörte Brust mir.

Ihr guten Götter! arm ist, wer euch nicht kennt,
   Im rohen Busen ruhet der Zwist ihm nie,
      Und Nacht ist ihm die Welt und keine
         Freude gedeihet und kein Gesang ihm.

Nur ihr, mit eurer ewigen Jugend, nährt
   In Herzen die euch lieben, den Kindersinn,
      Und laßt in Sorgen und in Irren
         Nimmer den Genius sich vertrauern.

The Gods

Silent Upper Air! You're always on guard
    Against the pain in my soul, and often
        My heart is moved and ennobled, Helios,
            By the brightness of your light!

Most excellent gods! Those who don't know you
    Are poorer for it, their crude hearts always in discord,
        And the world is night for them,
            And no song or joy goes out to them.

Only you, with your eternal youth, grow
    In the hearts of those who love you,
        Childlike in mind, and never let
            Sorrow and error diminish genius.

Der Nekar

In deinen Thälern wachte mein Herz mir auf
    Zum Leben, deine Wellen umspielten mich,
        Und all der holden Hügel, die dich
            Wanderer! kennen, ist keiner fremd mir.

Auf ihren Gipfeln löste des Himmels Luft
    Mir oft der Knechtschaft Schmerzen; und aus dem Thal,
        Wie Leben aus dem Freudebecher,
            Glänzte die bläuliche Silberwelle.

Der Berge Quellen eilten hinab zu dir,
    Mit ihnen auch mein Herz und du nahmst uns mit,
        Zum stillerhabnen Rhein, zu seinen
            Städten hinunter und lustgen Inseln.

Noch dünkt die Welt mir schön, und das Aug entflieht
    Verlangend nach den Reizen der Erde mir,
        Zum goldenen Paktol, zu Smirnas
            Ufer, zu Ilions Wald. Auch möcht ich

Bei Sunium oft landen, den stummen Pfad
    Nach deinen Säulen fragen, Olympion!
        Noch eh der Sturmwind und das Alter
            Hin in den Schutt der Athenertempel

Und ihrer Gottesbilder auch dich begräbt,
    Denn lang schon einsam stehst du, o Stolz der Welt,
        Die nicht mehr ist. Und o ihr schönen
            Inseln Ioniens! wo die Meerluft

The Neckar

In your valleys my heart awakened to life,
    Your small waves played around me,
        And of all the gracious hills that know you,
           Wanderer! not one is foreign to me.

Often on your peaks, the air of heaven
    Relieved the pain of my labors; and from the valley,
        Like life from the cup of original joy,
           A silver and blue wave glittered.

The mountain streams hurried down to you;
    With them came my heart, and you carried us along
        The calm and lofty Rhine, to his
           Cities below and pleasure-giving islands.

The world still looks lovely, and my sight
    Is drawn away by earth's many enticements,
        To golden Pactoclus, the coast of Smyrna,
           Or Ilium's forest. I'd also like to land

At Sunium, to ask the silent path
    About your pillars, Olympion!
        Before age and storm-winds
           Bury you too in the rubble

Of Athens' temple and her images of God,
    For a long time you stand alone, o pride
        Of a vanished world, and you o lovely
           Ionian islands, where the sea-breeze

Die heißen Ufer kühlt und den Lorbeerwald
  Durchsäuselt, wenn die Sonne den Weinstok wärmt,
    Ach! wo ein goldner Herbst dem armen
      Volk in Gesänge die Seufzer wandelt,

Wenn sein Granatbaum reift, wenn aus grüner Nacht
  Die Pomeranze blinkt, und der Mastyxbaum
    Von Harze träuft und Pauk und Cymbel
      Zum labyrintischen Tanze klingen.

Zu euch, ihr Inseln! bringt mich vielleicht, zu euch
  Mein Schuzgott einst; doch weicht mir aus treuem Sinn
    Auch da mein Nekar nicht mit seinen
      Lieblichen Wiesen und Uferweiden.

Cools the hot shore and rustles through
    The laurel trees, when sunlight heats the vines,
        Oh! where the golden autumn changes
            The sighing of the poor to songs,

When the pomegranate ripens, when in the green night
    An orange shines, resin drips from mastic trees
        And the kettledrum and cymbal
            Resound throughout the labyrinth-dances.

Perhaps to you, my islands, my guardian god
    One day will take me. But still I won't surrender
        My true feelings for this river, with its
            Lovely meadows and shoreline willows.

Die Liebe

Wenn ihr Freunde vergeßt, wenn ihr die Euern all,
  O ihr Dankbaren, sie, euere Dichter schmäht,
    Gott vergeb' es, doch ehret
      Nur die Seele der Liebenden.

Denn o saget, wo lebt menschliches Leben sonst,
  Da die knechtische jezt alles, die Sorge zwingt?
    Darum wandelt der Gott auch
      Sorglos über dem Haupt uns längst.

Doch, wie immer das Jahr kalt und gesanglos ist
  Zur beschiedenen Zeit, aber aus weißem Feld
    Grüne Halme doch sprossen,
      Oft ein einsamer Vogel singt,

Wenn sich mälig der Wald dehnet, der Strom sich regt,
  Schon die mildere Luft leise von Mittag weht
    Zur erlesenen Stunde,
      So ein Zeichen der schönern Zeit,

Die wir glauben, erwächst einziggenügsam noch,
  Einzig edel und fromm über dem ehernen,
    Wilden Boden die Liebe,
      Gottes Tochter, von ihm allein.

Sei geseegnet, o sei, himmlische Pflanze, mir
  Mit Gesange gepflegt, wenn des ätherischen
    Nektars Kräfte dich nähren,
      Und der schöpfrische Stral dich reift.

Love

When you forget a friend who was everything to you,
    You grateful ones, when you slight your poets,
        May God forgive you, but always
           Respect the souls of lovers.

Where do men live humanly, I ask,
    Now that we're slaves to worry?
        Likewise, the gods have wandered
           Indifferently over our heads.

Yet no matter how cold and songless the year,
    At the right time and in season
        Spring grass turns the white field green,
           And often a lonely bird sings,

As the woods fills in with leaves and the river stirs,
    At the appointed hour milder winds
        Blow gently from the South,
           Sign of a better season,

We believe that from the virgin, unshakeable
    Soil, proud and self-satisfied,
        Noble and pious, Love, God's daughter,
           Comes from him alone.

As the ethereal powers of nature
    Nourish you like nectar, and you ripen
        From highest light, let me bless you,
           Love, with my song.

Wachs und werde zum Wald! eine beseeltere,
Vollentblühende Welt! Sprache der Liebenden
Sei die Sprache des Landes,
Ihre Seele der Laut des Volks!

Grow and become a wood! a living soul,
   A fully blossoming world! May the language
      Of lovers be our native tongue,
         Their souls the speech of men.

Lebenslauf

Größers wolltest auch du, aber die Liebe zwingt
   All uns nieder, das Laid beuget gewaltiger,
      Doch es kehret umsonst nicht
         Unser Bogen, woher er kommt.

Aufwärts oder hinab! herrschet in heil'ger Nacht,
   Wo die stumme Natur werdende Tage sinnt,
      Herrscht im schiefesten Orkus
         Nicht ein Grades, ein Recht noch auch?

Diß erfuhr ich. Denn nie, sterblichen Meistern gleich,
   Habt ihr Himmlischen, ihr Alleserhaltenden,
      Daß ich wüßte, mit Vorsicht
         Mich des ebenen Pfads geführt.

Alles prüfe der Mensch, sagen die Himmlischen,
   Daß er, kräftig genährt, danken für Alles lern',
      Und verstehe die Freiheit,
         Aufzubrechen, wohin er will.

The Course of Life

You too wanted more, but love
    Forces all of us under.
        Pain's necessary curve
            Returns us to our beginnings.

Whether up or down, in the holiness of night,
    Speechless nature determines all the days to come,
        Yet in the labyrinths of death
            Can't you also find a straight path?

I know this. Not once, like mortal instructors
    Did you heavenly, all-knowing gods
        Have the foresight to lead me
            Along a level path.

Everything's a test, say the gods.
    Having found his strength, a man gives thanks
        For everything he knows, and, knowing
            His freedom, goes where he wants to go.

Ihre Genesung

Sieh! dein Liebstes, Natur, leidet und schläft und du
    Allesheilende, säumst? oder ihr seids nicht mehr,
        Zarte Lüfte des Aethers,
            Und ihr Quellen des Morgenlichts?

Alle Blumen der Erd, alle die goldenen
    Frohen Früchte des Hains, alle sie heilen nicht
        Dieses Leben, ihr Götter,
            Das ihr selber doch euch erzogt?

Ach! schon athmet und tönt heilige Lebenslust
    Ihr im reizenden Wort wieder, wie sonst und schon
        Glänzt in zärtlicher Jugend
            Deine Blume, wie sonst, dich an,

Heilge Natur, o du, welche zu oft, zu oft,
    Wenn ich trauernd versank, lächelnd das zweifelnde
        Haupt mit Gaaben umkränzte,
            Jugendliche, nun auch, wie sonst!

Wenn ich altre dereinst, siehe so geb ich dir,
    Die mich täglich verjüngt, Allesverwandelnde,
        Deiner Flamme die Schlaken,
            Und ein anderer leb ich auf.

Her Recovery

Look, Nature, your most loved one suffers and sleeps,
And you hesitate, healer of all? Have you disappeared,
Sweet breath of the Upper Air,
And you wellsprings of morning light?

All the flowers of earth, all the golden
Happy fruits of the orchards, how can all this
Fail to heal her life, which you gods
Created as your own?

Ah, already the sacred will to live
Breathes and sounds again in her excited conversation.
How lovely as before the tender
Young flowers shine at you once again.

Holy Nature, you who too often, too often,
When I sank into sorrow, smiled as you
Would garland my head with gifts,
Youthful one, now also as before!

One day when I am old, remember how each day
You make me young again, alchemist of all things,
Therefore, I'll give to your flame my own embers
And live again as another.

Der Abschied

[Zweite Fassung]

Trennen wollten wir uns? wähnten es gut und klug?
   Da wirs thaten, warum schrökte, wie Mord, die That?
     Ach! wir kennen uns wenig,
       Denn es waltet ein Gott in uns.

Den verrathen? ach ihn, welcher uns alles erst,
   Sinn und Leben erschuff, ihn, den beseelenden
     Schuzgott unserer Liebe,
       Diß, diß Eine vermag ich nicht.

Aber anderen Fehl denket der Weltsinn sich,
   Andern ehernen Dienst übt er und anders Recht,
     Und es listet die Seele
       Tag für Tag der Gebrauch uns ab.

Wohl! ich wußt' es zuvor. Seit die gewurzelte
   Ungestalte die Furcht Götter und Menschen trennt,
     Muß, mit Blut sie zu sühnen,
       Muß der Liebenden Herz vergehn.

Laß mich schweigen! o laß nimmer von nun an mich
   Dieses Tödtliche sehn, daß ich im Frieden doch
     Hin ins Einsame ziehe,
       Und noch unser der Abschied sei!

Reich die Schaale mir selbst, daß ich des rettenden
   Heilgen Giftes genug, daß ich des Lethetranks
     Mit dir trinke, daß alles
       Haß und Liebe vergessen sei!

The Farewell

[Second Version]

So we wanted to part? Thought it good and clever?
    Then why did the act horrify us like a murder?
        Oh, we know ourselves so little,
            For within us a god holds sway.

Betray him then? He who first created
    All meaning and life, he who inspired
        And protected our love,
            This, this one thing I cannot do.

But the world's mind makes a different error,
    Practices another servitude, other laws,
        And through craft and custom,
            Day by day, takes away our souls.

I knew this already. Ever since rooted,
    Misshapen fear has divided men from God;
        To appease the gods with blood,
            The hearts of lovers must wither.

Let me be silent! Don't let me ever be guilty
    Of knowing this deadly truth, that I in peace
        Can hide myself in loneliness,
            The farewell at least will be ours.

So pass me the cup, that of the rescuing,
    Holy poison enough, so I can drink
        Death with you, so that all
            Hate and love be forgotten.

Hingehn will ich. Vieleicht seh' ich in langer Zeit
Diotima! dich hier. Aber verblutet ist
Dann das Wünschen und friedlich
Gleich den Seeligen, fremde gehn

Wir umher, ein Gespräch führet uns ab und auf,
Sinnend, zögernd, doch izt mahnt die Vergessenen
Hier die Stelle des Abschieds,
Es erwarmet ein Herz in uns,

Staunend seh' ich dich an, Stimmen und süßen Sang,
Wie aus voriger Zeit hör' ich und Saitenspiel,
Und die Lilie duftet
Golden über dem Bach uns auf.

I want to pass away. Perhaps after a long time,
    I'll see you here, Diotima, but by then
        Our desires will have bled away, and, peaceful
            As the blessed, we'll walk around like strangers

As our talk takes us here and there;
    Thoughtful, hesitant, we who have forgotten
        Will recall the place of our parting,
            And a heart will warm in us;

Astonished I look at you, voices and sweet song;
    As in previous times, I hear the music of strings,
        And the lily gives off her fragrance,
            Golden over the brook.

Das Ahnenbild

Ne virtus ulla pereat!

Alter Vater! Du blikst immer, wie ehmals, noch,
    Da du gerne gelebt unter den Sterblichen,
        Aber ruhiger nur, und
            Wie die Seeligen, heiterer

In die Wohnung, wo dich, Vater! das Söhnlein nennt,
    Wo es lächelnd vor dir spielt und den Mutwill übt,
        Wie die Lämmer im Feld', auf
            Grünem Teppiche, den zur Lust

Ihm die Mutter gegönnt. Ferne sich haltend, sieht
    Ihm die Liebende zu, wundert der Sprache sich
        Und des jungen Verstandes
            Und des blühenden Auges schon.

Und an andere Zeit mahnt sie der Mann, dein Sohn;
    An die Lüfte des Mais, da er geseufzt um sie,
        An die Bräutigamstage,
            Da der Stolze die Demuth lernt.

Doch es wandte sich bald: Sicherer, denn er war,
    Ist er, herrlicher ist unter den Seinigen
        Nun der Zweifachgeliebte,
            Und ihm gehet sein Tagewerk.

Stiller Vater! auch du lebtest und liebtest so;
    Darum wohnest du nun, als ein Unsterblicher,
        Bei den Kindern, und Leben,
            Wie vom schweigenden Aether, kommt

Ancestral Portrait

Ne virtus ulla pereat!

Grandfather, ancient one, you gaze out as before,
    When happily you lived among us,
        But quietly now, and,
            Like the blessed, more calmly,

In the room where still your little son speaks of you, father!
    Where he smiles mischievously as he plays at your feet,
        Like lambs in the field
            On the green carpet which his mother

Provides for his pleasure. Keeping her distance,
    She looks on with love, marvels at his words
        And the youthful wisdom that even now
            Blossoms from his eyes.

And her husband, your son; recalls another time to her,
    There in the May breezes, when he sighed for her,
        In the days of courtship,
            When the proud man learned to be humble.

But soon that was changed: he'd grown surer
    Than before, more admired among his people,
        Now doubly loved,
            And his daily work goes forward.

Silent father! You also lived and loved,
    And now, through your children, you live
        As one who never dies, and a life
            Like that of the speechless Upper Air comes

Öfters über das Haus, ruhiger Mann! von dir,
　Und es mehrt sich, es reift, edler von Jahr zu Jahr,
　　In bescheidenem Glüke,
　　　Was mit Hoffnungen du gepflanzt.

Die du liebend erzogst, siehe! sie grünen dir,
　Deine Bäume, wie sonst, breiten ums Haus den Arm,
　　Voll von dankenden Gaaben;
　　　Sichrer stehen die Stämme schon;

Und am Hügel hinab, wo du den sonnigen
　Boden ihnen gebaut, neigen und schwingen sich
　　Deine freudigen Reben,
　　　Trunken, purpurner Trauben voll.

Aber unten im Haus ruhet, besorgt von dir,
　Der gekelterte Wein. Theuer ist der dem Sohn',
　　Und er sparet zum Fest das
　　　Alte, lautere Feuer sich.

Dann beim nächtlichen Mahl, wenn er, in Lust und Ernst,
　Von Vergangenem viel, vieles von Künftigem
　　Mit den Freunden gesprochen
　　　Und der lezte Gesang noch hallt,

Hält er höher den Kelch, siehet dein Bild und spricht:
　Deiner denken wir nun, dein, und so werd' und bleib'
　　Ihre Ehre des Haußes
　　　Guten Genien, hier und sonst!

From you, calm man, often over the house,
 And it grows nobler and more mature each year,
  In its allotment of good fortune,
   That with hopes you planted.

Look, your trees, which you reared with love,
 Turn green for you! They spread their branches
  Around the house; full of grateful gifts,
   Their trunks have grown stronger.

And on the hillside, where you plotted
 Sunny ground, the pleasant grapevines
  Bend and sway, weighed down
   With their drunken, purple fruit.

But down in the peaceful house, due to your care,
 The wine you pressed is stored. Precious to your son,
  He saves its old, pure fire
   For a special feast.

Then at an evening meal, when he's both grave and glad,
 When much time has passed and much is to come,
  And he has spoken with his friends,
   And the last of their songs are sung,

He raises his goblet high, looks at your portrait and says:
 We're thinking of you now, and so it always will be
  That the good spirits of the house be honored,
   Now and in the future!

Und es tönen zum Dank hell die Krystalle dir;
   Und die Mutter, sie reicht, heute zum erstenmal,
      Daß es wisse vom Feste,
         Auch dem Kinde von deinem Trank.

In gratitude, we toast you with bright crystal.
   And his mother allows today, for the first time,
      Our child to drink from your cup
         So he may share in the celebration."

Die Dioskuren

Ihr edeln Brüder droben, unsterbliches
   Gestirn, euch frag ich Helden woher es ist,
     Daß ich so unterthan ihm bin und
       So der Gewaltige sein mich nennet?

Denn wenig, aber Eines hab ich daheim, das ich
   Da niemand mag soll tauschen, ein gutes Glük
     Ein lichtes, reines, zum Gedächtniß
       Lebender Tage zurükgeblieben.

So aber er gebietet, diß Eine doch
   Wohin ers wollte, wagt' ich mein Saitenspiel
     Samt dem Gesange folgt ich, selbst ins
       Dunkel der Tapferen ihm hinunter.

Mit Wolken, säng ich, tränkt das Gewitter dich
   Du spöttichser Boden, aber mit Blut der Mensch
     So schweigt, so heiligt, der sein Gleiches
       Droben und drunten umsonst erfragte.

The Dioscuri

You noble brothers, immortal stars,
    I ask you heroes above, why is
        The Strong One so able to command me
           And why am I so subject to him?

There's one small thing I have at home,
    Of which no one can cheat me, a happiness
        That's bright and pure, lasting
           Reminder of the living days.

If he demanded one thing of me,
    I'd wager my lyre along with
        My song and follow him down myself,
           To the darkness of the brave.

I would sing with clouds. Scornful soil, it's not storms
    That soak you through, but rather the blood of men.
        Your equal above and below seeks for you
           In vain, thus silenced and made holy.

Unter den Alpen gesungen

Heilige Unschuld, du der Menschen und der
Götter liebste vertrauteste! du magst im
Hauß oder draußen ihnen zu Füßen
     Sizen, den Alten,

Immerzufriedner Weisheit voll; denn manches
Gute kennet der Mann, doch staunet er, dem
Wild gleich, oft zum Himmel, aber wie rein ist
     Reine, dir alles!

Siehe! das rauhe Thier des Feldes, gerne
Dient und trauet es dir, der stumme Wald spricht
Wie vor Alters, seine Sprüche zu dir, es
     Lehren die Berge

Heil'ge Geseze dich, und was noch jezt uns
Vielerfahrenen offenbar der große
Vater werden heißt, du darfst es allein uns
     Helle verkünden.

So mit den Himmlischen allein zu seyn, und
Geht vorüber das Licht, und Strom und Wind, und
Zeit eilt hin zum Ort, vor ihnen ein stetes
     Auge zu haben,

Seeliger weiß und wünsch' ich nichts, so lange
Nicht auch mich, wie die Weide, fort die Fluth nimmt,
Daß wohl aufgehoben, schlafend dahin ich
     Muß in den Woogen;

Sung Beneath the Alps

Holy innocence, that men and gods
Love the most! either inside the house
Or out of doors, you sit at the feet
        Of the ancients,

Always full of contented wisdom; for man knows
Much that's good, but astonished as the animals
He looks toward heaven, but how pure everything is
        To you, Pure One!

Look! The rough beast of the field gladly
Serves and trusts you, the voiceless forest
Speaks to you of the ancients, the mountains
        Teach you

Holy laws, and even now what the Great Father
Wants to name for us, who have
Much experience, only you can clarify
        And brighten.

To be alone with the gods, and when
The light passes over, and wind and flood, and
When time hurries to its place, you have a steady
        Eye for them,

Nothing is holier that I know and want,
As long as the flood doesn't take me, like
The willows, well cared for, sleeping as I must
        On the waves;

Aber es bleibt daheim gern, wer in treuem
Busen Göttliches hält, und frei will ich, so
Lang ich darf, euch all', ihr Sprachen des Himmels!
Deuten und singen.

He who holds divine things in his heart
Will gladly stay home, however, and I'll be free,
As long as needed, to translate and sing
                    In the tongues of heaven.

Dichterberuf

Des Ganges Ufer hörten des Freudengotts
   Triumph, als allerobernd vom Indus her
     Der junge Bacchus kam mit heilgem
       Weine vom Schlafe die Völker wekend.

Und du, des Tages Engel! erwekst sie nicht,
   Die jezt noch schlafen? gieb die Geseze, gieb
     Uns Leben, siege, Meister, du nur
       Hast der Eroberung Recht, wie Bacchus.

Nicht, was wohl sonst des Menschen Geschik und Sorg'
   Im Haus und unter offenem Himmel ist,
     Wenn edler, denn das Wild, der Mann sich
       Wehret und nährt! denn es gilt ein anders,

Zu Sorg' und Dienst den Dichtenden anvertraut!
   Der Höchste, der ists, dem wir geeignet sind
     Daß näher, immerneu besungen
       Ihn die befreundete Brust vernehme.

Und dennoch, o ihr Himmlischen all, und all
   Ihr Quellen und ihr Ufer und Hain' und Höhn,
     Wo wunderbar zuerst, als du die
       Loken ergriffen, und unvergeßlich

Der unverhoffte Genius über uns
   Der schöpferische, göttliche kam, daß stumm
     Der Sinn uns ward und, wie vom
       Strale gerührt das Gebein erbebte,

The Poet's Vocation

The banks of the Ganges heard how the god of joy
    Triumphed, when all-conquering the young
        Bacchus came from Indus and with holy
            Wine awoke the people from sleep.

And you, angel of our day! Don't you awaken
    Those still sleeping? Give us laws, give
        Us life, triumph, master, only you,
            Like Bacchus, have the right to conquer.

Nothing else within the care and skill of man
    Is in the house and under the open sky,
        When, nobler than wild beasts, men
            Work to provide for themselves, but

A different task and calling is given to poets!
    We serve the gods alone, so that,
        More closely and always freshly sung,
            They will hear our friendly heartbeats.

And yet, all you heavenly powers, and all
    You fountains and banks and groves and peaks,
        Where wonderful at first, you grabbed us
            By the hair and unexpectedly

Our imaginations overcame us
    Like a god, silencing our senses,
        And left us struck as if by lightning
            Down to our trembling bones,

Ihr ruhelosen Thaten in weiter Welt!
　Ihr Schiksaalstag', ihr reißenden, wenn der Gott
　　Stillsinnend lenkt, wohin zorntrunken
　　　Ihn die gigantischen Rosse bringen,

Euch sollten wir verschweigen, und wenn in uns
　Vom stetigstillen Jahre der Wohllaut tönt,
　　So sollt' es klingen, gleich als hätte
　　　Muthig und müßig ein Kind des Meisters

Geweihte, reine Saiten im Scherz gerührt?
　Und darum hast du, Dichter! des Orients
　　Propheten und den Griechensang und
　　　Neulich die Donner gehört, damit du

Den Geist zu Diensten brauchst und die Gegenwart
　Des Guten übereilest, in Spott, und den Albernen
　　Verläugnest, herzlos, und zum Spiele
　　　Feil, wie gefangenes Wild, ihn treibest?

Bis aufgereizt vom Stachel im Grimme der
　Des Ursprungs sich erinnert und ruft, daß selbst
　　Der Meister kommt, dann unter heißen
　　　Todesgeschossen entseelt dich lässet.

Zu lang ist alles Göttliche dienstbar schon
　Und alle Himmelskräfte verscherzt, verbraucht
　　Die Gütigen, zur Lust, danklos, ein
　　　Schlaues Geschlecht und zu kennen wähnt es

You restless deeds in the wide world!
   You fateful, rapacious days, when the god,
      Calm and thoughtful, drives wherever
         The gigantic rage-drunk horses take him.

We should keep quiet about you, and when in us
   The constant, quiet year rings sweetly out,
      Then should it sound, as if a capricious child
         Had been idly strumming, just for fun,

The master's pure and sacred strings?
   And for that alone, poet, you heard
      Greek songs and the prophets of the East
         And lately heard divine thunder, by which

You exploit the spirit and thoughtlessly
   Mock his kind presence, heartlessly deny
      This good soul and, for a few coins,
         Bait him like a captured animal?

Until provoked to anger by those fierce stings,
   The spirit recalls his origins and cries out, then
      The master himself appears, to leave you
         Lifeless beneath his hot death-charges.

For too long all that was godly and all
   The powers of heaven have been cheapened
      And good things wasted by a thankless,
         Cunning generation, who believe that he, the highest,

Wenn ihnen der Erhabne den Aker baut,
  Das Tagslicht und den Donnerer, und es späht
    Das Sehrohr wohl sie all und zählt und
      Nennet mit Namen des Himmels Sterne.

Der Vater aber deket mit heilger Nacht,
  Damit wir bleiben mögen, die Augen zu.
    Nicht liebt er Wildes! Doch es zwinget
      Nimmer die weite Gewalt den Himmel.

Noch ists auch gut, zu weise zu seyn. Ihn kennt
  Der Dank. Doch nicht behält er es leicht allein,
    Und gern gesellt, damit verstehn sie
      Helfen, zu anderen sich ein Dichter.

Furchtlos bleibt aber, so er es muß, der Mann
  Einsam vor Gott, es schüzet die Einfalt ihn,
    Und keiner Waffen brauchts und keiner
      Listen, so lange, bis Gottes Fehl hilft.

Tills their fields for them in person, that only
   They know daylight and the Thunderer
      And gaze through a telescope to count
         And name the stars of heaven.

But the father covers us with holy night,
   So we may endure on earth, eyes wide open.
      He loves nothing wild! Never will
         Our broad powers overwhelm his heaven.

Nor is it good to know too much. Our gratitude
   Knows him. But the poet can't keep
      His knowledge to himself and likes to join
         With others, who help him understand it.

But if he must, the man remains fearless,
   Alone before God, simplicity keeps him safe,
      He needs no weapons and no cunning,
         As long as God's absence comes to his aid.

Der blinde Sänger

Ελυσεν αινον αχος απ’ ομματων Αρης
                    Sophokles

Wo bist du, Jugendliches! das immer mich
    Zur Stunde wekt des Morgens, wo bist du, Licht!
        Das Herz ist wach, doch bannt und hält in
            Heiligem Zauber die Nacht mich immer.

Sonst lauscht’ ich um die Dämmerung gern, sonst harrt’
    Ich gerne dein am Hügel, und nie umsonst!
        Nie täuschten mich, du Holdes, deine
            Boten, die Lüfte, denn immer kamst du,

Kamst allbeseeligend den gewohnten Pfad
    Herein in deiner Schöne, wo bist du, Licht!
        Das Herz ist wieder wach, doch bannt und
            Hemmt die unendliche Nacht mich immer.

Mir grünten sonst die Lauben; es leuchteten
    Die Blumen, wie die eigenen Augen, mir;
        Nicht ferne war das Angesicht der
            Meinen und leuchtete mir und droben

Und um die Wälder sah ich die Fittige
    Des Himmels wandern, da ich ein Jüngling war;
        Nun siz ich still allein, von einer
            Stunde zur anderen und Gestalten

The Blind Singer

Ελυσεν αινον αχος απ' ομματων Αρης

Sophocles

Where are you, young one, who would always
    Wake me in the morning, where are you, light?
        My heart is awake, but the night always
            Holds and binds me in its holy magic.

Once near dawn I listened, glad to wait
    For you on the hill, and never for nothing!
        Not once did your messengers, the sweet breezes,
            Deceive me, for always you came,

All-inspiring in your loveliness,
    Down the usual path; where are you, light?
        Once again, my heart is awake, but always
            The endless night binds and constrains me.

Once the leaves greened for me; the flowers
    Would shine like my own eyes;
        Not far away, familiar faces
            Shone for me, and, when I

Was a child, I saw the wings of heaven
    Traveling above and around the woods;
        Now I sit silent and alone, from one
            Hour to the next, making shapes

Aus Lieb und Laid der helleren Tage schafft
Zur eignen Freude nun mein Gedanke sich,
Und ferne lausch' ich hin, ob nicht ein
Freundlicher Retter vieleicht mir komme.

Dann hör ich oft die Stimme des Donnerers
Am Mittag, wenn der eherne nahe kommt,
Wenn ihm das Haus bebt und der Boden
Unter ihm dröhnt und der Berg es nachhallt.

Den Retter hör' ich dann in der Nacht, ich hör'
Ihn tödtend, den Befreier, belebend ihn,
Den Donnerer vom Untergang zum
Orient eilen und ihm nach tönt ihr,

Ihm nach, ihr meine Saiten! es lebt mit ihm
Mein Lied und wie die Quelle dem Strome folgt,
Wohin er denkt, so muß ich fort und
Folge dem Sicheren auf der Irrbahn.

Wohin? wohin? ich höre dich da und dort
Du Herrlicher! und rings um die Erde tönts.
Wo endest du? und was, was ist es
Über den Wolken und o wie wird mir?

Tag! Tag! du über stürzenden Wolken! sei
Willkommen mir! es blühet mein Auge dir.
O Jugendlicht! o Glük! das alte
Wieder! doch geistiger rinnst du nieder,

Of love and pain from brighter days,
   Taking comfort only in my thoughts,
      And strain far to hear if perhaps
         A kindly rescuer comes to me.

Then I often hear the voice of the Thunderer
   At midday, when the brazen one comes near,
      When he shakes his house, and under him
         The foundation quakes, and the mountain resounds.

Then I hear my rescuer in the night, I hear
   Him kill, this liberator, to give new life;
      From sunrise to sunset I hear the Thunderer
         Hurry on, and you call in his direction,

My strings! My song lives with him,
   And, as the stream follows the source,
      Wherever he has a thought, I must also go,
         Follow the sure one on his erratic path.

Where to? Where to? I hear you here and there,
   Majestic one! And all around the earth it sounds.
      Where do you end? And what, what is there,
         Beyond the clouds, and what will become of me?

Day! Day! Above the tumbling clouds, I will
   Welcome you back! my eyes will flower for you,
      O light of youth, o joy, returning once again,
         Yet now more spiritually the golden source

Du goldner Quell aus heiligem Kelch! und du,
 Du grüner Boden, friedliche Wieg'! und du,
  Haus meiner Väter! und ihr Lieben,
   Die mir begegneten einst, o nahet,

O kommt, daß euer, euer die Freude sei,
 Ihr alle, daß euch seegne der Sehende!
  O nimmt, daß ichs ertrage, mir das
   Leben, das Göttliche mir vom Herzen.

Flows from its holy chalice, and you,
    Green earth, in your peaceful cradle, and you,
        House of my fathers! and you, loved ones
            I met once in the past, o draw near,

O come, that the joy will be yours,
    That you all will receive the seeing man's blessing!
        O take this life from me, that I may
            Endure it, take the godly from my heart.

Chiron

Wo bist du, Nachdenkliches! das immer muß
  Zur Seite gehn, zu Zeiten, wo bist du, Licht?
    Wohl ist das Herz wach, doch mir zürnt, mich
      Hemmt die erstaunende Nacht nun immer.

Sonst nemlich folgt' ich Kräutern des Walds und lauscht'
  Ein waiches Wild am Hügel; und nie umsonst.
    Nie täuschten, auch nicht einmal deine
      Vögel; denn allzubereit fast kamst du,

So Füllen oder Garten dir labend ward,
  Rathschlagend, Herzens wegen; wo bist du, Licht?
    Das Herz ist wieder wach, doch herzlos
      Zieht die gewaltige Nacht mich immer.

Ich war's wohl. Und von Krokus und Thymian
  Und Korn gab mir die Erde den ersten Straus.
    Und bei der Sterne Kühle lernt' ich,
      Aber das Nennbare nur. Und bei mir

Das wilde Feld entzaubernd, das traur'ge, zog
  Der Halbgott, Zeus Knecht, ein, der gerade Mann;
    Nun siz' ich still allein, von einer
      Stunde zur anderen, und Gestalten

Aus frischer Erd' und Wolken der Liebe schafft,
  Weil Gift ist zwischen uns, mein Gedanke nun;
    Und ferne lausch' ich hin, ob nicht ein
      Freundlicher Retter vieleicht mir komme.

Chiron

Where are you, thoughtful one, who now
    Must move beside me, where are you, light?
        The heart is awake but angry, always now
            The astounding night confines me.

For I searched for herbs in the woods,
    And heard soft game on the hillside,
        And never once did your birds disappoint me,
            Never; for almost too quickly you'd come,

When foal or garden comforted you,
    Advising, for the heart's sake; where are you, light?
        The heart is awake once more, but, heartless,
            Night's power wins my affection.

Yes, it's really me. For me, earth picked the first
    Bouquet of crocus, thyme, and grain, and in
        The coolness of the stars I learned, but
            Only what can be named. Disenchanting,

Now mournful, the wild meadow, Zeus's helper,
    Half a god, sat directly down beside me.
        But now I sit alone in silence,
            Hour after hour, and, since poison stands

Between us, my mind makes shapes
    From fresh earth and the clouds of love;
        And I strain to hear at a distance if
            A kindly savior is coming in my direction.

Dann hör' ich oft den Wagen des Donnerers
    Am Mittag, wenn er naht, der bekannteste,
      Wenn ihm das Haus bebt und der Boden
        Reiniget sich, und die Quaal Echo wird.

Den Retter hör' ich dann in der Nacht, ich hör'
    Ihn tödtend, den Befreier, und drunten voll
      Von üpp'gem Kraut, als in Gesichten
        Schau ich die Erd', ein gewaltig Feuer;

Die Tage aber wechseln, wenn einer dann
    Zusiehet denen, lieblich und bös', ein Schmerz,
      Wenn einer zweigestalt ist, und es
        Kennet kein einziger nicht das Beste;

Das aber ist der Stachel des Gottes; nie
    Kann einer lieben göttliches Unrecht sonst.
      Einheimisch aber ist der Gott dann
        Angesichts da, und die Erd' ist anders.

Tag! Tag! Nun wieder athmet ihr recht; nun trinkt,
    Ihr meiner Bäche Weiden! ein Augenlicht,
      Und rechte Stapfen gehn, und als ein
        Herrscher, mit Sporen, und bei dir selber

Örtlich, Irrstern des Tages, erscheinest du,
    Du auch, o Erde, friedliche Wieg', und du,
      Haus meiner Väter, die unstädtisch
        Sind, in den Wolken des Wilds, gegangen.

Often I hear the Thunderer's clattering wagon
　　At noon, when the famous man comes near,
　　　　When his own house is cleansed to its
　　　　　　Shaken foundations, and anguish becomes an echo.

Then I hear my savior in the night, I hear
　　Him kill, this liberator, and down below
　　　　As in visions filled with dense vegetation,
　　　　　　I see the earth, a storm of fire;

But the days pass, lovely and awful, and
　　When one looks closely, there's suffering,
　　　　Since people are of two natures,
　　　　　　And no one knows what is best;

But that's the gods' sting; otherwise,
　　No one could love divine injustice.
　　　　But God feels at home there and when
　　　　　　He shows his face, the earth is changed.

Day! Day! Once more you can breathe, then drink,
　　Willow of the stream, light of the eyes,
　　　　And footsteps are sure and true
　　　　　　As a king in spurs, and, caught

In your own orbit, planet of days, you appear,
　　Peaceful cradle, earth, and you also,
　　　　House of my rustic fathers, who
　　　　　　Traveled among clouds with forest creatures.

Nimm nun ein Roß, und harnische dich und nimm
Den leichten Speer, o Knabe! Die Wahrsagung
Zerreißt nicht, und umsonst nicht wartet,
Bis sie erscheinet, Herakles Rükkehr.

Now take a horse and armor and take
A light spear, son. The prophecy
Will not tear, and not in vain
Heracles' return awaits its fulfillment.

Thränen

Himmlische Liebe! zärtliche! wenn ich dein
   Vergäße, wenn ich, o ihr geschiklichen,
     Ihr feur'gen, die voll Asche sind und
       Wüst und vereinsamet ohnediß schon,

Ihr lieben Inseln, Augen der Wunderwelt!
   Ihr nemlich geht nun einzig allein mich an,
     Ihr Ufer, wo die abgöttische
       Büßet, doch Himmlischen nur, die Liebe.

Denn allzudankbar haben die Heiligen
   Gedienet dort in Tagen der Schönheit und
     Die zorn'gen Helden; und viel Bäume
       Sind, und die Städte daselbst gestanden,

Sichtbar, gleich einem sinnigen Mann; izt sind
   Die Helden todt, die Inseln der Liebe sind
     Entstellt fast. So muß übervortheilt,
       Albern doch überall seyn die Liebe.

Ihr waichen Thränen, löschet das Augenlicht
   Mir aber nicht ganz aus; ein Gedächtniß doch,
     Damit ich edel sterbe, laßt ihr
       Trügrischen, Diebischen, mir nachleben.

Tears

Heavenly love, so tender, if I should
    Forget you, you who are marked by fate,
        You who are fiery, full of ash and waste,
            And even before that, you were lonely and desolate,

Dear islands, eyes of the world-in-wonder!
    Since only you matter now, you banks
        On which, for the sake of love and to heaven
            Alone, the godless say their prayers.

For almost too gratefully in the days of beauty
    Furious heroes and the holy served there
        And there were many trees,
            And the cities stood there at one time,

Visible like a man lost in thought; now
    The heroes are dead, the islands of love defaced,
        Almost disfigured. So forever love
            Is outwitted and utterly absurd.

Yet, soft tears, don't completely extinguish
    The light of vision for me; still, to help me
        Die nobly, you frauds and thieves,
            Let one memory live on in me.

An die Hofnung

O Hofnung! holde! gütiggeschäfftige!
 Die du das Haus der Trauernden nicht verschmähst,
  Und gerne dienend, Edle! zwischen
   Sterblichen waltest und Himmelsmächten,

Wo bist du? wenig lebt' ich; doch athmet kalt
 Mein Abend schon. Und stille, den Schatten gleich,
  Bin ich schon hier; und schon gesanglos
   Schlummert das schaudernde Herz im Busen.

Im grünen Thale, dort, wo der frische Quell
 Vom Berge täglich rauscht, und die liebliche
  Zeitlose mir am Herbsttag aufblüht,
   Dort, in der Stille, du Holde, will ich

Dich suchen, oder wenn in der Mitternacht
 Das unsichtbare Leben im Haine wallt,
  Und über mir die immerfrohen
   Blumen, die blühenden Sterne, glänzen,

O du des Aethers Tochter! erscheine dann
 Aus deines Vaters Gärten, und darfst du nicht,
  Ein Geist der Erde, kommen, schrök', o
   Schröke mit anderem nur das Herz mir.

To Hope

Hope! Sweet industrious one
    Who doesn't scorn the house of grief,
        Serves happily, noble one, to form ties
            Between mortals and the powers of heaven.

Where are you? I have lived little; but my evening
    Already breathes cold. And silent as the shadows
        I am already here; and, without a song,
            My shivering heart lies quietly in my chest.

In the green valley, there, where the fresh spring
    Rushes daily from the mountain, and the lovely
        Meadow saffron blooms for me on a fall day,
            There, in the quiet, I will search for you,

My dear, or when at midnight
    Invisible lives stir in the forest,
        And above me the ever-joyful
            Flowering stars are shining,

Daughter of the Upper Air, you appear to me
    Out of your father's gardens, and if you cannot
        Draw near as a spirit of the earth, frighten, o
            Frighten my heart with a different face.

Vulkan

Jezt komm und hülle, freundlicher Feuergeist,
 Den zarten Sinn der Frauen in Wolken ein,
  In goldne Träum’ und schüze sie, die
   Blühende Ruhe der Immerguten.

Dem Manne laß sein Sinnen, und sein Geschäfft,
 Und seiner Kerze Schein, und den künftgen Tag
  Gefallen, laß des Unmuths ihm, der
   Häßlichen Sorge zu viel nicht werden,

Wenn jezt der immerzürnende Boreas,
 Mein Erbfeind, über Nacht mit dem Frost das Land
  Befällt, und spät, zur Schlummerstunde,
   Spottend der Menschen, sein schröklich Lied singt,

Und unsrer Städte Mauren und unsern Zaun,
 Den fleißig wir gesezt, und den stillen Hain
  Zerreißt, und selber im Gesang die
   Seele mir störet, der Allverderber,

Und rastlos tobend über den sanften Strom
 Sein schwarz Gewölk ausschüttet, daß weit umher
  Das Thal gährt, und, wie fallend Laub, vom
   Berstenden Hügel herab der Fels fällt.

Wohl frömmer ist, denn andre Lebendige,
 Der Mensch; doch zürnt es draußen, gehöret der
  Auch eigner sich, und sinnt und ruht in
   Sicherer Hütte, der Freigeborne.

Vulcan

Come now, friendly spirit of fire,
    And veil the tender minds of women in clouds,
        In golden dreams, and keep safe
            The blossoming calm of the always good.

Let man be content with his thoughts, and his work,
    And his shining candles, and the future day.
        Let him be free of annoyances
            And too many hateful worries,

When now the ever-raging Boreas,
    My old rival, strikes the land with frost
        Overnight, and late, past the hour of sleep,
            Mocking at men, sings his frightening war-song,

And tears down our city walls and the fences
    We built with effort and the quiet grove,
        And even disturbs my soul in the middle
            Of its song, the destroyer of all,

And restlessly he roars over the gentle stream
    And throws down his black clouds, until, far and wide,
        They shred the valley to pieces, and, like falling leaves,
            Rocks fall from the fractured hills.

Man is more pious than all other living
    Things; yet, angry with the world outside,
        He becomes more himself, free-born,
            And, safe in his cottage, rests and wonders.

Und immer wohnt der freundlichen Genien
    Noch Einer gerne seegnend mit ihm, und wenn
        Sie zürnten all', die ungelehrgen
            Geniuskräfte, doch liebt die Liebe.

And there's always at least one friendly spirit
Who gladly blesses him, and even when
The fierce, uneducated spirit-powers
Are angry, love still loves.

Dichtermuth
[Erste Fassung]

Sind denn dir nicht verwandt alle Lebendigen?
    Nährt zum Dienste denn nicht selber die Parze dich?
        Drum! so wandle nur wehrlos
            Fort durch's Leben und sorge nicht!

Was geschiehet, es sei alles gesegnet dir,
    Sei zur Freude gewandt! oder was könnte denn
        Dich belaidigen, Herz! was
            Da begegnen, wohin du sollst?

Denn, wie still am Gestad, oder in silberner
    Fernhintönender Fluth, oder auf schweigenden
        Wassertiefen der leichte
            Schwimmer wandelt, so sind auch wir,

Wir, die Dichter des Volks, gerne, wo Lebendes
    Um uns athmet und wallt, freudig, und jedem hold,
        Jedem trauend; wie sängen
            Sonst wir jedem den eignen Gott?

Wenn die Wooge denn auch einen der Muthigen,
    Wo er treulich getraut, schmeichlend hinunterzieht,
        Und die Stimme des Sängers
            Nun in blauender Halle schweigt;

Freudig starb er und noch klagen die Einsamen,
    Seine Haine, den Fall ihres Geliebtesten;
        Öfters tönet der Jungfrau
            Vom Gezweige sein freundlich Lied.

The Poet's Courage

[First Version]

Isn't everything alive already in your blood?
    Doesn't Fate herself keep you in her service?
        Wander defenseless, through life,
            Therefore, and don't worry!

Whatever happens will be sacred to you,
    Be expert in joy! For what could
        Harm you, heart! What could
            You suffer, where you must go?

For, as on quiet shores, or in the silver
    Distantly echoing flood, or upon the silent
        Deep-running water the effortless
            Swimmer travels, that's how we are,

We, the poets of the people, who like to be
    Where people live and breathe around us,
        And, trusting in each one; how else
            To sing for him in the voice of his god?

When the wave smashes a courageous man under,
    Where he truly dares to go,
        And the voice of that singer
            Falls silent as the hall turns blue;

He dies there gladly, but still his lonely groves
    Lament the fall of the one they loved most;
        Often his cheerful song resounds
            To the maiden from distant branches.

Wenn des Abends vorbei Einer der Unsern kömmt,
  Wo der Bruder ihm sank, denket er manches wohl
    An der warnenden Stelle,
      Schweigt und gehet gerüsteter.

When at evening a man like us passes
    The place where his brother drowned
        He'll think many things in the way of warning
          And silently walk on, all the wiser.

Blödigkeit

Sind denn dir nicht bekannt viele Lebendigen?
   Geht auf Wahrem dein Fuß nicht, wie auf Teppichen?
      Drum, mein Genius! tritt nur
         Baar in's Leben, und sorge nicht!

Was geschiehet, es sei alles gelegen dir!
   Sei zur Freude gereimt, oder was könnte denn
      Dich belaidigen, Herz, was
         Da begegnen, wohin du sollst?

Denn, seit Himmlischen gleich Menschen, ein einsam Wild
   Und die Himmlischen selbst führet, der Einkehr zu,
      Der Gesang und der Fürsten
         Chor, nach Arten, so waren auch

Wir, die Zungen des Volks, gerne bei Lebenden,
   Wo sich vieles gesellt, freudig und jedem gleich,
      Jedem offen, so ist ja
         Unser Vater, des Himmels Gott,

Der den denkenden Tag Armen und Reichen gönnt,
   Der, zur Wende der Zeit, uns die Entschlafenden
      Aufgerichtet an goldnen
         Gängelbanden, wie Kinder, hält.

Gut auch sind und geschikt einem zu etwas wir,
   Wenn wir kommen, mit Kunst, und von den Himmlischen
      Einen bringen. Doch selber
         Bringen schikliche Hände wir.

Timidness

Aren't many of the living well known to you?
   Don't your feet tread on truth as on carpets?
      Therefore, my genius, step straight into life
         And don't worry so much!

Whatever happens will work out for you.
   If you're ready to feel joy, what then
      Can harm you, heart, where
         Then must you go to find offense?

Since the gods became like men, lonely as beasts,
   Song and the sovereign choir, each in its way,
      Brought the gods back to earth,
         So we too, the tongues of men,

Live happily among the living,
   Where many are brought together, equally open,
      Equally delighted, as is our father
         The god of heaven, who grants

The thinking day to rich and poor,
   Holds the sleepy ones upright, at the turning
      Of time, as one restrains children
         By means of a golden leash.

We are also good and have a knack for things
   When we come with our art and bring
      One of the gods along. But we ourselves
         Have hands as skillful as fate.

Der gefesselte Strom

Was schläfst und träumst du, Jüngling, gehüllt in dich,
   Und säumst am kalten Ufer, Geduldiger,
      Und achtest nicht des Ursprungs, du, des
         Oceans Sohn, des Titanenfreundes!

Die Liebesboten, welche der Vater schikt,
   Kennst du die lebenathmenden Lüfte nicht?
      Und trift das Wort dich nicht, das hell von
         Oben der wachende Gott dir sendet?

Schon tönt, schon tönt es ihm in der Brust, es quillt,
   Wie, da er noch im Schoose der Felsen spielt',
      Ihm auf, und nun gedenkt er seiner
         Kraft, der Gewaltige, nun, nun eilt er,

Der Zauderer, er spottet der Fesseln nun,
   Und nimmt und bricht und wirft die Zerbrochenen
      Im Zorne, spielend, da und dort zum
         Schallenden Ufer und an der Stimme

Des Göttersohns erwachen die Berge rings,
   Es regen sich die Wälder, es hört die Kluft
      Den Herold fern und schaudernd regt im
         Busen der Erde sich Freude wieder.

Der Frühling kommt; es dämmert das neue Grün;
   Er aber wandelt hin zu Unsterblichen;
      Denn nirgend darf er bleiben, als wo
         Ihn in die Arme der Vater aufnimmt.

The River in Chains

Why do you sleep and dream, young one, so wrapped up
    In yourself, and linger patiently by the cold bank,
        And pay no attention to your place of birth, you
            Son of Oceans, friend of titans!

The messengers of love, sent by your father,
    Don't you recognize their life-breathing winds?
        And doesn't the word strike you, which the watchful
            God sends you, bright from above?

Already it sounds in his breast, wells up,
    As when he played in a womb of stone,
        And as he weighs his force and strength,
            Now, now, he hurries,

This slacker, and now mocks his chains
    And takes and breaks and throws the broken pieces
        Down in anger, playing here and there
            On the echoing banks, and the voice

Of that god's son wakes the mountains all around,
    The woods begin to stir, the deep ravine can hear
        The distant herald, and shivering joy
            Stirs in the earth's bosom.

Spring arrives; a new green dawns;
    But he wanders toward the immortals;
        For he has no place to stay, except
            To be received into his father's arms.

Ganymed

Was schläfst du, Bergsohn, liegest in Unmuth, schief,
  Und frierst am kahlen Ufer, Gedultiger!
    Denkst nicht der Gnade du, wenn's an den
      Tischen die Himmlischen sonst gedürstet?

Kennst drunten du vom Vater die Boten nicht,
  Nicht in der Kluft der Lüfte geschärfter Spiel?
    Trift nicht das Wort dich, das voll alten
      Geists ein gewanderter Mann dir sendet?

Schon tönet's aber ihm in der Brust. Tief quillt's,
  Wie damals, als hoch oben im Fels er schlief,
    Ihm auf. Im Zorne reinigt aber
      Sich der Gefesselte nun, nun eilt er

Der Linkische; der spottet der Schlaken nun,
  Und nimmt und bricht und wirft die Zerbrochenen
    Zorntrunken, spielend, dort und da zum
      Schauenden Ufer, und bei des Fremdlings

Besondrer Stimme stehen die Heerden auf,
  Es regen sich die Wälder, es hört tief Land
    Den Stromgeist fern, und schaudernd regt im
      Nabel der Erde der Geist sich wieder.

Der Frühling kömmt. Und jedes, in seiner Art,
  Blüht. Der ist aber ferne; nicht mehr dabei.
    Irr gieng er nun; denn allzugut sind
      Genien; himmlisch Gespräch ist sein nun.

Ganymede

Why do you sleep, son of the mountains, so crookedly,
 Ill-tempered, and freeze on the bare banks?
  Too patient, don't you think of grace when
   Even the gods are thirsty at the table?

Don't you recognize your father's messengers,
 Where sharper winds cut through the ravine?
  Doesn't the invitation of that well-traveled man
   Strike home its ancient meaning?

Now it resounds in his breast, deeply welling up,
 As when he slept high upon the rock.
  In anger now, the one in chains
   Bathes himself, and now he hurries,

Clumsily; now he mocks his chains and
 Takes and breaks and throws them down,
  Drunk with anger, playing here and there,
   As the riverbanks observe him, and at this stranger's

Peculiar voice, the resting herds rise,
 The woods awaken, and deep in the land
  You can hear the river god's voice, and stirring
   At the earth's core the spirit shudders once more.

Spring comes. And everything, in its own way,
 Blossoms. But he is distant; no longer there.
  Now he strays off; geniuses are all
   Too good; he chats away in heaven now.

Elegies and Hymns

Menons Klagen um Diotima

1

Täglich geh' ich heraus, und such' ein Anderes immer,
    Habe längst sie befragt alle die Pfade des Lands;
Droben die kühlenden Höhn, die Schatten alle besuch' ich,
    Und die Quellen; hinauf irret der Geist und hinab,
Ruh' erbittend; so flieht das getroffene Wild in die Wälder,
    Wo es um Mittag sonst sicher im Dunkel geruht;
Aber nimmer erquikt sein grünes Lager das Herz ihm,
    Jammernd und schlummerlos treibt es der Stachel umher.
Nicht die Wärme des Lichts, und nicht die Kühle der Nacht hilft,
    Und in Woogen des Stroms taucht es die Wunden umsonst.
Und wie ihm vergebens die Erd' ihr fröhliches Heilkraut
    Reicht, und das gährende Blut keiner der Zephyre stillt,
So, ihr Lieben! auch mir, so will es scheinen, und niemand
    Kann von der Stirne mir nehmen den traurigen Traum?

2

Ja! es frommet auch nicht, ihr Todesgötter! wenn einmal
    Ihr ihn haltet, und fest habt den bezwungenen Mann,
Wenn ihr Bösen hinab in die schaurige Nacht ihn genommen,
    Dann zu suchen, zu flehn, oder zu zürnen mit euch,
Oder geduldig auch wohl im furchtsamen Banne zu wohnen,
    Und mit Lächeln von euch hören das nüchterne Lied.
Soll es seyn, so vergiß dein Heil, und schlummere klanglos!
    Aber doch quillt ein Laut hoffend im Busen dir auf,
Immer kannst du noch nicht, o meine Seele! noch kannst du's
    Nicht gewohnen, und träumst mitten im eisernen Schlaf!
Festzeit hab' ich nicht, doch möcht' ich die Loke bekränzen;
    Bin ich allein denn nicht? aber ein Freundliches muß
Fernher nahe mir seyn, und lächeln muß ich und staunen,
    Wie so seelig doch auch mitten im Leide mir ist.

Menon's Lament for Diotima

1

I go out every day, always searching in a different place,
    For a long time I have questioned the roads of the land;
Up on the cool hilltops, I visit the wellsprings
    And shadows; my mind roams here and there,
Begging for rest, as a wounded deer will hide in the woods,
    Where he lies in the dark toward midday,
But his green hiding place can never soothe his heart;
    Miserable and sleepless, he moves on, pricked by a thorn.
Neither the warmth of light nor the cool of night helps him,
    And in the current of the stream he soothes his wounds in vain.
And as the earth offers herbal remedies to cheer him,
    And none of the winds can cool his feverish blood,
So, dear ones, it is with me, too, and can no one lift
    This tragic dream from my brow?

2

Indeed, it is in vain, gods of death, when once
    You have caught and bound a man,
When your evil ones come down in the terrible night
    To take him, then to want, to implore, or be angry
With you, to show patience, or to live timidly when constrained,
    And smile to hear you sing him the sobering song.
If so, then forget your health and slumber tunelessly!
    But if a sound rises up with hope in your heart,
You can never relent, my soul, no never can you live
    And dream in the midst of iron sleep!
While I have no cause to be festive, I long for a wreath
    In my hair; am I not alone then? But something gentle
Must be near me, and, smiling, I must wonder
    How I can feel so blessed in the middle of my grief.

3

Licht der Liebe! scheinest du denn auch Todten, du goldnes!
　　Bilder aus hellerer Zeit leuchtet ihr mir in die Nacht?
Liebliche Gärten seid, ihr abendröthlichen Berge,
　　Seid willkommen und ihr, schweigende Pfade des Hains,
Zeugen himmlischen Glüks, und ihr, hochschauende Sterne,
　　Die mir damals so oft seegnende Blike gegönnt!
Euch, ihr Liebenden auch, ihr schönen Kinder des Maitags,
　　Stille Rosen und euch, Lilien, nenn' ich noch oft!
Wohl gehn Frühlinge fort, ein Jahr verdränget das andre,
　　Wechselnd und streitend, so tost droben vorüber die Zeit
Über sterblichem Haupt, doch nicht vor seeligen Augen,
　　Und den Liebenden ist anderes Leben geschenkt.
Denn sie alle die Tag' und Jahre der Sterne, sie waren
　　Diotima! um uns innig und ewig vereint;

4

Aber wir, zufrieden gesellt, wie die liebenden Schwäne,
　　Wenn sie ruhen am See, oder, auf Wellen gewiegt,
Niedersehn in die Wasser, wo silberne Wolken sich spiegeln,
　　Und ätherisches Blau unter den Schiffenden wallt,
So auf Erden wandelten wir. Und drohte der Nord auch,
　　Er, der Liebenden Feind, klagenbereitend, und fiel
Von den Ästen das Laub, und flog im Winde der Reegen,
　　Ruhig lächelten wir, fühlten den eigenen Gott
Unter trautem Gespräch; in Einem Seelengesange,
　　Ganz in Frieden mit uns kindlich und freudig allein.
Aber das Haus ist öde mir nun, und sie haben mein Auge
　　Mir genommen, auch mich hab' ich verloren mit ihr.
Darum irr' ich umher, und wohl, wie die Schatten, so muß ich
　　Leben, und sinnlos dünkt lange das Übrige mir.

3

Light of love, golden one, do you shine also for the dead?
    Do images of brilliant times shine out to me in the night?
Pleasant gardens and mountains red with evening,
    I call to welcome you, silent paths of the grove,
Witness to heavenly joy, and you, high-shining stars,
    Who else would grant me the grace of your gaze!
And you lovers, too, you pretty children of May,
    Quiet roses and you, lilies, I often speak your names!
It's true, spring goes by, one year supplanting the next,
    Changing things and causing strife, so over our mortal heads,
Time rushes by, but not in the blessed one's eyes,
    And not to lovers, who are given a different life,
For these, since all the days and years of the stars,
    Diotima, are around us closely and forever joined;

4

But we, contented with each other like loving swans
    When they rest on the lake, cradled in its waves,
They look down into the water where the clouds reflect silver,
    And an ethereal blue travels beneath the voyagers
As we used to wander on this earth. And though the North Wind
    Rages, an enemy of lovers, full of lamentation,
Down come leaves from the bough, and rain fills the wind,
    We still smiled calmly, sensing our guardian god
In intimate conversation, in one song of our souls,
    Completely at peace with ourselves, childishly and
Happily alone. Now my house is desolate, and they've taken
    Even my eyes, and I have lost myself by losing her.
That is why I live like a wandering shadow, and so I must
    Live, and for a long time the rest has seemed senseless.

5

Feiern möcht' ich; aber wofür? und singen mit Andern,
  Aber so einsam fehlt jegliches Göttliche mir.
Diß ist's, diß mein Gebrechen, ich weiß, es lähmet ein Fluch mir
  Darum die Sehnen, und wirft, wo ich beginne, mich hin,
Daß ich fühllos size den Tag, und stumm wie die Kinder,
  Nur vom Auge mir kalt öfters die Thräne noch schleicht,
Und die Pflanze des Felds, und der Vögel Singen mich trüb macht,
  Weil mit Freuden auch sie Boten des Himmlischen sind,
Aber mir in schaudernder Brust die beseelende Sonne,
  Kühl und fruchtlos mir dämmert, wie Stralen der Nacht.
Ach! und nichtig und leer, wie Gefängnißwände, der Himmel
  Eine beugende Last über dem Haupte mir hängt!

6

Sonst mir anders bekannt! o Jugend, und bringen Gebete
  Dich nicht wieder, dich nie? führet kein Pfad mich zurük?
Soll es werden auch mir, wie den Götterlosen, die vormals
  Glänzenden Auges doch auch saßen an seeligem Tisch',
Aber übersättiget bald, die schwärmenden Gäste,
  Nun verstummet, und nun, unter der Lüfte Gesang,
Unter blühender Erd' entschlafen sind, bis dereinst sie
  Eines Wunders Gewalt sie, die Versunkenen, zwingt,
Wiederzukehren, und neu auf grünendem Boden zu wandeln.—
  Heiliger Othem durchströmt göttlich die lichte Gestalt,
Wenn das Fest sich beseelt, und Fluthen der Liebe sich regen,
  Und vom Himmel getränkt, rauscht der lebendige Strom,
Wenn es drunten ertönt, und ihre Schäze die Nacht zollt,
  Und aus Bächen herauf glänzt das begrabene Gold.—

5

I should celebrate, but what for? And sing with others,
    But, because I feel so alone, nothing godlike seems true.
This, I know, this is my weakness, I'm crippled to the bone
    By this curse and lose everything as I gain it,
So that I sit all day, numb as a child, without feeling,
    Though often a tear falls coldly from my eyes,
And flowers of the field and the singing birds make
    Me sad now, for they are messengers of heavenly joy,
But to me, the sun that gives forth the soul dawns cool
    And infertile, like rays of night in my shuddering breast.
Oh, and futile and empty, like walls of a prison,
    The heavens heap a smothering weight on my head!

6

How different it once was! o, youth, can no prayer bring
    You back, ever again? Can no path lead me back
Once more? Shall it be my fate, as it was for the godless,
    To sit with bright eyes at a heavenly table, and to
Remain unsatisfied, one of the dreamlike guests, now
    Fallen silent, and now under the winds' song,
Under the blooming and sleeping earth, until the power
    Of a miracle shall force them one day to return,
Those lost ones, and wander again on the green earth.—
    Holy breath will flow through their bright, god-like shapes
While the feast is inspired and love gathers like a flood-tide,
    Nourished by the heavens themselves; the living river
Sweeps on when the deep places resound, and Night gives forth
    Her treasure and drowned gold glimmers up from the streams.—

7

Aber o du, die schon am Scheidewege mir damals,
  Da ich versank vor dir, tröstend ein Schöneres wies,
Du, die Großes zu sehn, und froher die Götter zu singen,
  Schweigend, wie sie, mich einst stille begeisternd gelehrt;
Götterkind! erscheinest du mir, und grüßest, wie einst, mich,
  Redest wieder, wie einst, höhere Dinge mir zu?
Siehe! weinen vor dir, und klagen muß ich, wenn schon noch,
  Denkend edlerer Zeit, dessen die Seele sich schämt.
Denn so lange, so lang auf matten Pfaden der Erde
  Hab' ich, deiner gewohnt, dich in der Irre gesucht,
Freudiger Schuzgeist! aber umsonst, und Jahre zerrannen,
  Seit wir ahnend um uns glänzen die Abende sahn.

8

Dich nur, dich erhält dein Licht, o Heldinn! im Lichte,
  Und dein Dulden erhält liebend, o Gütige, dich;
Und nicht einmal bist du allein; Gespielen genug sind,
  Wo du blühest und ruhst unter den Rosen des Jahrs;
Und der Vater, er selbst, durch sanftumathmende Musen
  Sendet die zärtlichen Wiegengesänge dir zu.
Ja! noch ist sie es ganz! noch schwebt vom Haupte zur Sohle,
  Stillherwandelnd, wie sonst, mir die Athenerinn vor.
Und wie, freundlicher Geist! von heitersinnender Stirne
  Seegnend und sicher dein Stral unter die Sterblichen fällt;
So bezeugest du mir's, und sagst mir's, daß ich es andern
  Wiedersage, denn auch Andere glauben es nicht,
Daß unsterblicher doch, denn Sorg' und Zürnen, die Freude
  Und ein goldener Tag täglich am Ende noch ist.

7

O, but you, who were even then at the crossroads when I
    Sank down before you, and you, comforting and consoling,
Showed me the way, you taught me to see what was great
    And to sing with serene joy, quietly like the gods;
Child of the gods! Will you appear to me, greet me once again,
    Talk to me a little longer, as before, about higher things?
Look! I weep in your presence, I must lament when I think further
    Of the noble times of the past; deep in my soul there is shame.
For so long, so long, though accustomed to you, I have sought you
    In all the wrong directions on the earth's dim paths,
Guardian spirit! But all in vain, and the years have come to nothing
    Since we walked and the evening bathed us in its uneasy glow.

8

Only you in the light, o heroine, you preserve the light,
    And your long suffering keeps you loving and kind;
Never are you lonely; there are playmates enough
    Where you bloom and rest under the year's roses;
And the Father himself, by means of the Muses'
    Soft exhalations, sends you gentle lullabies.
Yes, she is still there! From head to foot the Athenian,
    Quiet and poised as before, hovers in front of me.
And how, friendly spirit! From her clear contemplative brow,
    Blessed and sure, your radiance falls upon mortals;
So you proved to me, and you tell me, that I should repeat it
    To others, for others also question it, that joy
Is more immortal than care and anger
    And, in the end, the day shines golden.

9

So will ich, ihr Himmlischen! denn auch danken, und endlich
    Athmet aus leichter Brust wieder des Sängers Gebet.
Und wie, wenn ich mit ihr, auf sonniger Höhe mit ihr stand,
    Spricht belebend ein Gott innen vom Tempel mich an.
Leben will ich denn auch! schon grünt's! wie von heiliger Leier
    Ruft es von silbernen Bergen Apollons voran!
Komm! es war wie ein Traum! Die blutenden Fittige sind ja
    Schon genesen, verjüngt leben die Hoffnungen all.
Großes zu finden, ist viel, ist viel noch übrig, und wer so
    Liebte, gehet, er muß, gehet zu Göttern die Bahn.
Und geleitet ihr uns, ihr Weihestunden! ihr ernsten,
    Jugendlichen! o bleibt, heilige Ahnungen, ihr
Fromme Bitten! und ihr Begeisterungen und all ihr
    Guten Genien, die gerne bei Liebenden sind;
Bleibt so lange mit uns, bis wir auf gemeinsamem Boden
    Dort, wo die Seeligen all niederzukehren bereit,
Dort, wo die Adler sind, die Gestirne, die Boten des Vaters,
    Dort, wo die Musen, woher Helden und Liebende sind,
Dort uns, oder auch hier, auf thauender Insel begegnen,
    Wo die Unsrigen erst, blühend in Gärten gesellt,
Wo die Gesänge wahr, und länger die Frühlinge schön sind,
    Und von neuem ein Jahr unserer Seele beginnt.

9

So, heavenly one, I thank you once more and finally
    Breathe from a lighter breast as I offer my song again.
And, as before, when I stood with her on a sunny hill,
    A god speaks within me as if from a temple.
I will live then! Newly green! As if from a holy lyre,
    Apollo's silver mountains call us forward! Come!
It was like a dream, the wounds in your wings have already
    Healed, and, restored to new life, all your hopes come alive.
To find what's important is much, but there's still much
    Remaining, and when one loved as you did, he can only
Move on to the gods. You lead us, earnest ones, you consecrated hours!
    Youthful ones! o, stay with us, holy hints of the future,
Pious prayers, and you, inspirations, and all your good spirits,
    Who like to protect lovers; stay so long with us until,
Reunited on common ground where, when all blessed and
    Holy souls return to earth, there where the eagles are,
The planets, messengers of the fathers, there where the
    Muses and heroes and lovers still are, there we,
Or also here, will meet again on the dew-covered island,
    Where that which for once is ours will join like flowering
Gardens, all our poems are true, and spring stays lovely longer,
    And in another new year our souls can be born.

Stutgard
An Siegfried Schmidt

1

Wieder ein Glük ist erlebt. Die gefährliche Dürre geneset,
    Und die Schärfe des Lichts senget die Blüthe nicht mehr.
Offen steht jezt wieder ein Saal, und gesund ist der Garten,
    Und von Reegen erfrischt rauschet das glänzende Thal,
Hoch von Gewächsen, es schwellen die Bäch' und alle gebundnen
    Fittige wagen sich wieder ins Reich des Gesangs.
Voll ist die Luft von Fröhlichen jezt und die Stadt und der Hain ist
    Rings von zufriedenen Kindern des Himmels erfüllt.
Gerne begegnen sie sich, und irren untereinander,
    Sorgenlos, und es scheint keines zu wenig, zu viel.
Denn so ordnet das Herz es an, und zu athmen die Anmuth,
    Sie, die geschikliche, schenkt ihnen ein göttlicher Geist.
Aber die Wanderer auch sind wohlgeleitet und haben
    Kränze genug und Gesang, haben den heiligen Stab
Vollgeschmükt mit Trauben und Laub bei sich und der Fichte
    Schatten; von Dorfe zu Dorf jauchzt es, von Tage zu Tag,
Und wie Wagen, bespannt mit freiem Wilde, so ziehn die
    Berge voran und so träget und eilet der Pfad.

2

Aber meinest du nun, es haben die Thore vergebens
    Aufgethan und den Weg freudig die Götter gemacht?
Und es schenken umsonst zu des Gastmahls Fülle die Guten
    Nebst dem Weine noch auch Beeren und Honig und Obst?
Schenken das purpurne Licht zu Festgesängen und kühl und
    Ruhig zu tieferem Freundesgespräche die Nacht?
Hält ein Ernsteres dich, so spars dem Winter und willst du
    Freien, habe Gedult, Freier beglüket der Mai.

Stuttgart

To Siegfried Schmidt

1

Joy is lived once more. The dangerous dryness is healed
    And the sharpness of the light no longer singes the flower.
Again the great hall stands open, and the garden is healthy,
    And the glistening valley is refreshed by rain,
Its banks overgrown, the brook swells and the all-constricted
    Wings set forth again into the kingdom of song.
The air is full of glad beings now and the city and the grove
    Are surrounded and filled with the children of heaven.
They are happy to meet each other and get lost together
    Without a care, and nothing to them seems too much or too little.
For thus has the heart decreed, and to breathe the grace
    That is destined for them, sent as a gift by a godly spirit.
But the travelers also have good maps and possess
    Enough garlands and songs and have a holy staff
Richly decorated with grapes and leaves in the fir tree's
    Shadows; from town to town, day to day, there is rejoicing,
And like wagons drawn by wild beasts, the mountains
    Are pulled forward, and so the path hurries along.

2

But could it be that the gods, in subsiding, have thrown
    Open the doors and made a pathway for joy? And not
For nothing do they send to the banquet a bounty of good things,
    Not only wine but also berries and honey and fruit?
They give us the purple light of festival songs and coolness
    And calmness for the deeper conversations of friends at night?
If you have deep cares, save them for winter, and if you want
    To marry, have patience, courtship works better in May.

Jezt ist Anderes Noth, jezt komm' und feire des Herbstes
  Alte Sitte, noch jezt blühet die Edle mit uns.
Eins nur gilt für den Tag, das Vaterland und des Opfers
  Festlicher Flamme wirft jeder sein Eigenes zu.
Darum kränzt der gemeinsame Gott umsäuselnd das Haar uns,
  Und den eigenen Sinn schmelzet, wie Perlen, der Wein.
Diß bedeutet der Tisch, der geehrte, wenn, wie die Bienen,
  Rund um den Eichbaum, wir sizen und singen um ihn,
Diß der Pokale Klang, und darum zwinget die wilden
  Seelen der streitenden Männer zusammen der Chor.

3

Aber damit uns nicht, gleich Allzuklugen, entfliehe
  Diese neigende Zeit, komm' ich entgegen sogleich,
Bis an die Grenze des Lands, wo mir den lieben Geburtsort
  Und die Insel des Stroms blaues Gewässer umfließt.
Heilig ist mir der Ort, an beiden Ufern, der Fels auch,
  Der mit Garten und Haus grün aus den Wellen sich hebt.
Dort begegnen wir uns; o gütiges Licht! wo zuerst mich
  Deiner gefühlteren Stralen mich einer betraf.
Dort begann und beginnt das liebe Leben von neuem;
  Aber des Vaters Grab seh' ich und weine dir schon?
Wein' und halt' und habe den Freund und höre das Wort, das
  Einst mir in himmlischer Kunst Leiden der Liebe geheilt.
Andres erwacht! ich muß die Landesheroën ihm nennen,
  Barbarossa! dich auch, gütiger Kristoph, und dich,
Konradin! wie du fielst, so fallen Starke, der Epheu
  Grünt am Fels und die Burg dekt das bacchantische Laub,
Doch Vergangenes ist, wie Künftiges heilig den Sängern,
  Und in Tagen des Herbsts sühnen die Schatten wir uns.

Now there is another need, come now and celebrate fall's
    Old ritual, still now the noble blooms with us.
Only one thing counts for today, the native land; each to
    His own ability throws offerings to the festive flame.
In that way, the god of the people musses our hair with a garland,
    And our own consciousness melts like pearls in wine.
This is what the table means, so honored among us, when,
    Like bees around the oak tree, we sit and sing,
This the clanging of goblets, and in this way the wild souls
    Of quarrelsome men are forced to join in chorus.

3

But unlike those who are all too clever, though this
    Declining season flees, I come at once to meet it,
As far as the land's border, where the beloved birthplace
    Encircles the island of the river's blue water that I love.
On both banks including the stones, the place is holy to me,
    Which rises green from the waves along with garden and house.
There we meet each other, o gracious light, where first
    Your rays of consciousness touched my senses!
There began and now begins anew the love of life;
    But I see my father's grave and soon start to cry?
Cry and hold to a friend for support and hear the word, that
    Once through heavenly art healed all love's sufferings.
Other things awaken! I must name the heroes of the land,
    Barbarossa! You too, good Christoph, and you,
Conradin, fell as strong men fall, the ivy green
    On the rock and the castle covered with drunken leaves,
But the past, like days to come, are holy to singers,
    And we soothe ourselves in days of autumn shadows.

4

So der Gewaltgen gedenk und des herzerhebenden Schiksaals,
  Thatlos selber, und leicht, aber vom Aether doch auch
Angeschauet und fromm, wie die Alten, die göttlicherzognen
  Freudigen Dichter ziehn freudig das Land wir hinauf.
Groß ist das Werden umher. Dort von den äußersten Bergen
  Stammen der Jünglinge viel, steigen die Hügel herab.
Quellen rauschen von dort und hundert geschäfftige Bäche,
  Kommen bei Tag und Nacht nieder und bauen das Land.
Aber der Meister pflügt die Mitte des Landes, die Furchen
  Ziehet der Nekarstrom, ziehet den Seegen herab.
Und es kommen mit ihm Italiens Lüfte, die See schikt
  Ihre Wolken, sie schikt prächtige Sonnen mit ihm.
Darum wächset uns auch fast über das Haupt die gewaltge
  Fülle, denn hieher ward, hier in die Ebne das Gut
Reicher den Lieben gebracht, den Landesleuten, doch neidet
  Keiner an Bergen dort ihnen die Gärten, den Wein
Oder das üppige Gras und das Korn und die glühenden Bäume,
  Die am Wege gereiht über den Wanderern stehn.

5

Aber indeß wir schaun und die mächtige Freude durchwandeln,
  Fliehet der Weg und der Tag uns, wie den Trunkenen, hin.
Denn mit heiligem Laub umkränzt erhebet die Stadt schon
  Die gepriesene, dort leuchtend ihr priesterlich Haupt.
Herrlich steht sie und hält den Rebenstab und die Tanne
  Hoch in die seeligen purpurnen Wolken empor.
Sei uns hold! dem Gast und dem Sohn, o Fürstin der Heimath!
  Glükliches Stutgard, nimm freundlich den Fremdling mir auf!
Immer hast du Gesang mit Flöten und Saiten gebilligt,
  Wie ich glaub' und des Lieds kindlich Geschwäz und der Mühn
Süße Vergessenheit bei gegenwärtigem Geiste,

4

Thinking about the powerful ones and the fate that lifts
    Our hearts, ourselves slight and without deeds, but obvious
To the Upper Air and pious as the ancients, joyful poets
    Instructed by God, we joyously roam the land. The growth
All around us is vast. Many young people who are born there,
    Near the outermost mountains, descend from the hills.
Wellsprings rush from there, and a hundred busy brooks,
    Come down by day and night to cultivate the land.
But the Master plows at the land's center, shapes furrows
    In the Neckar's stream and draws down all blessings.
And the Italian breezes come along with him, the sea sends
    Its clouds, it sends glorious sunshine with him.
It is here that the mighty abundance grows almost over
    Our heads, for it is here, in the lowlands, that cherished
Wealth is brought to our country's people, but none
    Of the mountain people begrudge them wine,
Gardens, or luxurious grass and corn, and shining trees
    Stand along the road above the travelers.

5

But while we look on and experience powerful joy,
    Our path and our day flee us like a drunk,
For the city raises her priestly head to be
    Exalted with garlands of holy leaves.
Glorious, she stands with wine staff and fir tree
    Raised high in the holy purple clouds. Be gracious
To us, to guest and son, o prince of the land!
    Fortunate Stuttgart, for me, receive the stranger with kindness!
You have always approved of songs on flute or strings,
    So I believe, and the song's childish babbling
And labor's sweet forgetfulness among actual minds,

Drum erfreuest du auch gerne den Sängern das Herz.
Aber ihr, ihr Größeren auch, ihr Frohen, die allzeit
    Leben und walten, erkannt, oder gewaltiger auch,
Wenn ihr wirket und schafft in heiliger Nacht und allein herrscht
    Und allmächtig empor ziehet ein ahnendes Volk,
Bis die Jünglinge sich der Väter droben erinnern,
    Mündig und hell vor euch steht der besonnene Mensch —

6

Engel des Vaterlands! o ihr, vor denen das Auge,
    Sei's auch stark und das Knie bricht dem vereinzelten Mann,
Daß er halten sich muß an die Freund' und bitten die Theuern,
    Daß sie tragen mit ihm all die beglükende Last,
Habt, o Gütige, Dank für den und alle die Andern,
    Die mein Leben, mein Gut unter den Sterblichen sind.
Aber die Nacht kommt! laß uns eilen, zu feiern das Herbstfest
    Heut noch! voll ist das Herz, aber das Leben ist kurz,
Und was uns der himmlische Tag zu sagen geboten,
    Das zu nennen, mein Schmidt! reichen wir beide nicht aus.
Trefliche bring' ich dir und das Freudenfeuer wird hoch auf
    Schlagen und heiliger soll sprechen das kühnere Wort.
Siehe! da ist es rein! und des Gottes freundliche Gaaben
    Die wir theilen, sie sind zwischen den Liebenden nur.
Anderes nicht – o kommt! o macht es wahr! denn allein ja
    Bin ich und niemand nimmt mir von der Stirne den Traum?
Kommt und reicht, ihr Lieben, die Hand! das möge genug seyn,
    Aber die größere Lust sparen dem Enkel wir auf.

Therefore you always please singers and gladden the heart.
Yet you still greater ones, you the glad, who live at all times
    And hold sway, known, or powerful still,
When you work and strive in holy night and rule alone
    And with your almighty power lift a people through signs,
Until the young people remember their forefathers above them
    And shining before you stands the thoughtful man—

6

Angel of our native country, o you, before whom the vision
    Is equally strong, and the knees of a man in solitude buckle,
So he must look to his friends for support and ask the dear ones
    To help him bear all the burden of his joy,
O good ones, accept my thanks for him and all the others,
    Who are my life and wealth among mortals.
But the night comes! Let us hurry to celebrate this very day
    The autumn festival! The heart is full, but life is short,
And what the heavenly day has commanded, we must speak of.
    To make them known, my dear Schmidt, is too much for you and me.
I bring you excellent people and a festival fire that strikes on high,
    And audacious words that should be spoken with more reverence.
Look! There it's pure! And God's generous gifts,
    Which we share, when joined by love, remain together.
Nothing else can—come, make it true! For I am alone.
    Can no one lift the dreams from my brow?
Come and hold out your hands, loved ones! May that be enough
    For us, but for the grandson we save the greatest pleasure.

Brod und Wein
An Heinze

1

Rings um ruhet die Stadt; still wird die erleuchtete Gasse,
    Und, mit Fakeln geschmükt, rauschen die Wagen hinweg.
Satt gehn heim von Freuden des Tags zu ruhen die Menschen,
    Und Gewinn und Verlust wäget ein sinniges Haupt
Wohlzufrieden zu Haus; leer steht von Trauben und Blumen,
    Und von Werken der Hand ruht der geschäfftige Markt.
Aber das Saitenspiel tönt fern aus Gärten; vieleicht, daß
    Dort ein Liebendes spielt oder ein einsamer Mann
Ferner Freunde gedenkt und der Jugendzeit; und die Brunnen
    Immerquillend und frisch rauschen an duftendem Beet.
Still in dämmriger Luft ertönen geläutete Gloken,
    Und der Stunden gedenk rufet ein Wächter die Zahl.
Jezt auch kommet ein Wehn und regt die Gipfel des Hains auf,
    Sieh! und das Schattenbild unserer Erde, der Mond
Kommet geheim nun auch; die Schwärmerische, die Nacht kommt,
    Voll mit Sternen und wohl wenig bekümmert um uns,
Glänzt die Erstaunende dort, die Fremdlingin unter den Menschen
    Über Gebirgeshöhn traurig und prächtig herauf.

2

Wunderbar ist die Gunst der Hocherhabnen und niemand
    Weiß von wannen und was einem geschiehet von ihr.
So bewegt sie die Welt und die hoffende Seele der Menschen,
    Selbst kein Weiser versteht, was sie bereitet, denn so
Will es der oberste Gott, der sehr dich liebet, und darum
    Ist noch lieber, wie sie, dir der besonnene Tag.
Aber zuweilen liebt auch klares Auge den Schatten
    Und versuchet zu Lust, eh' es die Noth ist, den Schlaf,

Bread and Wine

To Heinse

1

Around us the town is quiet, quiet the street in lamplight,
  And with torches flaming, coaches run here and there.
Satisfied with the pleasures of their day, men go home to rest,
  And weighing in their pensive heads the profit and loss,
They're happy to be home; empty now of grapes and flowers
  And goods made by hand, the market stands are quiet.
But the music of strings can be heard from distant gardens;
  Perhaps one in love is playing, or a lonesome man thinking
Of distant friends and the days of his youth; and the fountains
  Always welling new murmurs among fragrant beds of flowers.
Softly in the twilight air, the church bells ring,
  And the time is called by a watcher of the hours.
Now a breeze rises, and stirs the tips of the grove,
  Look! And the moon, the shadow image of our world,
Secretly rises also; and the visionary night approaches,
  Replete with stars and indifferent to us entirely,
The astonishing one, a stranger to all things human,
  Mournful and brilliant, shines over the mountain tops.

2

It's wonderful to share this exalted one's favors, and no one
  Knows the source of all that flows from her,
So she excites the world and the hopeful souls of men,
  Not even a wise man understands what she's preparing, for this
God the Highest has willed, who loves you so much, therefore
  Is clearer to you than the common sense of day.
But there are times when the clearest eye also loves shadows
  And tasting sleep for pleasure before sleep demands,

Oder es blikt auch gern ein treuer Mann in die Nacht hin,
 Ja, es ziemet sich ihr Kränze zu weihn und Gesang,
Weil den Irrenden sie geheiliget ist und den Todten,
 Selber aber besteht, ewig, in freiestem Geist.
Aber sie muß uns auch, daß in der zaudernden Weile,
 Daß im Finstern für uns einiges Haltbare sei,
Uns die Vergessenheit und das Heiligtrunkene gönnen,
 Gönnen das strömende Wort, das, wie die Liebenden, sei,
Schlummerlos und vollern Pokal und kühneres Leben,
 Heilig Gedächtniß auch, wachend zu bleiben bei Nacht.

3

Auch verbergen umsonst das Herz im Busen, umsonst nur
 Halten den Muth noch wir, Meister und Knaben, denn wer
Möcht' es hindern und wer möcht' uns die Freude verbieten?
 Göttliches Feuer auch treibet, bei Tag und bei Nacht,
Aufzubrechen. So komm! daß wir das Offene schauen,
 Daß ein Eigenes wir suchen, so weit es auch ist.
Fest bleibt Eins; es sei um Mittag oder es gehe
 Bis in die Mitternacht, immer bestehet ein Maas,
Allen gemein, doch jeglichem auch ist eignes beschieden,
 Dahin gehet und kommt jeder, wohin er es kann.
Drum! und spotten des Spotts mag gern frohlokkender Wahnsinn,
 Wenn er in heiliger Nacht plözlich die Sänger ergreift.
Drum an den Isthmos komm! dorthin, wo das offene Meer rauscht
 Am Parnaß und der Schnee delphische Felsen umglänzt,
Dort ins Land des Olymps, dort auf die Höhe Cithärons,
 Unter die Fichten dort, unter die Trauben, von wo
Thebe drunten und Ismenos rauscht im Lande des Kadmos,
 Dorther kommt und zurük deutet der kommende Gott.

Or a faithful man will also look gladly into the night,
    Yes, it's fitting to dedicate songs to her starry diadem,
Since she is holy to the dead and those who've lost their way,
    But by herself she stands, eternally free in spirit,
But to us also, so that, in the moment's hesitation,
    Something at least endures for us in the dark,
She grants us forgetfulness and holy drunkenness,
    Grants us the rushing word, sleepless as lovers,
With our wine cups full, and full, audacious lives,
    Holy memory, too, keeps us wide-eyed at night.

3

And, in vain, we hide our hearts in our breasts, in vain
    We hold our courage in check, master and boy,
For who would hinder us, who forbid our joy?
    By day and night, divine fire drives us on,
Cracks us open. So come! to gaze at the Open,
    To seek what is ours, remote as it may be.
One thing remains; at noon or just before midnight,
    A measure always endures, common to all,
Though everyone is apportioned his own,
    Each coming and going according to his reach.
Well! Let jubilant madness mock at the scorners
    When holy night suddenly seizes the poets.
Off to the Isthmus, therefore, where the open sea roars
    Near Parnassus and snow glistens on Delphic stones,
There in Olympian lands, to the heights of Cithaeron,
    Under the pine trees, under grape clusters, from which
Thebes and Ismenos descend, in the land of Cadmus,
    From there the approaching god comes and points back.

4

Seeliges Griechenland! du Haus der Himmlischen alle,
    Also ist wahr, was einst wir in der Jugend gehört?
Festlicher Saal! der Boden ist Meer! und Tische die Berge,
    Wahrlich zu einzigem Brauche vor Alters gebaut!
Aber die Thronen, wo? die Tempel, und wo die Gefäße,
    Wo mit Nectar gefüllt, Göttern zu Lust der Gesang?
Wo, wo leuchten sie denn, die fernhintreffenden Sprüche?
    Delphi schlummert und wo tönet das große Geschik?
Wo ist das schnelle? wo brichts, allgegenwärtigen Glüks voll
    Donnernd aus heiterer Luft über die Augen herein?
Vater Aether! so riefs und flog von Zunge zu Zunge
    Tausendfach, es ertrug keiner das Leben allein;
Ausgetheilet erfreut solch Gut und getauschet, mit Fremden,
    Wirds ein Jubel, es wächst schlafend des Wortes Gewalt
Vater! heiter! und hallt, so weit es gehet, das uralt
    Zeichen, von Eltern geerbt, treffend und schaffend hinab.
Denn so kehren die Himmlischen ein, tiefschütternd gelangt so
    Aus den Schatten herab unter die Menschen ihr Tag.

5

Unempfunden kommen sie erst, es streben entgegen
    Ihnen die Kinder, zu hell kommet, zu blendend das Glük,
Und es scheut sie der Mensch, kaum weiß zu sagen ein Halbgott,
    Wer mit Nahmen sie sind, die mit den Gaaben ihm nahn.
Aber der Muth von ihnen ist groß, es füllen das Herz ihm
    Ihre Freuden und kaum weiß er zu brauchen das Gut,
Schafft, verschwendet und fast ward ihm Unheiliges heilig,
    Das er mit seegnender Hand thörig und gütig berührt.
Möglichst dulden die Himmlischen diß; dann aber in Wahrheit
    Kommen sie selbst und gewohnt werden die Menschen des Glüks
Und des Tags und zu schaun die Offenbaren, das Antliz

4

Blessed land of the Greeks! Home of all the gods,
    So it is true then, what we first heard in youth?
Festive hall whose floor is the sea, whose tables are
    Mountains truly built in ancient times for a singular need!
But where are the thrones, the temple, and where the vessels,
    Filled with nectar, to delight the gods with songs?
Where, where then, do they shine, the far-reaching truths?
    Delphi is asleep, and where does the great fate resound?
Where is the quick? Where breaks through the full, all-pervasive joy,
    Out of clear skies, thundering to us above our eyes?
Father Aether! one cried, and it flew from tongue to tongue
    A thousand fold, for no one could bear such a life alone;
Shared, such wealth gives joy, and when traded with strangers
    Turns to exaltation, and its power grows in sleep,
Father! Clear one! The cry resounds as far as it travels, ancient
    Signs handed down from elders, creating and striking down
From above. As the heavenly enter, deeply shaking,
    So their day travels out from shadows and down to man.

5

Unnoticed at first, they come, and the children gravitate
    Toward them, the joy too bright, too dazzling,
And the men become afraid, a demigod hardly knows what to say
    Their names might be, who come so near with gifts.
But their courage is very great, they fill his heart with their joy,
    And he hardly knows what to do with such wealth,
Made and then squandered, the holy quickly becomes unholy,
    On which he, with consecrating hand, foolishly, indulgently
Depended. The heavenly bear it as long as they can, but when
    In fact they arrive, men grow accustomed to joy,
To day, to the gods stripped bare, and to their faces,

Derer, welche, schon längst Eines und Alles genannt,
Tief die verschwiegene Brust mit freier Genüge gefüllet,
Und zuerst und allein alles Verlangen beglükt;
So ist der Mensch; wenn da ist das Gut, und es sorget mit Gaaben
Selber ein Gott für ihn, kennet und sieht er es nicht.
Tragen muß er, zuvor; nun aber nennt er sein Liebstes,
Nun, nun müssen dafür Worte, wie Blumen, entstehn.

6

Und nun denkt er zu ehren in Ernst die seeligen Götter,
Wirklich und wahrhaft muß alles verkünden ihr Lob.
Nichts darf schauen das Licht, was nicht den Hohen gefället,
Vor den Aether gebührt müßigversuchendes nicht.
Drum in der Gegenwart der Himmlischen würdig zu stehen,
Richten in herrlichen Ordnungen Völker sich auf
Untereinander und baun die schönen Tempel und Städte
Vest und edel, sie gehn über Gestaden empor—
Aber wo sind sie? wo blühn die Bekannten, die Kronen des Festes?
Thebe welkt und Athen; rauschen die Waffen nicht mehr
In Olympia, nicht die goldnen Wagen des Kampfspiels,
Und bekränzen sich denn nimmer die Schiffe Korinths?
Warum schweigen auch sie, die alten heilgen Theater?
Warum freuet sich denn nicht der geweihete Tanz?
Warum zeichnet, wie sonst, die Stirne des Mannes ein Gott nicht,
Drükt den Stempel, wie sonst, nicht dem Getroffenen auf?
Oder er kam auch selbst und nahm des Menschen Gestalt an
Und vollendet' und schloß tröstend das himmlische Fest.

Which once and for all, finally have names.
Their breasts were filled deeply with quiet contentment,
    And alone and from the start, every desire was met;
Such is man; when wealth is present and he's tended with gifts
    By no less than a god, he sees and understands nothing.
First he must suffer; but now he names his most loved things,
    Now, now, he must instead find words arising like flowers.

6

And now he thinks to honor the holy gods in earnest,
    In truth and in deed, all must repeat their praise.
Nothing must see the light but what pleases the high ones.
    The Upper Air was never made for such idle endeavors.
So to stand proudly in the gods' presence, nations rise up
    And build in glorious order, competing with each other,
Gracious temples and cities; noble and firm,
    They tower high above shores—but where are they?
Laurels of the festival, where do the famous ones bloom?
    Thebes is withered, and Athens;
No more do weapons ring out in Olympia,
    Nor the games' golden chariots, and are
Corinthian ships no longer covered in garlands?
    Where are they, too, the old holy theaters?
Why is the sacred, holy dance no longer celebrated?
    Why, as never before, is the brow of man unmarked by a god?
Or he would come as himself and take a human shape,
    And, comforting everyone, bring an end to the heavenly feast.

7

Aber Freund! wir kommen zu spät. Zwar leben die Götter,
    Aber über dem Haupt droben in anderer Welt.
Endlos wirken sie da und scheinens wenig zu achten,
    Ob wir leben, so sehr schonen die Himmlischen uns.
Denn nicht immer vermag ein schwaches Gefäß sie zu fassen,
    Nur zu Zeiten erträgt göttliche Fülle der Mensch.
Traum von ihnen ist drauf das Leben. Aber das Irrsaal
    Hilft, wie Schlummer und stark machet die Noth und die Nacht,
Biß daß Helden genug in der ehernen Wiege gewachsen,
    Herzen an Kraft, wie sonst, ähnlich den Himmlischen sind.
Donnernd kommen sie drauf. Indessen dünket mir öfters
    Besser zu schlafen, wie so ohne Genossen zu seyn,
So zu harren und was zu thun indeß und zu sagen,
    Weiß ich nicht und wozu Dichter in dürftiger Zeit?
Aber sie sind, sagst du, wie des Weingotts heilige Priester,
    Welche von Lande zu Land zogen in heiliger Nacht.

8

Nemlich, als vor einiger Zeit, uns dünket sie lange,
    Aufwärts stiegen sie all, welche das Leben beglükt,
Als der Vater gewandt sein Angesicht von den Menschen,
    Und das Trauern mit Recht über der Erde begann,
Als erschienen zu lezt ein stiller Genius, himmlisch
    Tröstend, welcher des Tags Ende verkündet' und schwand,
Ließ zum Zeichen, daß einst er da gewesen und wieder
    Käme, der himmlische Chor einige Gaaben zurük,
Derer menschlich, wie sonst, wir uns zu freuen vermöchten,
    Denn zur Freude, mit Geist, wurde das Größre zu groß
Unter den Menschen und noch, noch fehlen die Starken zu höchsten
    Freuden, aber es lebt stille noch einiger Dank.
Brod ist der Erde Frucht, doch ists vom Lichte gesegnet,

7

But, friend, we've come too late. Though the gods are living,
    Over our heads, above in a different world,
Endlessly they do their work, and seem so to protect us
    They pay little attention to whether we live or die.
For a delicate vessel can't always contain them,
    Only at times can men bear the gods' fullness.
Even after life, we dream of them. But that labyrinth helps,
    Like sleep; distress and the night make us strong,
Until the heroes grow large enough in their steel cradles,
    And only when our hearts are strong, as before, can we match
The heavenly. Then they come thundering. Meanwhile, I often
    Think it's better to sleep than to be without friends,
Always waiting, and what to say or do in the meantime,
    I don't know, and of what use are poets in such meager times?
But they are, as you say, like the holy priests of the wine god,
    Who roam from land to land in the holiness of night.

8

For some time, to us it seems long,
    Everyone rose up whose light had blessed us
When the father turned his face away from men,
    And all over the earth, quite rightly, they began to mourn;
It appeared that at last a genius had come, offering heavenly
    Comfort, and he who named the day's end then disappeared,
Leaving a token that once they were here and once would
    Come again; the heavenly chorus left gifts behind,
For, to spiritual joy, the great had become too great
    Among men, and still, still, lacking the strength
For God's joy, they still offer silent thanksgiving.
    Bread is the fruit of earth, yet touched by the blessings
Of light, and from the thundering god, comes the joy of wine.

Und vom donnernden Gott kommet die Freude des Weins.
Darum denken wir auch dabei der Himmlischen, die sonst
  Da gewesen und die kehren in richtiger Zeit,
Darum singen sie auch mit Ernst die Sänger den Weingott
  Und nicht eitel erdacht tönet dem Alten das Lob.

9

Ja! sie sagen mit Recht, er söhne den Tag mit der Nacht aus,
  Führe des Himmels Gestirn ewig hinunter, hinauf,
Allzeit froh, wie das Laub der immergrünenden Fichte,
  Das er liebt, und der Kranz, den er von Epheu gewählt,
Weil er bleibet und selbst die Spur der entflohenen Götter
  Götterlosen hinab unter das Finstere bringt.
Was der Alten Gesang von Kindern Gottes geweissagt,
  Siehe! wir sind es, wir; Frucht von Hesperien ists!
Wunderbar und genau ists als an Menschen erfüllet,
  Glaube, wer es geprüft! aber so vieles geschieht,
Keines wirket, denn wir sind herzlos, Schatten, bis unser
  Vater Aether erkannt jeden und allen gehört.
Aber indessen kommt als Fakelschwinger des Höchsten
  Sohn, der Syrier, unter die Schatten herab.
Seelige Weise sehns; ein Lächeln aus der gefangnen
  Seele leuchtet, dem Licht thauet ihr Auge noch auf.
Sanfter träumet und schläft in Armen der Erde der Titan,
  Selbst der neidische, selbst Cerberus trinket und schläft.

Thereby, partaking of them, we think of the heavenly,
Who once were here and will return at the moment prepared,
 Therefore poets sing earnest songs to the wine god
And never idly compose songs of praise for the ancients.

9

Yes, they say rightly, he reconciles day with night,
 Drives the heaven's stars endlessly up and down,
As glad always as the green boughs of the evergreen,
 Which he loves, and the wreath made of ivy
Chosen because it lasts and, to the godless below
 In their gloom, contains the vanished god's essence.
The ancient song foretells what God knows of his children.
 Look! We are those very same ones; it is Hesperian fruit!
And so quite perfectly it has been fulfilled in man.
 Believe, since it has been proven! But so much happens,
Nothing succeeds, because we're heartless, mere shadows
 Until our Father Aether is known and heard by all.
Meanwhile, however, the son of the highest, the Syrian,
 Comes down through the shadows bearing his torch.
The wise men are happy to see it, in their captive souls
 A radiant smile, and the light thaws out their eyes.
The Titans sleep gently and dream in the arms of earth;
 Even Cerberus, that envious one, drinks and goes to sleep.

Heimkunft

An die Verwandten

1

Drinn in den Alpen ists noch helle Nacht und die Wolke,
    Freudiges dichtend, sie dekt drinnen das gähnende Thal.
Dahin, dorthin toset und stürzt die scherzende Bergluft,
    Schroff durch Tannen herab glänzet und schwindet ein Stral.
Langsam eilt und kämpft das freudigschauernde Chaos,
    Jung an Gestalt, doch stark, feiert es liebenden Streit
Unter den Felsen, es gährt und wankt in den ewigen Schranken,
    Denn bacchantischer zieht drinnen der Morgen herauf.
Denn es wächst unendlicher dort das Jahr und die heilgen
    Stunden, die Tage, sie sind kühner geordnet, gemischt.
Dennoch merket die Zeit der Gewittervogel und zwischen
    Bergen, hoch in der Luft weilt er und rufet den Tag.
Jezt auch wachet und schaut in der Tiefe drinnen das Dörflein
    Furchtlos, Hohem vertraut, unter den Gipfeln hinauf.
Wachstum ahnend, denn schon, wie Blize, fallen die alten
    Wasserquellen, der Grund unter den Stürzenden dampft,
Echo tönet umher, und die unermeßliche Werkstatt
    Reget bei Tag und Nacht, Gaaben versendend, den Arm.

2

Ruhig glänzen indeß die silbernen Höhen darüber,
    Voll mit Rosen ist schon droben der leuchtende Schnee.
Und noch höher hinauf wohnt über dem Lichte der reine
    Seelige Gott vom Spiel heiliger Stralen erfreut.
Stille wohnt er allein und hell erscheinet sein Antlitz,
    Der ätherische scheint Leben zu geben geneigt,
Freude zu schaffen, mit uns, wie oft, wenn, kundig des Maases,
    Kundig der Athmenden auch zögernd und schonend der Gott

Homecoming
To his Relatives

1

There in the Alps is another bright night, and the clouds,
    As they cover the wide-open valley, are intent on joy.
This way and that, the playful mountain air plunges and roars,
    Steeply through the pine forest, a beam of light falls and is lost.
Slowly it hurries and struggles, this chaos shaking with joy,
    With youthful shape, yet strong, celebrates love's strife;
Seething amid the rocks, it staggers within its eternal boundaries,
    More drunkenly now, morning approaches within.
For more infinitely there, the year grows and the holy
    Hours, and the days are various and well-ordered.
Yet the bird of thunder marks the time between mountains,
    High in the air, he waits and announces the day.
Deep inside now, the little village also awakens and fearlessly
    Looks far off, where they see the high familiar peaks.
Growing, they know when the ancient welling-up waters
    Fall like lightning and the ground below is soaked by the plunge,
Echoes sound all around, and the measureless workshop,
    Always in motion, sends gifts out day and night.

2

In the meantime, quietly above, the silvery peaks gleam,
    The luminous snow up there is filled with roses.
And even higher, over the light, there is the pure
    Blessed God, whose holy beams are joyful in play.
He lives alone in silence, and his bright face now shines,
    The ethereal one seems inclined to give forth life,
To create joy with us as often, when, aware of the measure,
    Aware of those who breathe, also hesitating and modest,

Wohlgediegenes Glük den Städten und Häußern und milde
    Reegen, zu öffnen das Land, brütende Wolken, und euch,
Trauteste Lüfte dann, euch, sanfte Frühlinge, sendet,
    Und mit langsamer Hand Traurige wieder erfreut,
Wenn er die Zeiten erneut, der Schöpferische, die stillen
    Herzen der alternden Menschen erfrischt und ergreifft,
Und hinab in die Tiefe wirkt, und öffnet und aufhellt,
    Wie ers liebet, und jezt wieder ein Leben beginnt,
Anmuth blühet, wie einst, und gegenwärtiger Geist kömmt,
    Und ein freudiger Muth wieder die Fittige schwellt.

3

Vieles sprach ich zu ihm, denn, was auch Dichtende sinnen
    Oder singen, es gilt meistens den Engeln und ihm;
Vieles bat ich, zu lieb dem Vaterlande, damit nicht
    Ungebeten uns einst plözlich befiele der Geist;
Vieles für euch auch, die im Vaterlande besorgt sind,
    Denen der heilige Dank lächelnd die Flüchtlinge bringt,
Landesleute! für euch, indessen wiegte der See mich,
    Und der Ruderer saß ruhig und lobte die Fahrt.
Weit in des Sees Ebene wars Ein freudiges Wallen
    Unter den Seegeln und jezt blühet und hellet die Stadt
Dort in der Frühe sich auf, wohl her von schattigen Alpen
    Kommt geleitet und ruht nun in dem Hafen das Schiff.
Warm ist das Ufer hier und freundlich offene Thale,
    Schön von Pfaden erhellt grünen und schimmern mich an.
Gärten stehen gesellt und die glänzende Knospe beginnt schon,
    Und des Vogels Gesang ladet den Wanderer ein.
Alles scheinet vertraut, der vorübereilende Gruß auch
    Scheint von Freunden, es scheint jegliche Miene verwandt.

God sends well-apportioned fortune to cities and houses
    And mild rain to open the land and brooding clouds, and you,
Most loved breezes, you, sweet spring, are sent,
    And, once again, with a slow hand, the creative one
Makes sad ones glad when he renews the seasons,
    He refreshes and embraces the quiet hearts of the old,
And works to open and brighten the lower depths,
    As he loves to do, and now life begins again,
And beauty blossoms as before, and a more courageous spirit
    Comes to be among us, wings again unfurled.

3

I said much to him, for whatever poets know
    And sing, it mostly concerns the angels or him;
Much I asked for love of my country, so the spirit,
    Without warning, would not set upon us one day;
To whom, countrymen, holy gratitude brings exiles
    Back with a smile! Meanwhile, the sea rocked me,
And the rudder-man sat peacefully, praising the journey.
    Out on the even lake, pleasant waves lifted beneath
The sails, and now the town brightened and flourished,
    There in early morning shadows cast by the Alps,
And now the boat calmly comes into its harbor.
    The shore is warm here, and the valleys friendly
And open, paths shine at me, illuminated in greenness.
    Gardens are located next to other gardens,
And already the glistening buds begin to open,
    And a bird's song welcomes the traveler home.
Everything feels familiar, even a hasty greeting seems
    That of a friend, every face resembles one of the family.

4

Freilich wohl! das Geburtsland ists, der Boden der Heimath,
    Was du suchest, es ist nahe, begegnet dir schon.
Und umsonst nicht steht, wie ein Sohn, am wellenumrauschten
    Thor' und siehet und sucht liebende Nahmen für dich,
Mit Gesang ein wandernder Mann, glükseeliges Lindau!
    Eine der gastlichen Pforten des Landes ist diß,
Reizend hinauszugehn in die vielversprechende Ferne,
    Dort, wo die Wunder sind, dort, wo das göttliche Wild
Hoch in die Ebnen herab der Rhein die verwegene Bahn bricht,
    Und aus Felsen hervor ziehet das jauchzende Thal,
Dort hinein, durchs helle Gebirg, nach Komo zu wandern,
    Oder hinab, wie der Tag wandelt, den offenen See;
Aber reizender mir bist du, geweihete Pforte!
    Heimzugehn, wo bekannt blühende Wege mir sind,
Dort zu besuchen das Land und die schönen Thale des Nekars,
    Und die Wälder, das Grün heiliger Bäume, wo gern
Sich die Eiche gesellt mit stillen Birken und Buchen,
    Und in Bergen ein Ort freundlich gefangen mich nimmt.

5

Dort empfangen sie mich. O Stimme der Stadt, der Mutter!
    O du triffest, du regst Langegelerntes mir auf!
Dennoch sind sie es noch! noch blühet die Sonn' und die Freud' euch,
    O ihr Liebsten! und fast heller im Auge, wie sonst.
Ja! das Alte noch ists! Es gedeihet und reifet, doch keines
    Was da lebet und liebt, lässet die Treue zurük.
Aber das Beste, der Fund, der unter des heiligen Friedens
    Bogen lieget, er ist Jungen und Alten gespart.
Thörig red ich. Es ist die Freude. Doch morgen und künftig
    Wenn wir gehen und schaun draußen das lebende Feld
Unter den Blüthen des Baums, in den Feiertagen des Frühlings

4

And, of course, your native country, the soil of home,
    Which you seek, is near, will meet you soon.
And not by chance, like a son, stands gazing by the gate
    Surrounded by the sound of waves, seeking loving names
For you in his poem, a wandering man, the blissful Lindau!
    It's not the least of our land's welcoming gateways,
Urging men to go out into the promised distance,
    There, where the wonders are, there, where the godlike
Wild animals, far up the Rhine, break their way through thickets
    And paths, and out of rocks comes the exultant valley,
Wander there, through the brightly lit mountain range
    Toward Como, or, as the day drifts on, to the open lake;
But you are alluring to me, sacred gateway!
    Urging me home, where I know blossoming paths,
There to visit the land and the lovely valleys of the Neckar
    And the woods' green trees so holy to me, where the oak
Happily meets the quiet birch and beech trees, and in
    The mountains, one place holds me agreeably captive.

5

They receive me there, voice of my town, my mother!
    Things I learned long ago which move and stir me!
But they are still themselves, still their sun and joy
    Blossom to me, o my dear ones, radiantly as ever.
Yes, it's all as it used to be. It thrives and grows ripe,
    Yet nothing that lives and loves there ever loses its faith.
But the best thing of all, the underlying discovery beneath
    The radiant arc of peace, is reserved for young and old.
In my joy, I speak like a fool. Yet tomorrow and in the future,
    When we go outside to see the living field,
Under the trees in blossom, on holidays in spring,

Red' und hoff' ich mit euch vieles, ihr Lieben! davon.
Vieles hab' ich gehört vom großen Vater und habe
   Lange geschwiegen von ihm, welcher die wandernde Zeit
Droben in Höhen erfrischt, und waltet über Gebirgen
   Der gewähret uns bald himmlische Gaaben und ruft
Hellern Gesang und schikt viel gute Geister. O säumt nicht,
   Kommt, Erhaltenden ihr! Engel des Jahres! und ihr,

6

Engel des Haußes, kommt! in die Adern alle des Lebens,
   Alle freuend zugleich, theile das Himmlische sich!
Adle! verjünge! damit nichts Menschlichgutes, damit nicht
   Eine Stunde des Tags ohne die Frohen und auch
Solche Freude, wie jezt, wenn Liebende wieder sich finden,
   Wie es gehört für sie, schiklich geheiliget sei.
Wenn wir seegnen das Mahl, wen darf ich nennen und wenn wir
   Ruhn vom Leben des Tags, saget, wie bring' ich den Dank?
Nenn' ich den Hohen dabei? Unschikliches liebet ein Gott nicht,
   Ihn zu fassen, ist fast unsere Freude zu klein.
Schweigen müssen wir oft; es fehlen heilige Nahmen,
   Herzen schlagen und doch bleibet die Rede zurük?
Aber ein Saitenspiel leiht jeder Stunde die Töne,
   Und erfreuet vieleicht Himmlische, welche sich nahn.
Das bereitet und so ist auch beinahe die Sorge
   Schon befriediget, die unter das Freudige kam.
Sorgen, wie diese, muß, gern oder nicht, in der Seele
   Tragen ein Sänger und oft, aber die anderen nicht.

I'll speak and hope many such things with you, dear ones.
  For much I have heard of him, the Great Father, and have
    Long kept silent about him, who, on summits up above,
  Refreshes Time as it passes, and rules over the high mountain
    Ranges, who will soon grant heavenly gifts and call forth
  Luminous songs and send us many good spirits. Delay no more,
    Come now, preservers, angels of the year! And you,

6

Angels of our house, come! In the veins of all life,
  Re-enter now, gladdening all, share the heavenly with us!
Noble and new! Until nothing is humanly good,
  No hour of the day lacks joy or only such joy
Known by lovers when they find each other again,
  As it belongs to them, fateful as that made sacred is.
When we bless the meal, whom shall I name and when we rest
  From the life of days, tell me, to whom shall I give thanks?
Should I therefore name the most holy? A god doesn't love
  What's out of place, and our joy is too small to embrace him.
We must often be silent; we lack holy names, hearts
  May pound, yet why do our words fall short?
But a lyre lends every hour the right mood, and perhaps
  It will please the holy ones when they draw near. ·
This made ready, there is nothing of the worry
  That made our days dark and undermined our joy.
Whether he likes it or not, in his soul a singer must often
  Hold these cares, but not, however, the others.

Die Entschlafenen

Einen vergänglichen Tag lebt' ich und wuchs mit den Meinen,
  Eins um's andere schon schläft mir und fliehet dahin.
Doch ihr Schlafenden wacht am Herzen mir, in verwandter
  Seele ruhet von euch mir das entfliehende Bild.
Und lebendiger lebt ihr dort, wo des göttlichen Geistes
  Freude die Alternden all, alle die Todten verjüngt.

The Departed

In a day that passed swiftly, I lived and grew with my family.
  One by one, they go from me into their sleep.
Yet you sleepers awaken in my heart, and a fleeting image
  Of each fugitive one rests in my kindred soul.
More alive, you live there, where the godly spirit of joy
  Makes young once more the aging and the dead.

Lebensalter

Ihr Städte des Euphrats!
Ihr Gassen von Palmyra!
Ihr Säulenwälder in der Eb'ne der Wüste,
Was seid ihr?
Euch hat die Kronen,
Dieweil ihr über die Gränze
Der Othmenden seid gegangen,
Von Himmlischen der Rauchdampf und
Hinweg das Feuer genommen;
Jezt aber siz' ich unter Wolken, darin
Ein jedes eine Ruh' hat eigen unter
Wohleingerichteten Eichen, auf
Der Heide des Rehs, und fremd
Erscheinen und gestorben mir
Der Seeligen Geister.

The Ages of Life

Cities of the Euphrates!
Streets of Palmyra!
Forests of pillars on a waste plain,
What are you?
As you passed beyond the limits
Of those who merely breathe,
Your glory was consumed
By the fires and smoke of heaven.
But now I sit under clouds (as a strange
Quiet comes upon each one) beneath
A pleasant row of oaks, on
The heath where roe-deer graze,
And it seems so strange to me
How truly dead
The souls of these ghosts are.

Der Winkel von Hahrdt

Hinunter sinket der Wald,
Und Knospen ähnlich, hängen
Einwärts die Blätter, denen
Blüht unten auf ein Grund,
Nicht gar unmündig.
Da nemlich ist Ulrich
Gegangen; oft sinnt, über den Fußtritt,
Ein groß Schiksaal
Bereit, an übrigem Orte.

The Shelter at Hardt

The forest slopes down,
And, like buds, its leaves
Hang inward, toward which
A ground below blossoms,
Not entirely silent.
There Ulrich himself
Once walked; over that footprint, it often seems,
A great fate is ready,
At the abandoned site.

Hälfte des Lebens

Mit gelben Birnen hänget
Und voll mit wilden Rosen
Das Land in den See,
Ihr holden Schwäne,
Und trunken von Küssen
Tunkt ihr das Haupt
Ins heilignüchterne Wasser.

Weh mir, wo nehm' ich, wenn
Es Winter ist, die Blumen, und wo
Den Sonnenschein,
Und Schatten der Erde?
Die Mauern stehn
Sprachlos und kalt, im Winde
Klirren die Fahnen.

Half of Life

Weighted with yellow pears
And full of wild roses,
The land flows into the lake,
Drunk with kisses,
You lovely swans
Dip your heads
Into calm and holy water.

But, oh, where shall I find flowers
When winter is here, and where
The sunshine,
And earth's shadows?
The walls stand
Speechless and cold, in wind
The weathervanes clatter.

Wie wenn am Feiertage…

Wie wenn am Feiertage, das Feld zu sehn
Ein Landmann geht, des Morgens, wenn
Aus heißer Nacht die kühlenden Blize fielen
Die ganze Zeit und fern noch tönet der Donner,
In sein Gestade wieder tritt der Strom,
Und frisch der Boden grünt
Und von des Himmels erfreuendem Reegen
Der Weinstok trauft und glänzend
In stiller Sonne stehn die Bäume des Haines:

So stehn sie unter günstiger Witterung
Sie die kein Meister allein, die wunderbar
Allgegenwärtig erzieht in leichtem Umfangen
Die mächtige, die göttlichschöne Natur.
Drum wenn zu schlafen sie scheint zu Zeiten des Jahrs
Am Himmel oder unter den Pflanzen oder den Völkern
So trauert der Dichter Angesicht auch,
Sie scheinen allein zu seyn, doch ahnen sie immer.
Denn ahnend ruhet sie selbst auch.

Jezt aber tagts! Ich harrt und sah es kommen,
Und was ich sah, das Heilige sei mein Wort.
Denn sie, sie selbst, die älter denn die Zeiten
Und über die Götter des Abends und Orients ist,
Die Natur ist jezt mit Waffenklang erwacht,
Und hoch vom Aether bis zum Abgrund nieder
Nach vestem Geseze, wie einst, aus heiligem Chaos gezeugt,
Fühlt neu die Begeisterung sich,
Die Allerschaffende wieder.

As when on holiday...

As when on holiday, to see the field
A countryman goes out in the morning, when
Out of the hot night the cooling lightning had fallen
For a long time, and in the distance thunder sounded,
And the stream once again fills its banks,
Fresh green covers the earth,
The reassuring rain falls from the heavens,
The grapevine drips, and the trees
Of the grove stand gleaming in the quiet sun:

So they stand in good weather,
Not brought up by one master alone,
But all-present, powerful, divinely beautiful nature,
So wonderfully in its light embrace.
So when she seems to sleep at certain times of the year,
In the sky or under the garden leaves, or among the world's people,
The poets' faces are also sad,
They seem to be alone, but they're always
Having a premonition, as Nature does when she rests.

Now day breaks! I attended to its coming,
And what I saw my words must convey as holy.
For she herself, who is older than Time
And higher than the gods of East and West,
Nature has now awakened to the clashing of armies
And from the upper air to the abyss below,
According to fixed law, as once produced from holy Chaos,
The All-Inspiring
Begins to stir once more.

Und wie im Aug' ein Feuer dem Manne glänzt,
Wenn Hohes er entwarf; so ist
Von neuem an den Zeichen, den Thaten der Welt jezt
Ein Feuer angezündet in Seelen der Dichter.
Und was zuvor geschah, doch kaum gefühlt,
Ist offenbar erst jezt,
Und die uns lächelnd den Aker gebauet,
In Knechtsgestalt, sie sind erkannt,
Die Allebendigen, die Kräfte der Götter.

Erfrägst du sie? im Liede wehet ihr Geist
Wenn es der Sonne des Tags und warmer Erd
Entwächst, und Wettern, die in der Luft, und andern
Die vorbereiteter in Tiefen der Zeit,
Und deutungsvoller, und vernehmlicher uns
Hinwandeln zwischen Himmel und Erd und unter den Völkern.
Des gemeinsamen Geistes Gedanken sind,
Still endend in der Seele des Dichters,

Daß schnellbetroffen sie, Unendlichem
Bekannt seit langer Zeit, von Erinnerung
Erbebt, und ihr, von heilgem Stral entzündet,
Die Frucht in Liebe geboren, der Götter und Menschen Werk
Der Gesang, damit er beiden zeuge, glükt.
So fiel, wie Dichter sagen, da sie sichtbar
Den Gott zu sehen begehrte, sein Bliz auf Semeles Haus
Und die göttlichgetroffne gebahr,
Die Frucht des Gewitters, den heiligen Bacchus.

And a fire gleams, as in that man's eye
When he makes great plans; so
Once more, with signs for kindling,
The deeds of the world stir fire in the souls of poets,
And what went before, barely noticed,
Is only now revealed,
And those who happily farm our land
In the form of workers are now known
As the gods' all-living powers.

You ask where they are? Their song grows out of
The sun of the day and the warm earth,
And storms in the air, and others
Prepared in the depths of time,
Full of meaning and murmuring to us,
Wander between heaven and earth and among the people.
They are everyone's thoughts together
And quietly find their lodging in the souls of poets,

So that suddenly dazed, long familiar
With the infinite, exalted by memory,
Brought to the kindling point by the holy radiance,
The fruit born of love, the work of God and men,
The song succeeds in testimony to both.
So it happened, as the poets say, when she wanted
To see the god made visible, his lightning fell
On Semele's house, and the one struck by God
Bore holy Bacchus, the fruit of the storm.

Und daher trinken himmlisches Feuer jezt
Die Erdensöhne ohne Gefahr.
Doch uns gebührt es, unter Gottes Gewittern,
Ihr Dichter! mit entblößtem Haupte zu stehen,
Des Vaters Stral, ihn selbst, mit eigner Hand
Zu fassen und dem Volk ins Lied
Gehüllt die himmlische Gaabe zu reichen.
Denn sind nur reinen Herzens,
Wie Kinder, wir, sind schuldlos unsere Hände,

Des Vaters Stral, der reine versengt es nicht
Und tieferschüttert, die Leiden des Stärkeren
Mitleidend, bleibt in den hochherstürzenden Stürmen
Des Gottes, wenn er nahet, das Herz doch fest.
Doch weh mir! wenn von

Weh mir!

Und sag ich gleich,

Ich sei genaht, die Himmlischen zu schauen,
Sie selbst, sie werfen mich tief unter die Lebenden
Den falschen Priester, ins Dunkel, daß ich
Das warnende Lied den Gelehrigen singe.
Dort

And so it is the sons of earth, without danger,
Now drink the fire of heaven.
Under God's thunderstorms, fellow poets,
We must stand bare-headed to grasp
The Father's radiance with our own hands,
Wrap the heavenly gift as song
And give it to the people.
For if only, like children,
We have pure hearts, and our hands are guiltless,

The Father's radiance won't burn us,
And, deeply shaken, taking the Strong One's sufferings
As our own, our hearts will stand fast
In God's high down-rushing storm as he approaches.
But woe is me! when of

Woe is me!

And let me confess

I approached to see the gods,
And they themselves threw me down beneath the living,
False priest that I am, into the dark, that I
Sing my warning song to those who can be taught.
There

Am Quell der Donau

Denn, wie wenn hoch von der herrlichgestimmten, der Orgel
Im heiligen Saal,
Reinquillend aus den unerschöpflichen Röhren,
Das Vorspiel, wekend, des Morgens beginnt
Und weitumher, von Halle zu Halle,
Der erfrischende nun, der melodische Strom rinnt,
Bis in den kalten Schatten das Haus
Von Begeisterungen erfüllt,
Nun aber erwacht ist, nun, aufsteigend ihr,
Der Sonne des Fests, antwortet
Der Chor der Gemeinde; so kam
Das Wort aus Osten zu uns,
Und an Parnassos Felsen und am Kithäron hör’ ich
O Asia, das Echo von dir und es bricht sich
Am Kapitol und jählings herab von den Alpen

Kommt eine Fremdlingin sie
Zu uns, die Erwekerin,
Die menschenbildende Stimme.
Da faßt’ ein Staunen die Seele
Der Getroffenen all und Nacht
War über den Augen der Besten.
Denn vieles vermag
Und die Fluth und den Fels und Feuersgewalt auch
Bezwinget mit Kunst der Mensch
Und achtet, der Hochgesinnte, das Schwerdt
Nicht, aber es steht
Vor Göttlichem der Starke niedergeschlagen,

At the Source of the Danube

For as when high from the splendidly voiced, the organ
In a holy hall,
Purely swelling forth from inexhaustible pipes,
The prelude awakening, the morning beginning,
And far and wide, from one great room to another,
Refreshing now, the melodic stream runs
Down to the cold shadows of the house,
Filling it with inspiration,
But now awake, rising to it,
The sun of celebration answers
In the voice of the choir united;
So the word came down to us from the East,
And by the rocks of Parnassus and by Cithaeron,
O Asia, I hear your echo and it breaks
Upon the capitol, and suddenly down from the Alps

    Comes to us as a stranger,
She who calls humans into their being.
Amazement took hold of the souls
Of all who were struck, and night
Passed over the eyes of the best men,
For we can accomplish much,
And flood and stone and even the power of fire
Are overcome by the art of man,
And the high-minded will not retreat
From the sword,
For, faced with divine powers,
The strong will stand in shame,

Und gleichet dem Wild fast; das,
Von süßer Jugend getrieben,
Schweift rastlos über die Berg'
Und fühlet die eigene Kraft
In der Mittagshizze. Wenn aber
Herabgeführt, in spielenden Lüften,
Das heilige Licht, und mit dem kühleren Stral
Der freudige Geist kommt zu
Der seeligen Erde, dann erliegt es, ungewohnt
Des Schönsten und schlummert wachenden Schlaf,
Noch ehe Gestirn naht. So auch wir. Denn manchen erlosch
Das Augenlicht schon vor den göttlichgesendeten Gaben,

Den freundlichen, die aus Ionien uns,
Auch aus Arabia kamen, und froh ward
Der theuern Lehr' und auch der holden Gesänge
Die Seele jener Entschlafenen nie,
Doch einige wachten. Und sie wandelten oft
Zufrieden unter euch, ihr Bürger schöner Städte,
Beim Kampfspiel, wo sonst unsichtbar der Heros
Geheim bei Dichtern saß, die Ringer schaut und lächelnd
Pries, der gepriesene, die müßigernsten Kinder.
Ein unaufhörlich Lieben wars und ists.
Und wohlgeschieden, aber darum denken
Wir aneinander doch, ihr Fröhlichen am Isthmos,
Und am Cephyß und am Taygetos,
Auch eurer denken wir, ihr Thale des Kaukasos,
So alt ihr seid, ihr Paradiese dort
Und deiner Patriarchen und deiner Propheten,

And nearly resemble wild beasts;
Which, driven by sweet youth,
Roam restlessly over mountains
And feel their own power in the noon-day heat,
But when led down by playful breezes,
And the holy light with its calm radiance,
The happy spirit descends to the holy earth;
Then, unfamiliar with the most beautiful, it succumbs
And slumbers in waking sleep,
Though stars are not yet out; so it is with us,
For the light of many eyes is extinguished
When it meets with gifts sent by God,

    The kindly one who came to us
From Ionia and from Arabia, too, and the souls
Who had gone to their rest were never made glad
By precious teachings nor gracious songs,
Yet some were awakened, and often, citizens
Of fine towns, they walked among you,
Contented by the games, where once, undetected, the hero
Sat secretly with poets, saw the wrestlers, and smilingly
Praised the happily loitering children, the praised one!
It was and is an endless love,
But now completely divided; yet still we think
Of one another, you happy ones of the Isthmus,
And by Cephissus and by Taygetus,
We think of you, valleys of the Caucasus,
As old as you are, there in paradise,
And of your patriarchs and your prophets,

O Asia, deiner Starken, o Mutter!
Die furchtlos vor den Zeichen der Welt,
Und den Himmel auf Schultern und alles Schiksaal,
Taglang auf Bergen gewurzelt,
Zuerst es verstanden,
Allein zu reden
Zu Gott. Die ruhn nun. Aber wenn ihr
Und diß ist zu sagen,
Ihr Alten all, nicht sagtet, woher?
Wir nennen dich, heiliggenöthiget, nennen,
Natur! dich wir, und neu, wie dem Bad entsteigt
Dir alles Göttlichgeborne.

Zwar gehn wir fast, wie die Waisen;
Wohl ists, wie sonst, nur jene Pflege nicht wieder;
Doch Jünglinge, der Kindheit gedenk,
Im Hauße sind auch diese nicht fremde.
Sie leben dreifach, eben wie auch
Die ersten Söhne des Himmels.
Und nicht umsonst ward uns
In die Seele die Treue gegeben.
Nicht uns, auch Eures bewahrt sie,
Und bei den Heiligtümern, den Waffen des Worts
Die scheidend ihr den Ungeschikteren uns
Ihr Schiksaalssöhne, zurükgelassen

Ihr guten Geister, da seid ihr auch,
Oftmals, wenn einen dann die heilige Wolk umschwebt,
Da staunen wir und wissens nicht zu deuten.
Ihr aber würzt mit Nectar uns den Othem
Und dann frohloken wir oft oder es befällt uns
Ein Sinnen, wenn ihr aber einen zu sehr liebt

O Asia, your strong ones, Mother!
Fearless in signs of the world,
Heaven and all fate heaped themselves on our shoulders,
For days we rooted down in the mountains,
And were the first to understand
How to speak
Alone to God. These are now at rest. But if,
And this must be said,
All you ancients, you would never tell us
How we're supposed to name you, under holy stricture,
Yet we name you, Nature, and new, as from a bath,
Emerges all that is born of God.

True, we nearly walk like orphans;
though much has stayed the same, all true care is lacking;
But youths who think of their childhood
Are not strangers in the house.
They live threefold, even as
The firstborn sons of heaven,
And not for nothing is faith
Given to us in our souls. Not ours alone,
But preserving everything that's yours
Along with holy relics, weapons of the word,
Which, when the Sons of Fate departed,
Were left behind for the fateless,

You, kindly spirits, are present in them, too,
And often, when one hovers in the holy cloud
Around someone, we are astounded
And don't know what it means.
But you spice our breath with nectar,
And then we can rejoice, or else we become pensive,

Er ruht nicht, bis er euer einer geworden.

Darum, ihr Gütigen! umgebet mich leicht,

Damit ich bleiben möge, denn noch ist manches zu singen,

Jezt aber endiget, seeligweinend,

Wie eine Sage der Liebe,

Mir der Gesang, und so auch ist er

Mir, mit Erröthen, Erblassen,

Von Anfang her gegangen. Doch Alles geht so.

But when you love someone too greatly,

There's no rest until he becomes one of you.

Therefore, good people! surround me lightly,

So that I may stay, for there is still much to sing,

But now like a myth of love weeping from my soul,

My song reaches its end,

And so, too, growing pale and blushing,

It's gone from the beginning. That's how it always goes.

Der Rhein

An Isaak von Sinclair

Im dunkeln Epheu saß ich, an der Pforte
Des Waldes, eben, da der goldene Mittag,
Den Quell besuchend, herunterkam
Von Treppen des Alpengebirgs,
Das mir die göttlichgebaute,
Die Burg der Himmlischen heißt
Nach alter Meinung, wo aber
Geheim noch manches entschieden
Zu Menschen gelanget; von da
Vernahm ich ohne Vermuthen
Ein Schiksaal, denn noch kaum
War mir im warmen Schatten
Sich manches beredend, die Seele
Italia zu geschweift
Und fernhin an die Küsten Moreas.

Jezt aber, drinn im Gebirg,
Tief unter den silbernen Gipfeln
Und unter fröhlichem Grün,
Wo die Wälder schauernd zu ihm,
Und der Felsen Häupter übereinander
Hinabschaun, taglang, dort
Im kältesten Abgrund hört'
Ich um Erlösung jammern
Den Jüngling, es hörten ihn, wie er tobt',
Und die Mutter Erd' anklagt',
Und den Donnerer, der ihn gezeuget,
Erbarmend die Eltern, doch
Die Sterblichen flohn von dem Ort,

The Rhine

To Isaak von Sinclair

    I was sitting in dark ivy, at the gate
Of the forest, just as the gold of noon
Visited the spring, coming down
The steps of the Alps,
Which, after ancient legend,
I call the gods' design,
The divinely built fortress of the gods,
From which many secrets
Are handed down to men; from there
Without expectation, I became aware
Of a fate, my soul still barely
Conversing with itself
In the warm shade,
Had already gone off to Italy
And beyond to the shores of Morea.

    But now, in the mountains
Deep below the silver peaks
And joyous green,
Where shivering woods
And the heads of rocks, one upon another,
Looked down at him all day,
There in the coldest abyss
I heard the young man
Beg to be released
And accuse Mother Nature and his father,
The Thunderer, and his parents
Who had been watching
Were moved to pity,

243

Denn furchtbar war, da lichtlos er
In den Fesseln sich wälzte,
Das Rasen des Halbgotts.

Die Stimme wars des edelsten der Ströme,
Des freigeborenen Rheins,
Und anderes hoffte der, als droben von den Brüdern,
Dem Tessin und dem Rhodanus,
Er schied und wandern wollt', und ungeduldig ihn
Nach Asia trieb die königliche Seele.
Doch unverständig ist
Das Wünschen vor dem Schiksaal.
Die Blindesten aber
Sind Göttersöhne. Denn es kennet der Mensch
Sein Haus und dem Thier ward, wo
Es bauen solle, doch jenen ist
Der Fehl, daß sie nicht wissen wohin?
In die unerfahrne Seele gegeben.

Ein Räthsel ist Reinentsprungenes. Auch
Der Gesang kaum darf es enthüllen. Denn
Wie du anfiengst, wirst du bleiben,
So viel auch wirket die Noth,
Und die Zucht, das meiste nemlich
Vermag die Geburt,
Und der Lichtstral, der
Dem Neugebornen begegnet.
Wo aber ist einer,
Um frei zu bleiben
Sein Leben lang, und des Herzens Wunsch
Allein zu erfüllen, so
Aus günstigen Höhn, wie der Rhein,

But mortals fled the place,
Fearful of the demigod
Who raged without light in his chains.

   It was the voice of the noblest of rivers,
Of the freeborn Rhine,
And he had other hopes when he left behind
His brothers Ticino and Rhône,
His regal soul departed and wanted to wander,
Impatiently driving toward Asia.
In the face of Fate,
It's unwise to wish.
But the sons of the gods
Are the blindest. For man knows his house
And the animals, where he must build,
But others fail, for in
Their souls' inexperience,
They don't know where to go.

   What springs from a pure source is a mystery.
Even song may barely reveal it.
For as you began, so you will remain,
As much as need and breeding
Have their effect, the important
Power is birth,
And that radiance of light
The newborn meets.
But where is one
Like the Rhine,
Who can stay free
His whole life long,
Fulfilling his heart's desire alone,

Und so aus heiligem Schoose
Glüklich geboren, wie jener?

    Drum ist ein Jauchzen sein Wort.
Nicht liebt er, wie andere Kinder,
In Wikelbanden zu weinen;
Denn wo die Ufer zuerst
An die Seit ihm schleichen, die krummen,
Und durstig umwindend ihn,
Den Unbedachten, zu ziehn
Und wohl zu behüten begehren
Im eigenen Zahne, lachend
Zerreißt er die Schlangen und stürzt
Mit der Beut und wenn in der Eil'
Ein Größerer ihn nicht zähmt,
Ihn wachsen läßt, wie der Bliz, muß er
Die Erde spalten, und wie Bezauberte fliehn
Die Wälder ihm nach und zusammensinkend die Berge.

    Ein Gott will aber sparen den Söhnen
Das eilende Leben und lächelt,
Wenn unenthaltsam, aber gehemmt
Von heiligen Alpen, ihm
In der Tiefe, wie jener, zürnen die Ströme.
In solcher Esse wird dann
Auch alles Lautre geschmiedet,
Und schön ists, wie er drauf,
Nachdem er die Berge verlassen,
Stillwandelnd sich im deutschen Lande
Begnüget und das Sehnen stillt
Im guten Geschäffte, wenn er das Land baut
Der Vater Rhein, und liebe Kinder nährt
In Städten, die er gegründet.

From such a favored height,
From such a sacred womb?

    And that is why his word is a shout of joy.
Unlike other children, he doesn't cry
In his swaddling clothes;
For when other riverbanks,
The crooked, creep up to him,
And thirstily wind around him,
Wishing to draw him unaware
Where they might devour him,
Laughing, he tears those serpents to pieces
And rushes on with his plunder,
And if no higher power
Tamed his momentum, he would grow
And split the earth like lightning,
And like dreaming companions
The forests join his flight, and mountains collapse together.

    But a god will spare his sons
Such a hasty life, and smiles,
When reckless but restrained
By holy Alps, rivers like this one
Rage at him from their depths.
In such a forge all that's pure
Is hammered into shape,
And it's nice to see
How, after leaving the mountains
And wandering German lands in peace,
Calming his longing
With useful work and tilling the land,
Father Rhine feeds the dear children
In cities he has founded.

Doch nimmer, nimmer vergißt ers.
Denn eher muß die Wohnung vergehn,
Und die Sazung und zum Unbild werden
Der Tag der Menschen, ehe vergessen
Ein solcher dürfte den Ursprung
Und die reine Stimme der Jugend.
Wer war es, der zuerst
Die Liebesbande verderbt
Und Strike von ihnen gemacht hat?
Dann haben des eigenen Rechts
Und gewiß des himmlischen Feuers
Gespottet die Trozigen, dann erst
Die sterblichen Pfade verachtend
Verwegnes erwählt
Und den Göttern gleich zu werden getrachtet.

Es haben aber an eigner
Unsterblichkeit die Götter genug, und bedürfen
Die Himmlischen eines Dings,
So sinds Heroën und Menschen
Und Sterbliche sonst. Denn weil
Die Seeligsten nichts fühlen von selbst,
Muß wohl, wenn solches zu sagen
Erlaubt ist, in der Götter Nahmen
Theilnehmend fühlen ein Andrer,
Den brauchen sie; jedoch ihr Gericht
Ist, daß sein eigenes Haus
Zerbreche der und das Liebste
Wie den Feind schelt' und sich Vater und Kind
Begrabe unter den Trümmern,
Wenn einer, wie sie, seyn will und nicht
Ungleiches dulden, der Schwärmer.

Yet he never, never forgets.

For sooner would the dwelling be destroyed
And all the laws and light of man
Be dismantled before one like him
Forget his origin
And the pure voice of his youth.
Who was it who first
Destroyed the bonds of love
And turned them into chains?
Which made the rebels
Scorn their own rights
And also heavenly fires,
And, hating the ways of mortals,
They chose insolence and tried
To become like gods.

But the gods are satisfied
By their immortality, and if
The heavenly need one thing,
It's heroes and men
And other mortals. For since
The gods feel nothing themselves,
If to say such a thing is permitted,
Someone else must share and feel
For them; yet it's the law
That he shall break
His own house and find fault
With one he loves, and hate him
Like an enemy and bury both father
And child under rubble
When he seeks to be like them,
And refuses to bear inequality, the fanatic.

Drum wohl ihm, welcher fand
Ein wohlbeschiedenes Schiksaal,
Wo noch der Wanderungen
Und süß der Leiden Erinnerung
Aufrauscht am sichern Gestade,
Daß da und dorthin gern
Er sehn mag bis an die Grenzen
Die bei der Geburt ihm Gott
Zum Aufenthalte gezeichnet.
Dann ruht er, seeligbescheiden,
Denn alles, was er gewollt,
Das Himmlische, von selber umfängt
Es unbezwungen, lächelnd
Jezt, da er ruhet, den Kühnen.

Halbgötter denk' ich jezt
Und kennen muß ich die Theuern,
Weil oft ihr Leben so
Die sehnende Brust mir beweget.
Wem aber, wie, Rousseau, dir,
Unüberwindlich die Seele
Die starkausdauernde ward,
Und sicherer Sinn
Und süße Gaabe zu hören,
Zu reden so, daß er aus heiliger Fülle
Wie der Weingott, thörig göttlich
Und gesezlos sie die Sprache der Reinesten giebt
Verständlich den Guten, aber mit Recht
Die Achtungslosen mit Blindheit schlägt
Die entweihenden Knechte, wie nenn ich den Fremden?

So he is happy who has found
A well-apportioned fate
Where sweetly the memory
Of his wandering and afflictions
Whispers on certain shores,
And he gladly looks this way and that
Toward the limits of the place
God gave him at birth.
There he rests, content in his soul,
For everything that he wanted
Of heaven surrounds
Him on its own, and smiles
Upon the bold one
Now that he rests.

I think of demigods now,
And I must know those dear ones
Because their existence has so often
Moved my yearning heart.
But when one like you, Rousseau,
Whose soul is strong and patient,
Endures and grows invincible,
Who has solid sense
And a sweet gift of hearing
And also of speech, so that out of holy ripeness,
Like the wine god in his folly, lawless
And godly, makes the language of the pure
Understandable to the good, but as he should,
Strikes blind the disrespectful, those profane
Common knaves, what shall I name such a stranger?

Die Söhne der Erde sind, wie die Mutter,
Allliebend, so empfangen sie auch
Mühlos, die Glüklichen, Alles.
Drum überraschet es auch
Und schrökt den sterblichen Mann,
Wenn er den Himmel, den
Er mit den liebenden Armen
Sich auf die Schultern gehäufft,
Und die Last der Freude bedenket;
Dann scheint ihm oft das Beste,
Fast ganz vergessen da,
Wo der Stral nicht brennt,
Im Schatten des Walds
Am Bielersee in frischer Grüne zu seyn,
Und sorglosarm an Tönen,
Anfängern gleich, bei Nachtigallen zu lernen.

Und herrlich ists, aus heiligem Schlafe dann
Erstehen und aus Waldes Kühle
Erwachend, Abends nun
Dem milderen Licht entgegenzugehn,
Wenn, der die Berge gebaut
Und den Pfad der Ströme gezeichnet,
Nachdem er lächelnd auch
Der Menschen geschäfftiges Leben
Das othemarme, wie Seegel
Mit seinen Lüften gelenkt hat,
Auch ruht und zu der Schülerin jezt,
Der Bildner, Gutes mehr
Denn Böses findend,
Zur heutigen Erde der Tag sich neiget.—

The sons of the earth, like their mother,
Love every thing. So the happy ones accept
Everything without effort.
And therefore it startles
And frightens mortal man
When he reflects on heaven,
Which with loving arms
He has heaped upon his shoulders,
And on the burden of joy;
So it often seems best
For him to remain forgotten,
Where no light burns
In the shade of the forest,
To be among the fresh greenery of Lake Bienne
And, careless, poor in tones,
Like a beginner, to learn from nightingales.

And it is glorious to rise
From holy sleep and, wake in
The forest's coolness
And walk at evening
Toward the softer light,
When he who built the mountains
And set the course of streams,
After which he laughed
At the lives of men,
Those short of breath, like sails
He has filled with winds,
And this day, the craftsman also rests,
And, finding more good than evil,
Bows to his student, the earth as it is.—

Dann feiern das Brautfest Menschen und Götter,
Es feiern die Lebenden all,
Und ausgeglichen
Ist eine Weile das Schiksaal.
Und die Flüchtlinge suchen die Heerberg,
Und süßen Schlummer die Tapfern,
Die Liebenden aber
Sind, was sie waren, sie sind
Zu Hauße, wo die Blume sich freuet
Unschädlicher Gluth und die finsteren Bäume
Der Geist umsäuselt, aber die Unversöhnten
Sind umgewandelt und eilen
Die Hände sich ehe zu reichen,
Bevor das freundliche Licht
Hinuntergeht und die Nacht kommt.

Doch einigen eilt
Diß schnell vorüber, andere
Behalten es länger.
Die ewigen Götter sind
Voll Lebens allzeit; bis in den Tod
Kann aber ein Mensch auch
Im Gedächtniß doch das Beste behalten,
Und dann erlebt er das Höchste.
Nur hat ein jeder sein Maas.
Denn schwer ist zu tragen
Das Unglük, aber schwerer das Glük.
Ein Weiser aber vermocht es
Vom Mittag bis in die Mitternacht,
Und bis der Morgen erglänzte,
Beim Gastmahl helle zu bleiben.

Then men and gods celebrate their marriage,
All living things rejoice,
And for a while
Fate is brought into balance.
And fugitives seek asylum,
The brave slumber sweetly,
But lovers
Are at home as always
Whenever flowers take pleasure
In harmless fire and the spirit moves
Through the dark trees, but while the unappeased
Are changed and rush
To take each other's hands
Before the benevolent light
Goes down and night comes.

For some, however,
This quickly passes; others
Bear it longer.
At all times, the eternal gods
Are full of life;
But until death
A man can keep the best in mind
And thus he lives the highest.
Yet each of us has his measure.
For misfortune is hard
To bear, harder is fortune,
But a wise man was able
To keep awake at the banquet,
From noon till midnight,
Until the break of dawn.

Dir mag auf heißem Pfade unter Tannen oder
Im Dunkel des Eichwalds gehüllt
In Stahl, mein Sinklair! Gott erscheinen oder
In Wolken, du kennst ihn, da du kennest, jugendlich,
Des Guten Kraft, und nimmer ist dir
Verborgen das Lächeln des Herrschers
Bei Tage, wenn
Es fieberhaft und angekettet das
Lebendige scheinet oder auch
Bei Nacht, wenn alles gemischt
Ist ordnungslos und wiederkehrt
Uralte Verwirrung.

To you, on the warm path under fir trees or
Beneath the oaks in darkness, sheathed
In steel, my Sinclair, may God appear, or
In clouds you will know him,
Since you know, in your youth, the power of good
Is never hidden from you
The smile of God is hidden
By day, when
All that lives seems feverish and chained,
Or also by night, when everything is mingled
In chaos and once again comes
Primordial confusion.

Germanien

Nicht sie, die Seeligen, die erschienen sind,
Die Götterbilder in dem alten Lande,
Sie darf ich ja nicht rufen mehr, wenn aber
Ihr heimatlichen Wasser! jezt mit euch
Des Herzens Liebe klagt, was will es anders,
Das Heiligtrauernde? Denn voll Erwartung liegt
Das Land und als in heißen Tagen
Herabgesenkt, umschattet heut
Ihr Sehnenden! uns ahnungsvoll ein Himmel.
Voll ist er von Verheißungen und scheint
Mir drohend auch, doch will ich bei ihm bleiben,
Und rükwärts soll die Seele mir nicht fliehn
Zu euch, Vegangene! Die zu lieb mir sind.
Denn euer schönes Angesicht zu sehn,
Als wärs, wie sonst, ich fürcht' es, tödtlich ists,
Und kaum erlaubt, Gestorbene zu weken.

Enflohene Götter! auch ihr, ihr gegenwärtigen, damals
Wahraftiger, ihr hattet eure Zeiten!
Nichts läugnen will ich hier und nichts erbitten.
Denn wenn es aus ist, und der Tag erloschen
Wohl trifts den Priester erst, doch liebend folgt
Der Tempel und das Bild ihm auch und seine Sitte
Zum dunkeln Land und keines mag noch scheinen.
Nur als von Grabesflammen, ziehet dann
Ein goldner Rauch, die Sage drob hinüber,
Und dämmert jezt uns Zweifelnden um das Haupt,
Und keiner weiß, wie ihm geschieht. Er fühlt
Die Schatten derer, so gewesen sind,
Die Alten, so die Erde neubesuchen.

Germania

Not them, the blessed who appeared,
Those images of gods in the old land,
I don't need to call them anymore, but if,
Waters of my homeland, the love of my heart
Laments with you now, what else does it want,
The sacredly grieving? For the land lies
Full of expectation and, as though
It had sunk closer on hot days, a heaven casts
An ominous shadow today, you yearners!
It's full of promises and seems
Menacing to me, too, but I will remain with it,
And now my soul won't flee back
To you, vanished ones, whom I love too much.
For to see your lovely face
As it was before is, I fear, deadly,
For it's scarcely allowed to awaken the dead.

Gods who have fled! Also you, who are present
And were once more genuine, you had your time!
I'll deny nothing and ask no favors here.
For when it's over and the day is extinguished,
The priest is the first one struck, but lovingly
The temple and image and also his practice
Follow him to the dark land, and none of them may shine.
Only like flames from a pyre, there drifts
A golden smoke, and the legend of it
Glimmers around our doubting heads,
And no one knows what's happening to him.
He feels the shadows of those who once were here,
The ancients newly visiting the earth,

Denn die da kommen sollen, drängen uns,
Und länger säumt von Göttermenschen
Die heilige Schaar nicht mehr im blauen Himmel.

  Schon grünet ja, im Vorspiel rauherer Zeit
Für sie erzogen das Feld, bereitet ist die Gaabe
Zum Opfermahl und Thal und Ströme sind
Weitoffen um prophetische Berge,
Daß schauen mag bis in den Orient
Der Mann und ihn von dort der Wandlungen viele bewegen.
Vom Aether aber fällt
Das treue Bild und Göttersprüche reegnen
Unzählbare von ihm, und es tönt im innersten Haine.
Und der Adler, der vom Indus kömmt,
Und über des Parnassos
Beschneite Gipfel fliegt, hoch über den Opferhügeln
Italias, und frohe Beute sucht
Dem Vater, nicht wie sonst, geübter im Fluge
Der Alte, jauchzend überschwingt er
Zulezt die Alpen und sieht die vielgearteten Länder.

  Die Priesterin, die stillste Tochter Gottes,
Sie, die zu gern in tiefer Einfalt schweigt,
Sie suchet er, die offnen Auges schaute,
Als wüßte sie es nicht, jüngst, da ein Sturm
Todtdrohend über ihrem Haupt ertönte;
Es ahnete das Kind ein Besseres,
Und endlich ward ein Staunen weit in Himmel
Weil Eines groß an Glauben, wie sie selbst,
Die seegnende, die Macht der Höhe sei;
Drum sandten sie den Boten, der, sie schnell erkennend,
Denkt lächelnd so: Dich, unzerbrechliche, muß

For we feel the pressure of those who should come,
And no longer will the holy multitude
Of gods incarnate remain in blue heaven.

    The field raised up for them already turns green
In the prelude of a rougher age, offerings are prepared
For the sacrifice, and valleys and streams
Lie wide open around the prophetic mountains,
That a man may gaze as far as the Orient
And be moved by life's many changes.
But the true image falls down
From the Upper Air itself, and words of gods
Rain immeasurably down, and the innermost grove resounds.
And the eagle that comes from the Indus
Flies over the snowy peaks of Parnassus
High above the sacrificial hills of Italy,
And seeks happy plunder for the Father,
Not as he used to, the ancient one
More practiced in flight at last triumphantly
Swings over the Alps and sees many different lands.

    The priestess, the quietest daughter of God,
All too happy to keep silent in the depths of innocence,
He seeks her, who looked up with open eyes,
As though she did not know when a storm
Threatening death resounded about her head;
The child prophesied for the better,
And astonishment finally spread in heaven,
Because one was as great in faith as the Holy Ones
Themselves, the blessed powers on high;
Therefore, they sent a messenger, who quickly recognized her,
And smilingly thought: You, the unbreakable one,

Ein ander Wort erprüfen und ruft es laut,
Der Jugendliche, nach Germania schauend:
»Du bist es, auswählt,
»Allliebend und ein schweres Glük
»Bist du zu tragen stark geworden,

Seit damals, da im Walde verstekt und blühendem Mohn
Voll süßen Schlummers, trunkene, meiner du
Nichet achtetest, lang, ehe noch auch geringere fühlten
Der Jungfrau Stolz und staunten weß du wärst und woher,
Doch du es selbst nicht wußtest. Ich miskannte dich nicht,
Und heimlich, da du träumtest, ließ ich
Am Mittag schneidend dir ein Freundeszeichen,
Die Blume des Mundes zurük und du redetest einsam.
Doch Fülle der goldenen Worte sandtest du auch
Glükseelige! mit den Strömen und sie quillen unerschöpflich
In die Gegenden all. Denn fast, wie der heiligen,
Die Mutter ist von allem,
Die Verborgene sonst genannt von Menschen,
So ist von Lieben und Leiden
Und voll von Ahnungen dir
Und voll von Frieden der Busen.

O trinke Morgenlüfte,
Biß daß du offen bist,
Und nenne, was vor Augen dir ist,
Nicht länger darf Geheimniß mehr
Das Ungesprochene bleiben,
Nachdem es lange verhüllt ist;
Denn Sterblichen geziemet die Schaam,
Und so zu reden die meiste Zeit,
Ist weise auch von Göttern.

The youthful one looking toward Germany, must
Try a different word and loudly cry:
"It is you, the chosen,
All-loving, who have grown strong
In bearing a difficult fortune,

  "Since, hidden in the woods and blooming poppies
Full of sweet slumber, you, drunken, paid no attention to me
For a long time, before others less worthy felt a young
Woman's pride and were amazed at who you were and where from,
But you yourself didn't know. But I didn't misjudge you,
And, secretly as you dreamed at mid-day, I left a token of friendship
     behind,
The flower of my mouth, and all alone you spoke.
For you also sent an abundance of golden words,
Fortunate soul, with your rivers, and they flowed unceasingly
Into all regions. For almost like the holy,
Of all things named by man,
The mother is the hidden one,
So it is with love and sorrow
And full of misgivings
And full of peace in her breast.

  "Drink, morning air,
Until you are opened,
And name what you see with your eyes,
No longer does the unspoken
Need to remain a mystery,
Although it is still disguised;
For we mortals are made for shame,
And most of the time it's wise
To speak of gods like this.

Wo aber überflüssiger, denn lautere Quellen
Das Gold und ernst geworden ist der Zorn an dem Himmel,
Muß zwischen Tag und Nacht
Einmals ein Wahres erscheinen.
Dreifach unschreibe du es,
Doch ungesprochen auch, wie es da ist,
Unschuldige, muß es bleiben.

O nenne Tochter du der heiligen Erd'
Einmal die Mutter. Es rauschen die Wasser am Fels
Und Wetter im Wald und bei dem Nahmen derselben
Tönt auf aus alter Zeit Vergangengöttliches wieder.
Wie anders ists! und rechthin glänzt und spricht
Zukünftiges auch erfreulich aus den Fernen.
Doch in der Mitte der Zeit
Lebt ruhig mit geweihter
Jungfräulicher Erde der Aether
Und gerne, zur Erinnerung, sind
Die unbedürftigen sie
Gastfreundlich bei den unbedürft'gen
Bei deinen Feiertagen
Germania, wo du Priesterin bist
Und wehrlos Rath giebst rings
Den Königen und den Völkern.

But where gold has become more over-abundant
Than the purest wellsprings, and heaven's anger is in earnest,
Between night and day
A truth needs for once to shine forth.
Even if you rewrite it three times,
Yet also unspoken, just as it was,
Innocent it must remain.

  "Speak of your mother once, daughter
Of Holy Earth. Water rustles over the stones,
And storms in the woods, and by their names alone
Sacred things of the past ring out once more.
How it all has changed! And to the right
Things of the future gleam and speak,
Bringing joy from the distance,
But at the center of time,
The virgin earth lives peacefully
And sacredly with the Upper Air
And gladly, for memory's sake, those never in need
Live hospitably with those never in need.
Among your holidays,
Germania, where you are priestess
And give disarming advice all around you
To kings and to the people."

Der Einzige

[Erste Fassung]

Was ist es, das
An die alten seeligen Küsten
Mich fesselt, daß ich mehr noch
Sie liebe, als mein Vaterland?
Denn wie in himmlische
Gefangenschaft verkaufft
Dort bin ich, wo Apollo gieng
In Königsgestalt,
Und zu unschuldigen Jünglingen sich
Herablies Zevs und Söhn' in heiliger Art
Und Töchter zeugte
Der Hohe unter den Menschen?

Der hohen Gedanken
Sind nemlich viel
Entsprungen des Vaters Haupt
Und große Seelen
Von ihm zu Menschen gekommen.
Gehöret hab' ich
Von Elis und Olympia, bin
Gestanden oben auf dem Parnaß,
Und über Bergen des Isthmus,
Und drüben auch
Bei Smyrna und hinab
Bei Ephesos bin ich gegangen;

Viel hab' ich schönes gesehn,
Und gesungen Gottes Bild,
Hab' ich, das lebet unter

The Only One

[First Version]

What is it that
Binds me to these blessed
Ancient shores, that I love
Them more than my own country?
For, as if sold into
Heavenly bondage,
I am where Apollo went
Appearing as a king,
And Zeus condescended
to innocent youths
And created, in godly fashion,
Sons and daughters among mortals.

Many sublime thoughts
Have sprung from
The Father's head
And great souls
Have come from him to men.
I have heard
Of Elis and Olympia,
Have stood above Parnassus,
And above the mountains of the Isthmus,
And over towards
Smyrna and down
By Ephesus, I've walked;

I've seen much of beauty
And sung the image of God
That lives among men,

Den Menschen, aber dennoch
Ihr alten Götter und all
Ihr tapfern Söhne der Götter
Noch Einen such ich, den
Ich liebe unter euch,
Wo ihr den lezten eures Geschlechts
Des Haußes Kleinod mir
Dem fremden Gaste verberget.

   Mein Meister und Herr!
O du, mein Lehrer!
Was bist du ferne
Geblieben? und da
Ich fragte unter den Alten,
Die Helden und
Die Götter, warum bliebest
Du aus? Und jezt ist voll
Von Trauern meine Seele
Als eifertet, ihr Himmlischen, selbst
Daß, dien' ich einem, mir
Das andere fehlet.

   Ich weiß es aber, eigene Schuld
Ists! Denn zu sehr,
O Christus! häng' ich an dir,
Wiewohl Herakles Bruder
Und kühn bekenn' ich, du
Bist Bruder auch des Eviers, der
An den Wagen spannte
Die Tyger und hinab
Bis an den Indus
Gebietend freudigen Dienst

And yet, you ancient gods, and all
You brave sons of gods,
There is one among you
That I love above all,
Who is the last of your kind,
Your house's treasure,
Which you hide
From me, a stranger.

My Lord and Master!
O you, my teacher!
Why have you kept
So distant? When I
Asked among ancients,
Heroes, and
Gods, why didn't you
Reveal yourself? And now,
My soul is filled with sadness,
As though you heavenly had zealously cried
That if I served one
I would lose the other.

And yet I know the fault is mine.
For too much, O Christ,
I cling to you,
Although Heracles' brother,
And I boldly confess
That you are the brother
Of Evius, too, who harnessed
Tigers to his chariot
And down to the Indus
Commanded glad worship,

Den Weinberg stiftet und
Den Grimm bezähmte der Völker.

   Es hindert aber eine Schaam
Mich dir zu vergleichen
Die weltlichen Männer. Und freilich weiß
Ich, der dich zeugte, dein Vater,
Derselbe der,

Denn nimmer herrscht er allein.

   Es hänget aber an Einem
Die Liebe. Diesesmal
Ist nemlich vom eigenen Herzen
Zu sehr gegangen der Gesang,
Gut machen will ich den Fehl

Established the vineyards,
And tamed the people's rage.

But shame keeps me
From associating with you,
The worldly men. And indeed I know
Who made you, Father,
The same one who,

For he never reigns alone

But love clings
To One. This time
The song has come
Too deeply from my heart,
I'll correct the error

Wenn ich noch andere singe.
Nie treff ich, wie ich wünsche,
Das Maas. Ein Gott weiß aber
Wenn kommet, was ich wünsche das Beste.
Denn wie der Meister
Gewandelt auf Erden
Ein gefangener Aar,

    Und viele, die
Ihn sahen, fürchteten sich,
Dieweil sein Äußerstes that
Der Vater und sein Bestes unter
Den Menschen wirkete wirklich,
Und sehr betrübt war auch
Der Sohn so lange, bis er
Gen Himmel fuhr in den Lüften,
Dem gleich ist gefangen die Seele der Helden.
Die Dichter müssen auch
Die geistigen weltlich seyn.

When I sing other songs.
No, as much as I wished to,
I never hit the mark. But a god knows
What best I wish for,
For like the Master
Who wandered on earth,
A captive bird of prey,

    And many who
Looked on him were afraid,
While the Father did
His utmost really to work
His best upon men,
And the son was very troubled
Until he ascended
On the breezes into heaven,
So it is for the captive souls of heroes.
The poets, men of spirit,
Must also be worldly.

Der Einzige

[Zweite Fassung]

Was ist es, das
An die alten seeligen Küsten
Mich fesselt, daß ich mehr noch
Sie liebe, als mein Vaterland?
Denn wie in himmlischer
Gefangenschaft gebükt, in flammender Luft
Dort bin ich, wo, wie Steine sagen, Apollo gieng
In Königsgestalt,
Und zu unschuldigen Jünglingen sich
Herablies Zevs und Söhn in heiliger Art
Und Töchter zeugte
Der Hohe unter den Menschen?

Der hohen Gedanken
Sind nemlich viel
Entsprungen des Vaters Haupt,
Und große Seelen
Von ihm zu Menschen gekommen.
Gehöret hab' ich
Von Elis und Olympia, bin
Gestanden oben auf dem Parnaß,
Und über Bergen des Isthmus,
Und drüben auch
Bei Smyrna und hinab
Bei Ephesos bin ich gegangen;

Viel hab' ich Schönes gesehn,
Und gesungen Gottes Bild
Hab' ich, das lebet unter

The Only One

[Second Version]

What is it that
Binds me to these blessed
Ancient shores, that I love
Them more than my own country?
For, as if cowering in
Heavenly bondage,
I am in flaming air
Where the stones say Apollo went
Appearing as a king,
And Zeus condescended to innocent youths
And created, in godly fashion,
Sons and daughters among mortals.

Many sublime thoughts
Have sprung from
The Father's head
And great souls
Have come from him to men.
I have heard
Of Elis and Olympia,
Have stood above Parnassus,
And above the mountains of the Isthmus,
And also over
Towards Smyrna and down
By Ephesus, I've walked;

I've seen a lot of beauty
And sung the image of God
Which lives among men,

Den Menschen, denn sehr dem Raum gleich ist
Das Himmlische reichlich in
Der Jugend zählbar, aber dennoch
O du der Sterne Leben und all
Ihr tapfern Söhne des Lebens
Noch Einen such ich, den
Ich liebe unter euch,
Wo ihr den lezten eures Geschlechts
Des Haußes Kleinod mir
Dem fremden Gaste verberget

    Mein Meister und Herr!
O du, mein Lehrer!
Was bist du ferne
Geblieben? und da
Ich fragte unter den Alten,
Die Helden und
Die Götter, warum bliebest
Du aus? Und jezt ist voll
Von Trauern meine Seele
Als eifertet, ihr Himmlischen, selbst,
Daß, dien' ich einem, mir
Das andere fehlet.

    Ich weiß es aber, eigene Schuld ists! Denn zu sehr,
O Christus! Häng' ich an dir, wiewohl Herakles Bruder
Und kühn bekenn' ich, du bist Bruder auch des Eviers, der
Die Todeslust der Völker aufhält und zerreißet den Fallstrik,
Fein sehen die Menschen, daß sie
Nicht gehn den Weg des Todes und hüten das Maas, daß einer
Etwas für sich ist, den Augenblick,
Das Geschik der großen Zeit auch

For very much like space is the heavenly
Richly countable in youth,
And yet you, the life of stars, and all
You brave sons of life,
There is one among you
That I love above all,
Who is the last of your kind,
Your house's treasure,
Which you hide
From me, a stranger.

My Lord and Master!
O you, my teacher!
Why have you kept
So distant? and when I
Asked among ancients,
Heroes, and
Gods, why you didn't
Reveal yourself? And now,
My soul is filled with sadness,
As though you heavenly had zealously cried
That if I served one
I would lose the other.

And yet I know the fault is mine. For too much,
O Christ, I cling to you, although Heracles' brother,
And I boldly confess that you are the brother of Evius, too, who
Stems the mortal death wish and tears apart the snare
Men now see so well, so that
They do not go the way of death; by keeping the measure,
A man is something in himself, fearing
Both the moment and the destiny of great times, and

Ihr Feuer fürchtend, treffen sie, und wo
Des Wegs ein anderes geht, da sehen sie
Auch, wo ein Geschik sei, machen aber
Das sicher, Menschen gleichend oder Gesezen.

Es entbrennet aber sein Zorn; daß nemlich
Das Zeichen die Erde berührt, allmälich
Aus Augen gekommen, als an einer Leiter.
Dißmal. Eigenwillig sonst, unmäßig
Gränzlos, daß der Menschen Hand
Anficht das Lebende, mehr auch, als sich schiket
Für einen Halbgott, heiliggeseztes übergeht
Der Entwurf. Seit nemlich böser Geist sich
Bemächtiget des glüklichen Altertums, unendlich,
Langher währt Eines, gesangsfeind, klanglos, das
In Maasen vergeht, des Sinnes gewaltsames. Ungebundenes aber
Hasset Gott. Fürbittend aber

Hält ihn der Tag von dieser Zeit, stillschaffend,
Des Weges gehend, die Blüthe der Jahre.
Und Kriegsgetön, und Geschichte der Helden unterhält,
    hartnäkig Geschik,
Die Sonne Christi, Gärten der Büßenden, und
Der Pilgrime Wandern und der Völker ihn, und des Wächters
Gesang und die Schrift
Des Barden oder Afrikaners. Ruhmloser auch
Geschik hält ihn, die an den Tag
Jezt erst recht kommen, das sind väterliche Fürsten. Denn viel
    ist der Stand
Gottgleicher, denn sonst. Denn Männern mehr
Gehöret das Licht. Nicht Jünglingen.
Das Vaterland auch. Nemlich frisch

Faced with fires; where
Another goes that way, they also see
Where destiny lies, but make
It safe to resemble men or laws.

But his anger flares up; that is,
That its sign touches the earth,
This time gradually coming out of the eyes
Like a ladder. Willful otherwise,
In excess boundless, so that the hands of men
Challenge the living more than a
Demigod should, the design passes beyond
Divine law. For indeed bad spirits have
Usurped happy antiquity, endlessly
In the reign of One, an enemy of song, without sound, that
By means of measure transgresses the mind's powers. But God
Hates the unbound. But interceding

The day of this age holds him back, silently creating
The blossoms of the year, going on its way.
And sounds of war and stories of heroes keep
    destiny stiff-necked,
The sun of Christ, gardens of repentance and
The wanderings of pilgrims and the people and the watchman's
Song and the writings
Of the bards or Africans.
And the destiny holds him
Of those not famous, who are only now having their day,
That is, paternal princes. For much more godlike
Is that rank than before. For new light belongs
More to men. Not to youths.
Our fatherland also. Indeed fresh

Noch unerschöpfet und voll mit Loken.
Der Vater der Erde freuet nemlich sich deß
Auch, daß Kinder sind, so bleibet eine Gewißheit
Des Guten. So auch freuet
Das ihn, daß eines bleibet.
Auch einige sind, gerettet, als
Auf schönen Inseln. Gelehrt sind die.
Versuchungen sind nemlich
Gränzlos an die gegangen.
Zahllose gefallen. Also gieng es, als
Der Erde Vater bereitet ständiges
In Stürmen der Zeit. Ist aber geendet.

Still unexhausted, head full of curls.
For the Father of Earth is glad for this also;
As long as there are children, a proof of goodness
Remains. He is also glad
That one remains.
Also some are saved, as
On beautiful islands. They are the learned.
Indeed they've undergone
Temptations without end.
Countless fallen. So it went, when
The Father of Earth prepared what is constant
In the storms of time. But that is over.

Patmos

Dem Landgrafen von Homburg

Nah ist
Und schwer zu fassen der Gott.
Wo aber Gefahr ist, wächst
Das Rettende auch.
Im Finstern wohnen
Die Adler und furchtlos gehn
Die Söhne der Alpen über den Abgrund weg
Auf leichtgebaueten Brüken.
Drum, da gehäuft sind rings
Die Gipfel der Zeit, und die Liebsten
Nah wohnen, ermattend auf
Getrenntesten Bergen,
So gieb unschuldig Wasser,
O Fittige gieb uns, treuesten Sinns
Hinüberzugehn und wiederzukehren.

So sprach ich, da entführte
Mich schneller, denn ich vermuthet
Und weit, wohin ich nimmer
Zu kommen gedacht, ein Genius mich
Vom eigenen Hauß'. Es dämmerten
Im Zwielicht, da ich gieng
Der schattige Wald
Und die sehnsüchtigen Bäche
Der Heimath; nimmer kannt' ich die Länder;
Doch bald, in frischem Glanze,
Geheimnißvoll
Im goldenen Rauche, blühte
Schnellaufgewachsen,

Patmos

To the Landgrave of Homburg

    The god
Is near and difficult to grasp.
But where there is danger
The thing that rescues also grows.
The eagles live in darkness,
And without fear the sons of the Alps
Walk over chasms
On flimsy bridges.
Therefore, since the summits of time
Are heaped around us, and the most loved
Live near, grown weak
On separate mountains,
Give us blameless waters,
O winged ones, to travel over
And return with faithful minds.

    So I spoke, when
More quickly than I imagined,
And farther than ever
I thought I'd go, a spirit
Carried me from my own house.
As I went, the shadowy wood
And yearning streams
Of my homeland grew dim in the twilight;
I no longer recognized those places;
But soon, freshly growing
And in mystery,
In a golden haze,
Quickly grown up,

Mit Schritten der Sonne,
Mit tausend Gipfeln duftend,

   Mir Asia auf, und geblendet sucht'
Ich eines, das ich kennete, denn ungewohnt
War ich der breiten Gassen, wo herab
Vom Tmolus fährt
Der goldgeschmükte Pactol
Und Taurus stehet und Messogis,
Und voll von Blumen der Garten,
Ein stilles Feuer; aber im Lichte
Blüht hoch der silberne Schnee;
Und Zeug unsterblichen Lebens
An unzugangbaren Wänden
Uralt der Epheu wächst und getragen sind
Von lebenden Säulen, Cedern und Lorbeern
Die feierlichen,
Die göttlichgebauten Palläste.

   Es rauschen aber um Asias Thore
Hinziehend da und dort
In ungewisser Meeresebene
Der schattenlosen Straßen genug,
Doch kennt die Inseln der Schiffer.
Und da ich hörte
Der nahegelegenen eine
Sei Patmos,
Verlangte mich sehr,
Dort einzukehren und dort
Der dunkeln Grotte zu nahn.
Denn nicht, wie Cypros,
Die quellenreiche, oder

With every stride of the sun,
And with the fragrance of a thousand peaks,

   Now Asia blooms for me
And, blinded, I looked for one thing I knew,
For I wasn't accustomed to the broad streets,
Where Pactoclus, beaded in gold,
Drives down from Timolus
And Taurus stands, and Messogis,
And the flowers of the garden
Are a silent fire; but the silver snow
Blossoms high above in the light;
Witness to immortal life,
On private walls,
The ancient ivy grows, and supported
By living pillars of cedar and laurel,
There stand the solemn palaces
Built by the gods.

   But around Asia's gates, one hears
A murmur going this way and that
On the uncertain sea-plain,
Shadowless roads enough,
But the sailor knows the islands
And when I heard
One of those that lay close
Was Patmos,
I longed
To stay there
And approach the dark grotto.
For unlike Cyprus,
Rich in wellsprings,

Der anderen eine
Wohnt herrlich Patmos,

   Gastfreundlich aber ist
Im ärmeren Haußе
Sie dennoch
Und wenn vom Schiffbruch oder klagend
Um die Heimath oder
Den abgeschiedenen Freund
Ihr nahet einer
Der Fremden, hört sie es gern, und ihre Kinder
Die Stimmen des heißen Hains,
Und wo der Sand fällt, und sich spaltet
Des Feldes Fläche, die Laute
Sie hören ihn und liebend tönt
Es wieder von den Klagen des Manns. So pflegte
Sie einst des gottgeliebten,
Des Sehers, der in seeliger Jugend war

   Gegangen mit
Dem Sohne des Höchsten, unzertrennlich, denn
Es liebte der Gewittertragende die Einfalt
Des Jüngers und es sahe der achtsame Mann
Das Angesicht des Gottes genau,
Da, beim Geheimnisse des Weinstoks, sie
Zusammensaßen, zu der Stunde des Gastmals,
Und in der großen Seele, ruhigahnend den Tod
Aussprach der Herr und die lezte Liebe, denn nie genug
Hatt' er von Güte zu sagen
Der Worte, damals, und zu erheitern, da
Ers sahe, das Zürnen der Welt.
Denn alles ist gut. Drauf starb er. Vieles wäre

Or any of the others,
Patmos dwells in splendor,

   She is gracious
Nonetheless, in her
More impoverished house,
And she listens pleasantly
When after a shipwreck,
Or crying from homesickness
Or the loss of a friend,
A stranger draws near, and her children,
The voices of the hot grove,
And where the sand blows, and fields
Crack in the heat, the lute,
They hear him and the man's lament
Lovingly resounds. So once
She tended one beloved by God,
The seer who in his sacred youth

   Had walked with
The Son of God, inseparable, for
The Thunder-bearer loved the innocent
Youth and the mindful man
Saw the face of God,
When, by the mystery of the vine,
They sat together at supper,
And in his great soul, in peaceful knowledge of death,
The Lord spoke of the ultimate love,
For he could never find enough words
For goodness, and when he saw
The wrath of the world, he soothed it.
Then all was well. Then he died. Much more

Zu sagen davon. Und es sahn ihn, wie er siegend blikte
Den Freudigsten die Freunde noch zulezt,

    Doch trauerten sie, da nun
Es Abend worden, erstaunt,
Denn Großentschiedenes hatten in der Seele
Die Männer, aber sie liebten unter der Sonne
Das Leben und lassen wollten sie nicht
Vom Angesichte des Herrn
Und der Heimath. Eingetrieben war,
Wie Feuer im Eisen, das, und ihnen gieng
Zur Seite der Schatte des Lieben.
Drum sandt' er ihnen
Den Geist, und freilich bebte
Das Haus und die Wetter Gottes rollten
Ferndonnernd über
Die ahnenden Häupter, da, schwersinnend
Versammelt waren die Todeshelden,

    Izt, da er scheidend
Noch einmal ihnen erschien.
Denn izt erlosch der Sonne Tag
Der Königliche und zerbrach
Den geradestralenden,
Den Zepter, göttlichleidend, von selbst,
Denn wiederkommen sollt es
Zu rechter Zeit. Nicht wär es gut
Gewesen, später, und schroffabbrechend, untreu,
Der Menschen Werk, und Freude war es
Von nun an,
Zu wohnen in liebender Nacht, und bewahren
In einfältigen Augen, unverwandt

288

Could be said. Friends at the very last
Saw him looking up elated,

   Yet they were sad, for now
The evening had come, amazed,
For the men had great resolve
In their souls, but they loved life
Under the sun and could not relinquish
The face of the Lord
And their homeland. It was forced into them,
Like fire into iron, and the shadow
Of the one they loved walked beside them.
That's why the spirit sent them,
And shook their house
In every way, and the storms of God
Roared distantly over
Their expectant heads, as these heroes of death
Gathered in deep thought,

   Now that, departing,
He once again appeared to them.
For now the kingly one
Dimmed the sun's day
And broke the scepter-like
Beams of the sun, in godlike sorrow,
To return at the right moment
Of his own accord. Nor would it have been good,
Had it happened later, disloyally tearing men
Away from their work;
So from now on
It was a joy to live in loving night, and keep
In innocent eyes unchanging

Abgründe der Weisheit. Und es grünen
Tief an den Bergen auch lebendige Bilder,

    Doch furchtbar ist, wie da und dort
Unendlich hin zerstreut das Lebende Gott.
Denn schon das Angesicht
Der theuern Freunde zu lassen
Und fernhin über die Berge zu gehn
Allein, wo zweifach
Erkannt, einstimmig
War himmlischer Geist; und nicht geweissagt war es, sondern
Die Loken ergriff es, gegenwärtig,
Wenn ihnen plözlich
Ferneilend zurük blikte
Der Gott und schwörend,
Damit er halte, wie an Seilen golden
Gebunden hinfort
Das Böse nennend, sie die Hände sich reichten—

    Wenn aber stirbt alsdenn
An dem am meisten
Die Schönheit hieng, daß an der Gestalt
Ein Wunder war und die Himmlischen gedeutet
Auf ihn, und wenn, ein Räthsel ewig füreinander
Sie sich nicht fassen können
Einander, die zusammenlebten
Im Gedächtniß, und nicht den Sand nur oder
Die Weiden es hinwegnimmt und die Tempel
Ergreifft, wenn die Ehre
Des Halbgotts und der Seinen
Verweht und selber sein Angesicht
Der Höchste wendet

Wells of wisdom. And living images
Grow green in the mountains' depths,

    But it's terrible, how here and there,
God endlessly disperses all living things.
For already to leave the faces
Of true friends and travel
Alone over the mountains,
Where already
The heavenly spirit was twice perceived
By all who were there; and never was this prophesied,
But God seized them by their hair
When he suddenly
Looked behind him and swore
That he would stay, as if bound
By golden ropes,
Calling evil by its name,
As they stretched out their hands—

    But when he dies,
The one most draped with beauty,
So that his shape was judged
A wonder and the gods pointed at him,
And when they forever became
Mysteries to each other,
They couldn't understand one another,
Those who lived together
In his memory, and not only sand
But willows are blown away, and temples
Are seized, when the honor
Of the demigod and his followers
Is blown away, and even the face

Darob, daß nirgend ein
Unsterbliches mehr am Himmel zu sehn ist oder
Auf grüner Erde, was ist diß?

    Es ist der Wurf des Säemanns, wenn er faßt
Mit der Schaufel den Waizen,
Und wirft, dem Klaren zu, ihn schwingend über die Tenne.
Ihm fällt die Schaale vor den Füßen, aber
Ans Ende kommet das Korn,
Und nicht ein Übel ists, wenn einiges
Verloren gehet und von der Rede
Verhallet der lebendige Laut,
Denn göttliches Werk auch gleicht dem unsern,
Nicht alles will der Höchste zumal.
Zwar Eisen träget der Schacht,
Und glühende Harze der Aetna,
So hätt' ich Reichtum,
Ein Bild zu bilden, und ähnlich
Zu schaun, wie er gewesen, den Christ,

    Wenn aber einer spornte sich selbst,
Und traurig redend, unterweges, da ich wehrlos wäre
Mich überfiele, daß ich staunt' und von dem Gotte
Das Bild nachahmen möcht' ein Knecht—
Im Zorne sichtbar sah' ich einmal
Des Himmels Herrn, nicht, daß ich seyn sollt etwas, sondern
Zu lernen. Gütig sind sie, ihr Verhaßtestes aber ist,
So lange sie herrschen, das Falsche, und es gilt
Dann Menschliches unter Menschen nicht mehr.
Denn sie nicht walten, es waltet aber
Unsterblicher Schiksaal und es wandelt ihr Werk
Von selbst, und eilend geht es zu Ende.

Of the Most High turns away,
So that nothing more immortal can be seen
In the sky or on the green earth, what is this?

    It is the winnower when he scoops up
Wheat from his shovel, and, swinging it
over the barn floor, throws it into the clear.
The chaff falls at his feet, but
In the end the grain comes forth,
No harm when some of it
Gets lost, and the living sound
Of his speech grows fainter,
For the work of gods resembles ours,
The Almighty doesn't want everything at once.
Just as iron is pulled from the mine
And Aetna's glowing heart,
So I should have riches,
An image to shape, that looks
Like Christ as he was,

    But if someone spurs himself on
And speaks sadly along his way,
Unarmed, surprised as I was, that a mere servant
Could copy the image of God—
In anger surely I once saw
Heaven's master, not that I should be something,
But to learn. They are kind, but what they most hate,
As long as they reign, is falsehood, for then
Being human no longer counts among men.
For men don't govern; immortal Fate does,
And its work goes forward on its own,
Hurrying toward its end.

Wenn nemlich höher gehet himmlischer
Triumphgang, wird genennet, der Sonne gleich
Von Starken der frohlokende Sohn des Höchsten,

Ein Loosungszeichen, und hier ist der Stab
Des Gesanges, niederwinkend,
Denn nichts ist gemein. Die Todten weket
Er auf, die noch gefangen nicht
Vom Rohen sind. Es warten aber
Der scheuen Augen viele
Zu schauen das Licht. Nicht wollen
Am scharfen Strale sie blühn,
Wiewohl den Muth der goldene Zaum hält.
Wenn aber, als
Von schwellenden Augenbraunen
Der Welt vergessen
Stillleuchtende Kraft aus heiliger Schrift fällt, mögen
Der Gnade sich freuend, sie
Am stillen Blike sich üben.

Und wenn die Himmlischen jezt
So, wie ich glaube, mich lieben
Wie viel mehr Dich,
Denn Eines weiß ich,
Daß nemlich der Wille
Des ewigen Vaters viel
Dir gilt. Still ist sein Zeichen
Am donnernden Himmel. Und Einer stehet darunter
Sein Leben lang. Denn noch lebt Christus.
Es sind aber die Helden, seine Söhne
Gekommen all und heilige Schriften
Von ihm und den Bliz erklären

For when heaven's triumphant march
Goes even higher, the strong will give
The son on high a name like the sun,

    A sign of deliverance, here is the staff
Of song, calling down to us,
For nothing is common. He wakes up
The dead, who are not yet prisoners
Of even cruder forces. But many
Timid eyes wait to be shown
The light. They don't want to bloom
Under such harsh beams,
Though their courage is restrained by a golden leash.
But when a great strength
Falls from holy scripture,
The world is forgotten
Beyond one's jutting brows.
Practicing their quiet gazes,
They can rejoice in grace.

    And if the heavenly
Love me, as I now believe,
They will love you all the more.
For one thing I know,
Namely that the will
Of the Eternal Father
Means much to you. His sign is silent
In thundering heaven. And one stands beneath it
His whole life long. For Christ
Still lives, for the heroes, his sons,
Have all come, and the holy scriptures
About him, and lightning can be explained

Die Thaten der Erde bis izt,
Ein Wettlauf unaufhaltsam. Er ist aber dabei. Denn seine Werke sind
Ihm alle bewußt von jeher.

    Zu lang, zu lang schon ist
Die Ehre der Himmlischen unsichtbar.
Denn fast die Finger müssen sie
Uns führen und schmählich
Entreißt das Herz uns eine Gewalt.
Denn Opfer will der Himmlischen jedes,
Wenn aber eines versäumt ward,
Nie hat es Gutes gebracht.
Wir haben gedienet der Mutter Erd'
Und haben jüngst dem Sonnenlichte gedient,
Unwissend, der Vater aber liebt,
Der über allen waltet,
Am meisten, daß gepfleget werde
Der veste Buchstab, und bestehendes gut
Gedeutet. Dem folgt deutscher Gesang.

By the acts of the world until now,

An endless contest. But he takes part in it. For his works are

Known to him from the start.

   Too long, too long has

The glory of heaven remained unseen.

They must nearly guide

Our fingers and in shame,

Only by force, do we give up our hearts.

For every one of the gods wants sacrifices,

And when one of them is forgotten,

It never brings any good.

We have served our Mother Earth

And have lately served the sunlight,

Unaware that our Father, who reigns supreme,

Most loves that we keep

The letter firmly in our care

And interpret well what endures,

Which German song obeys.

Andenken

Der Nordost wehet,
Der liebste unter den Winden
Mir, weil er feurigen Geist
Und gute Fahrt verheißet den Schiffern.
Geh aber nun und grüße
Die schöne Garonne,
Und die Gärten von Bourdeaux
Dort, wo am scharfen Ufer
Hingehet der Steg und in den Strom
Tief fällt der Bach, darüber aber
Hinschauet ein edel Paar
Von Eichen und Silberpappeln;

Noch denket das mir wohl und wie
Die breiten Gipfel neiget
Der Ulmwald, über die Mühl',
Im Hofe aber wächset ein Feigenbaum.
An Feiertagen gehn
Die braunen Frauen daselbst
Auf seidnen Boden,
Zur Märzenzeit,
Wenn gleich ist Nacht und Tag,
Und über langsamen Stegen,
Von goldenen Träumen schwer,
Einwiegende Lüfte ziehen.

Es reiche aber,
Des dunkeln Lichtes voll,
Mir einer den duftenden Becher,
Damit ich ruhen möge; denn süß

Remembrance

The north-east wind blows,
Dear to me because of its fiery spirit
And the good voyage it promises sailors.
But go now and greet
The beautiful Garonne
And the gardens of Bordeaux,
Where on the steep bank
The path runs unevenly
And the brook falls
Deeply into the river, while above
A pair of noble oaks
And white poplars face the water;

I remember this so well, and how
The broad elm
With its leafy top
Leans over the mill, but a fig-tree
Grows in the courtyard.
On holidays the brown women
Walk on silken ground
In the month of March,
When night and day are the same,
And over slow paths
A light breeze blows
Heavy with dreams of gold.

Won't someone pass
A fragrant cup full of dark light
So I can rest sweetly
And sleep among shadows?

Wär' unter Schatten der Schlummer.
Nicht ist es gut,
Seellos von sterblichen
Gedanken zu seyn. Doch gut
Ist ein Gespräch und zu sagen
Des Herzens Meinung, zu hören viel
Von Tagen der Lieb',
Und Thaten, welche geschehen.

   Wo aber sind die Freunde? Bellarmin
Mit dem Gefährten? Mancher
Trägt Scheue, an die Quelle zu gehn;
Es beginnet nemlich der Reichtum
Im Meere. Sie,
Wie Mahler, bringen zusammen
Das Schöne der Erd' und verschmähn
Den geflügelten Krieg nicht, und
Zu wohnen einsam, jahrlang, unter
Dem entlaubten Mast, wo nicht die Nacht durchglänzen
Die Feiertage der Stadt,
Und Saitenspiel und eingeborener Tanz nicht.

   Nun aber sind zu Indiern
Die Männer gegangen,
Dort an der luftigen Spiz'
An Traubenbergen, wo herab
Die Dordogne kommt,
Und zusammen mit der prächt'gen
Garonne meerbreit
Ausgehet der Strom. Es nehmet aber
Und giebt Gedächtniß die See,
Und die Lieb' auch heftet fleißig die Augen,
Was bleibet aber, stiften die Dichter.

It's not good
To have mortal thoughts
But lack a soul.
But a little conversation is good
To express the heart's meaning,
To hear about
The days of love
And everything that's happened.

But where are our friends? Bellarmine
And his companions? Many
Are afraid of going to the source;
for wealth begins
In the sea. And like painters
They bring together
The beautiful things of the earth
And don't disdain war's outspread wings,
Nor years of solitude beneath the
Leafless mast, where the city's holidays
Don't gleam through the night
Nor the sound of violins or local dancers.

But now the men
Have gone to the Indians,
There on the windblown peak
And the vine-covered hills, where
The Dordogne flows from its source,
And together with the brilliant
Garonne, broad as the sea,
Its current flows out. But it's the sea
That offers memory and takes it back.
And love too fixes its attentive gaze,
But what endures comes from the poets.

Der Ister

Jezt komme, Feur!
Begierig sind wir
Zu schauen den Tag,
Und wenn die Prüfung
Ist durch die Knie gegangen,
Mag einer spüren das Waldgeschrei.
Wir singen aber vom Indus her
Fernangekommen und
Vom Alpheus, lange haben
Das Schikliche wir gesucht,
Nicht ohne Schwingen mag
Zum Nächsten einer greifen
Geradezu
Und kommen auf die andere Seite.
Hier aber wollen wir bauen.
Denn Ströme machen urbar
Das Land. Wenn nemlich Kräuter wachsen
Und an denselben gehn
Im Sommer zu trinken die Thiere,
So gehn auch Menschen daran.

Man nennet aber diesen den Ister.
Schön wohnt er. Es brennet der Säulen Laub,
Und reget sich. Wild stehn
Sie aufgerichtet, untereinander; darob
Ein zweites Maas, springt vor
Von Felsen das Dach. So wundert
Mich nicht, daß er
Den Herkules zu Gaste geladen,
Fernglänzend, am Olympos drunten,

The Ister

Come now, fire!
Impatient for the daylight,
And when the ordeal
Has passed through the knees,
It's then, in that silence,
We hear the woods' strange call.
But, we sing from the Indus,
Which comes from far away, and
From the Alpheus, we've
Long desired what's fitting.
Not without wings
May one seize
Straight on what is nearest
And reaches the other side.
But here we want to build.
For rivers make the land fertile
And allow the foliage to grow.
And if in the summer
Animals gather at a watering place
People will go there, too.

But this one is called the Ister.
It lives in beauty. Columns of leaves burn
And stir. They stand in the wild
Supporting each other; above,
A second mass juts out
A roof of rocks. So I'm
Not surprised that the distantly gleaming river
Made Hercules its guest,
When in search of shade

Da der, sich Schatten zu suchen
Vom heißen Isthmos kam,
Denn voll des Muthes waren
Daselbst sie, es bedarf aber, der Geister wegen,
Der Kühlung auch. Darum zog jener lieber
An die Wasserquellen hieher und gelben Ufer,
Hoch duftend oben, und schwarz
Vom Fichtenwald, wo in den Tiefen
Ein Jäger gern lustwandelt
Mittags, und Wachstum hörbar ist
An harzigen Bäumen des Isters,

    Der scheinet aber fast
Rükwärts zu gehen und
Ich mein, er müsse kommen
Von Osten.
Vieles wäre
Zu sagen davon. Und warum hängt er
An den Bergen gerad? Der andre
Der Rhein ist seitwärts
Hinweggegangen. Umsonst nich gehn
Im Troknen die Ströme. Aber wie? Ein Zeichen braucht es
Nichts anderes, schlecht und recht, damit es Sonn
Und Mond trag' im Gemüth', untrennbar,
Und fortgeh, Tag und Nacht auch, und
Die Himmlischen warm sich fühlen aneinander.
Darum sind jene auch
Die Freude des Höchsten. Denn wie käm er
Herunter? Und wie Hertha grün,
Sind sie die Kinder des Himmels. Aber allzugedultig
Scheint der mir, nicht
Freier, und fast zu spotten. Nemlich wenn

He came down by Olympus
And up from the hot Isthmus.
They were full of courage in that place,
But in the way of spirits
They also need the cool.
That's why the hero preferred
To come to the water's source, its fragrant yellow banks
Black with fir trees, in whose depths
The hunter likes to roam
At noon and the resinous trees
Moan as they grow.

    Yet the river almost seems
To flow backwards, and I
Think it must come
From the East.
Much more could
Be said about it. And why does
It cling to the mountain so upright? That other river,
The Rhine, has gone away
Sideways. Not for nothing rivers
Flow in dryness. But how? We need a sign,
Nothing other, something plain and simple,
To remind us of sun and moon, so inseparable,
Which go away, day and night also,
And warm each other in heaven.
They give joy to the highest god. For how
Can he descend to them?
And like Hertha's ancient greenness
They are the children of heaven. But he seems
Too indulgent to me, not freer,
And almost scornful. For when

Angehen soll der Tag
In der Jugend, wo er zu wachsen
Anfängt, es treibet ein anderer da
Hoch schon die Pracht, und Füllen gleich
In den Zaum knirscht er, und weithin hören
Das Treiben die Lüfte,
Is der zufrieden;
Es brauchet aber Stiche der Fels
Und Furchen die Erd',
Unwirthbar wär es, ohne Weile;
Was aber jener thuet der Strom,
Weis niemand.

Day begins in youth,
Where it commences growing,
Another is already there
To further enhance the beauty, and chafes
At the bit like foals, and if he is happy
Distant breezes
Hear the commotion;
But the rock needs engraving
And the earth needs furrows;
It would be unlivable, desolate.
But what a river will do,
Nobody knows.

Mnemosyne

[Dritte Fassung]

    Reif sind, in Feuer getaucht, gekochet
Die Frücht und auf der Erde geprüfet und ein Gesez ist
Daß alles hineingeht, Schlangen gleich,
Prophetisch, träumend auf
Den Hügeln des Himmels. Und vieles
Wie auf den Schultern eine
Last von Scheitern ist
Zu behalten. Aber bös sind
Die Pfade. Nemlich unrecht,
Wie Rosse, gehn die gefangenen
Element' und alten
Geseze der Erd. Und immer
Ins Ungebundene gehet eine Sehnsucht. Vieles aber ist
Zu behalten. Und Noth die Treue.
Vorwärts aber und rückwärts wollen wir
Nicht sehn. Uns wiegen lassen, wie
Auf schwankem Kahne der See.

    Wie aber Liebes? Sonnenschein
Am Boden sehen wir und trockenen Staub
Und heimatlich die Schatten der Wälder und es blühet
An Dächern der Rauch, bei alter Krone
Der Thürme, friedsam; gut sind nemlich,
Hat gegenredend die Seele
Ein Himmlisches verwundet, die Tageszeichen.
Denn Schnee, wie Majenblumen
Das Edelmüthige, wo
Es seie, bedeutend, glänzet auf
Der grünen Wiese .

Mnemosyne

[Third Version]

Dipped in fire, cooked to a ripeness,
Fruit falls to the judgment of earth,
And that's a prophetic law all must follow,
Like serpents dreaming on
The mounds of heaven. And heavy
As on the shoulders is a
Stack of wood to be kept.
But the paths are evil. For unjustly
the imprisoned elements and ancient laws
Of earth press forward like horses
In harness. Yearning always
seeks to be unrestrained. But there
Is much to keep.
And constancy is required.
We won't look forward and backward.
Let ourselves be rocked
As on a swaying boat at sea.

But how, my love? We see
Sunshine on the ground and dry dust
And the homely shadows of forests; smoke
Blossoms peacefully on rooftops, near the ancient
Crowns of turrets. For good indeed
Are the signs of day
When the soul in defiance
Has wounded one of the gods.
For snow, like lilies of the valley,
Pointing to the noble-minded where it is,
Shines brightly on the green

Der Alpen, hälftig, da, vom Kreuze redend, das
Gesezt ist unterwegs einmal
Gestorbenen, auf hoher Straß
Ein Wandersmann geht zornig,
Fern ahnend mit
Dem andern, aber was ist diß?

    Am Feigenbaum ist mein
Achilles mir gestorben,
Und Ajax liegt
An den Grotten der See,
An Bächen, benachbart dem Skamandros.
An Schläfen Sausen einst, nach
Der unbewegten Salamis steter
Gewohnheit, in der Fremd', ist groß
Ajax gestorben,
Patroklos aber in des Königes Harnisch. Und es starben
Noch andere viel. Am Kithäron aber lag
Elevtherä, der Mnemosyne Stadt. Der auch als
Ablegte den Mantel Gott, das abendliche nachher löste
Die Loken. Himmlische nemlich sind
Unwillig, wenn einer nicht die Seele schonend sich
Zusammengenommen, aber er muß doch; dem
Gleich fehlet die Trauer.

Alpine meadows, half-melted, where
High up, a traveler goes angrily,
Discussing with another
A cross once laid there for the dead,
And, and distantly surmising,
Says "But what is *this*?"

    Beside the fig-tree
My Achilles is dead to me,
And Ajax lies
Beside the grottoes of the sea
Near the streams of Scamander.
According to the changeless custom
Of pitiless Salamis, Great Ajax died
In a foreign land
Of a rushing noise in his head.
But Patroclus died in the king's own armor
And many others also. Eleutherae, however,
Mnemonsyne's town, lay near Cithaeron.
When God laid down his robe, the powers of evening
Soon cut a lock of her hair. For the gods
Are angry when someone fails to collect his soul
In order to save it; yet he must do so;
In equal measure, mourning bears the blame.

Die Nymphe
[Sattler Compilation]

Reif sind, in Feuer getaucht, gekochet
Die Frücht und auf der Erde geprüfet
Und ein Gesez, daß alles hineingeht,
Schlangen gleich ist
Prophetisch, träumend auf
Den Hügeln des Himmels. Und viel wie auf den Schultern eine
Last von Scheitern, ist
Zu behalten. Aber bös sind
Die Pfade. Nemlich
Wie Rosse, gehn unrecht die gefangenen
Element' und alten
Geseze der Erd. Und immer ins
Ungebundene gehet eine Sehnsucht.
Vieles aber ist
Zu behalten. Und Noth
Die Treue. Vorwärts aber und rükwärts wollen wir
Nicht sehn. Uns wiegen lassen, wie auf
Schwanken Kahne, auf der See.

Doch allzuscheu nicht, lieber sei
Unschiklich und gehe, mit der Erinnys, fort
Mein Leben. Denn alles fassen muß
Ein Halbgott oder ein Mensch, dem Leiden nach,
Indem er höret, allein, oder selber
Verwandelt wird, fernahnend die Rosse des Herrn, und
Das Horn des Wächters bei Tag
Und schenket das Liebste
Den Unfruchtbaren
Denn nimmer, von nun an

The Nymph

[Sattler Compilation]

Dipped in fire, cooked to a ripeness,
Fruit falls to the judgment of earth
And that's a prophetic law all must follow,
Like serpents dreaming on
The mounds of heaven. And heavy on the shoulders
Is a stack of logs
To be kept. But the paths
Are evil. That is,
Like horses, the captive
Elements and the ancient
Laws of earth go awry. And always
A yearning passes into the unbound.
But there is much
To keep. And constancy
Is required. Still we won't look forward
And backward. Let ourselves
Be rocked as on
A swaying boat at sea.

Better to be indecent, my life,
Than go away too timidly with the Furies.
For a man or demigod
Must apprehend everything in the way of suffering,
By obedience alone or going
Through change oneself, knowing from a distance the Master's horses
And the watchman's alarm by day
And giving away your most loved
To the fruitless,
For never, from now on,

Taugt zum Gebrauche das Heilge.
Ein Zeichen sind wir, deutungslos
Schmerzlos sind wir und haben fast
Die Sprache in der Fremde verloren.
Wenn nemlich ein Streit ist über Menschen
Am Himmel, und gewaltigen Schritt
Gestirne gehn, blind ist die Treue dann. Zweifellos
Ist aber Einer. Der

Kann täglich es ändern. Kaum bedarf er
Gesez, wie nemlich es
Bei Menschen bleiben soll und die Schrift tönt und
Es tönet das Blatt. Viel Männer möchten da
Seyn wahrer Sache.
Eichbäume wehn dann neben
Den Birnen. Denn nicht vermögen
Die Himmlischen alles. Nemlich es reichen
Die Sterbklichen eh' an den Abgrund.
Also wendet es sich,
Das Echo
Mit diesen. Schön ist
Der Brauttag, bange sind wir aber
Der Ehre wegen. Furchtbar gehet
Es ungestalt, wenn Eines uns
Zu gierig genommen. Lang ist
Die Zeit, es ereignet sich aber
Das Wahre.

Immer, Liebes! gehet
Die Erd', und der Himmel hält. Sonnenschein
Am Boden sehen wir und trokenen Staub
Und tief mit Schatten die Wälder und es blühet
An Dächern der Rauch, bei alter Krone

Is the holy fit for use.
We are but a meaningless sign,
Painless, and have nearly
Lost our speech so far from home.
For when there's a quarrel in heaven
Over man, and planets take
Great strides through space, then loyalty goes blind. But one
Is without doubt. Daily

He can change things. He hardly
Needs the laws, that's how it should be
With mortals, and a leaf makes sound
And writing resounds. Many men wish
To have a true cause.
Then oak trees sway
Next to pear trees. For the gods
Can't do everything. And mortals too
Come close to the abyss.
And even the echo
Turns around with them. The wedding day
Is beautiful, but we're anxious
About a point of honor. It goes terribly,
Grotesquely, when one has
Too greedily taken
Something of ours. Long is
Time, but the truth
Comes to pass.

Always, my dear, the earth
Moves and the sky holds firm. We see
Sunshine on the ground and dry dust
And the woods deep with shadows, and smoke
Blossoms peacefully on rooftops,

Der Thürme, friedsam, und es girren
Verloren in der Luft die Lerchen und unter dem Tage waiden
Wohlangeführt die Schaafe des Himmels.
Und Schnee, wie Majenblumen
Das Edelmüthige, wo
Es seie, bedeutend, glänzet mit
Der grünen Wiese
Der Alpen, dort
Vom Kreuze redend, das
Gesezt ist unterwegs einmal
Gestorbenen, geht auf der schroffen Straß'
Ein Wandersmann zornig, mit
Dem andern, aber was ist diß?

Am Feigenbaum ist mein
Achilles mir gestorben,
Und Ajax liegt
An Grotten der See,
An Bächen, benachbart dem Skamandros.
Bei Windessausen, nach
Der heimatlichen Samalis steter
Gewohnheit, in der Fremd', ist groß
Ajax gestorben.
Patroklos aber in des Königes Harnisch, und es starben
Noch andere viel. Mit eigener Hand
Viel traurige, wilden Muths, doch göttlich
Gezwungen, zulezt, die anderen aber
Im Geschike stehend, im Feld. Unwillig nemlich
Sind Himmlische, wenn einer nicht
Die Seele schonend sich
Zusammengenommen, aber er muß doch; dem gleich
Fehlet die Trauer.

Near the ancient
Crowns of turrets, and the call
Of larks is lost in the air and under day
The well-tended sheep of heaven graze.
And snow, like lilies of the valley,
Pointing to the noble-minded where it is,
Shines with the green
Alpine meadow, there
On a steep path, a traveler
angry with another,
Discusses a cross
Once laid there for the dead,
But what is *this?*

Beside the fig tree
My Achilles is dead to me,
And Ajax lies
Beside the grottoes of the sea
Near the streams of Scamandros.
In fierce windstorms, according to
The changeless customs of Salamis,
Great Ajax died in a
Foreign land,
But Patroclus died in the king's own armor
And many others also. By their own hand,
Wild with courage, many sad ones, [were] overcome
By god in the end, but the others,
Fast in their fate, stood on the field. For the gods
Are angry when someone fails
To collect his soul
In order to save it, but he must do so; in equal measure
Mourning bears the blame.

Fragments of Hymns

Heimath

Und niemand weiß

Indessen laß mich wandeln
Und wilde Beeren pflücken
Zu löschen die Liebe zu dir
An deinen Pfaden, o Erd'

Hier wo— — —
                und Rosendornen
Und süße Linden duften neben
Den Buchen, des Mittags, wenn im falben Kornfeld
Das Wachstum rauscht, an geradem Halm,
Und den Naken die Ähre seitwärts beugt
Dem Herbste gleich, jezt aber unter hohem
Gewölbe der Eichen, da ich sinn
Und aufwärts frage, der Glokenschlag
Mir wohlbekannt
Fernher tönt, goldenklingend, um die Stunde, wenn
Der Vogel wieder wacht. So gehet es wohl.

Home

And no one knows

But meanwhile let me walk
Along your paths, O Earth,
Picking wild berries
To quench my desire for you.

Here where— — —
         And the thorns of roses
And sweet linden is fragrant
Beside the beech trees at noon, when in the fallow cornfield
There's the rustle of growth on the stalk,
And the ear bends its neck to one side
Like autumn. But now beneath the high dome of oaks,
Where my thoughts and questions go upward,
The familiar
Sound of the bell
Rings a golden note in the distance
At the hour that birds awaken. And all is well.

Auf Falbem Laube…

Auf falbem Laube ruhet
Die Traube, des Weines Hoffnung, also ruhet der Wange
Der Schatten von dem goldenen Schmuk, der hängt
Am Ohre der Jungfrau.

Und ledig soll ich bleiben
Leicht fanget aber sich
In der Kette, die
Es abgerissen, das Kälblein.

Fleißig

Es liebet aber der Sämann
Zu sehen eine,
Des Tages schlafend über
Dem Strikstrumpf.

Nicht will wohllauten
Der deutsche Mund
Aber lieblich
Am stechenden Bart rauschen
Die Küsse.

On Yellow Leaves…

The grape rests
On dying leaves, a promise of wine,
As the shadow of a gold earring
Rests on a young woman's cheek.

And I must remain alone
But the little calf
Is entangled in the chain
Which it has torn loose.

So busy

But the sower
Loves to see a woman
Asleep at mid-day
Over a stocking half-knitted.

The German tongue
Is not easy on the ear
But lovingly
Plants its kisses
From a prickly beard.

Was ist der Menschen Leben…

Was ist der Menschen Leben   ein Bild der Gottheit.
Wie unter dem Himmel wandeln die Irrdischen alle, sehen
Sie diesen. Lesend aber gleichsam, wie
In einer Schrift, die Unendlichkeit nachahmen und den Reichtum
Menschen. Ist der einfältige Himmel
Denn reich? Wie Blüthen sind ja
Silberne Wolken. Es regent aber von daher
Der Thau und das Feuchte. Wenn aber
Das Blau ist ausgelöschet, das Einfältige, scheint
Das Matte, das dem Marmelstein gleichet, wie Erz,
Anzeige des Reichtums.

What is the Life of Men...

What is the life of men   a portrait of the godhead.
How far under heaven men wander the earth
To see this. Reading as in a script
An imitation of infinity and riches.
Is plain old heaven rich?
Like blossoms the silver clouds.
Dampness and dew
Rain down from them. But when
The blue is extinguished, the pallor of marble
Shines like an absence, like ore,
A sign of riches.

Was ist Gott?...

Was ist Gott? unbekannt, dennoch
Voll Eigenschaften ist das Angesicht
Des Himmels von ihm. Die Blize nemlich
Der Zorn sind eines Gottes. Jemehr ist eins
Unsichtbar,   schiket es sich in Fremdes. Aber der Donner
Der Ruhm ist Gottes. Die Liebe zur Unsterblichkeit
Das Eigentum auch, wie das unsere,
Ist eines Gottes.

What is God?...

What is God? Unknown, yet
His face has the qualities of heaven.
Of course, flashes of lightning
Are the anger of a god. The more
Invisible something is,   the stranger it becomes. Yet the thunder
Is the fame of God. Love of eternal life,
Property too, like our own,
Is a god's.

An die Madonna

Viel hab' ich dein
Und deines Sohnes wegen
Gelitten, o Madonna,
Seit ich gehöret von ihm
In süßer Jugend;
Denn nicht der Seher allein,
Es stehen unter einem Schiksaal
Die Dienenden auch. Denn weil ich

Und manchen Gesang, den ich
Dem höchsten zu singen, dem Vater
Gesonnen war, den hat
Mir weggezehret die Schwermuth.

Doch Himmlische, doch will ich
Dich feiern und nicht soll einer
Der Rede Schönheit mir
Die heimatliche, vorwerfen,
Dieweil ich allein
Zum Felde gehe, wo wild
Die Lilie wächst, furchtlos,
Zum unzugänglichen,
Uralten Gewölbe
Des Waldes,
     das Abendland,

       und gewaltet über
Den Menschen hat, statt anderer Gottheit sie
Die allvergessende Liebe.

To the Madonna

I have suffered much
O Madonna for your sake
And your son's,
Since I heard of him
In my tender youth;
For the seer is not alone
But stands under a fate
Of those who serve. For while I

And many songs, that I
Thought to sing to the Father
Most High, were stolen from me
And devoured by sadness.

Yet, Heavenly One, I will
Celebrate you and never should
Anyone reproach the beauty
Of my local speech,
As I go alone
To the fields, where
The lily grows wild, fearless,
Into the impenetrable
Primordial vault
Of the forest.
     The West,

          and having power
Over man, in place of other gods
The all-forgetting love

Denn damals sollt es beginnen
Als

Geboren dir im Schoose
Der göttliche Knabe und um ihn
Der Freundin Sohn, Johannes genannt
Vom stummen Vater, der kuhne
Dem war gegeben
Der Zunge Gewalt,
Zu deuten

Und die Furcht der Völker und
Die Donner und
Die stürzenden Wasser des Herrn.

Dem gut sind Sazungen, aber
Wie Drachenzähne, schneiden sie
Und tödten das Leben, wenn im Zorne sie schärft
Ein Geringer oder ein König.
Gleichmuth ist aber gegeben
Den Liebsten Gottes. So dann starben jene.
Die Beiden,   so auch sahst
Du göttlichtrauernd in der starken Seele sie sterben.
Und wohnst deswegen

                              und wenn in heiliger Nacht
Der Zukunft einer gedenkt und Sorge für
Die sorglosschlafenden trägt
Die frischaufblühenden Kinder
Kömmst lächelnd du, und fragst, was er, wo du
Die Königin seiest, befürchte.

For then it was to begin
When

Born from your womb
The godly boy, he who was
The son of your friend named John,
From his silent father, the brave one,
Whose tongue
Was given the power
To interpret

And the fear of the people and
The thunder and
The Lord's rushing waters

For statutes are good, but
Like dragons' teeth, they cut
And kill life, when sharpened in anger
By an ordinary man or king.
But a certain calm is given
To the best loved of God. So then they died.
Both,   so you saw
Them die, a godlike sadness in your heavy soul.
And therefore you dwell

                    and when in holy night
Someone happens to think of the future and worries for
The untroubled sleep
Of freshly blossoming children,
You come smiling, and ask him what
There is to fear, where you are Queen.

Denn nimmer vermagt du es
Die keimenden Tage zu neiden,
Denn lieb ist dirs, von je,
Wenn größer die Söhne sind,
Denn ihre Mutter. Und nimmer gefällt es dir
Wenn rükwärtsblikend
Ein Älteres spottet des Jungern.
Wer denkt der theuren Väter
Nicht gern und erzählet
Von ihren Thaten,

                       wenn aber Verwegnes geschach,
Und Undankbare haben
Das Ärgerniß   gegeben
Zu gerne blikt
Dann   zum
Und thatenscheu
Unendliche Reue und es haßt das Alte die Kinder.

Darum beschüze
Du Himmlische sie
Die jungen Pflanzen und wenn
Der Nord kömmt oder giftiger Thau weht oder
Zu lange dauert die Dürre
Und wenn sie üppigblühend
Versinken unter der Sense
Der allzuscharfen, gieb erneuertes Wachstum.
Und daß nur niemals nicht
Vielfältig, in schwachem Gezweige
Die Kraft mir vielversuchend
Zerstreue das frische Geschlecht, stark aber sei
Zu wählen aus Vielem das beste.

For you could never be guilty
Of envying the budding tendrils of the day,
For you have always liked it
When sons are greater
Than their mothers and you are never pleased
When an elder looks behind him
To mock a younger person.
Who doesn't think with pleasure
Of their precious fathers
And recount their deeds,

                            but when there is insolence
And the ungrateful ones
Instigate   scandal
To look too gladly
Then   toward
And fearful of action
Endless remorse and the elders hate the children.

Therefore protect
Them, Heavenly One,
The young plants, and when
The North Wind comes or poisonous dew drifts
Or a drought lasts too long,
And their abundant flowering
Sink under the scythe,
Which is all too sharp, grant them renewed growth.
And never, not once, let
The power in weak branches
Scatter the new generation,
But, looking in all directions, give it strength
To choose the best among the many.

Nichts ists, das Böse. Das soll
Wie der Adler den Raub
Mir eines begreifen.
Die Andren dabei. Damit sie nicht
Die Amme, die
Den Tag gebieret
Verwirren, falsch anklebend
Der Heimath und der Schwere spottend
Der Mutter ewig sizen
Im Schoose. Denn groß ist
Von dem sie erben den Reichtum.
Der

Vor allem, daß man schone
Der Wildniß göttlichgebaut
Im reinen Geseze, woher
Es haben die Kinder
Des Gotts, lustwandelnd unter
Den Felsen und Haiden purpurn blühn
Und dunkle Quellen
Dir, o Madonna und
Dem Sohne, aber den anderen auch
Damit nicht, als von Knechten,
Mit Gewalt das ihre nehmen
Die Götter.

An den Gränzen aber, wo stehet
Der Knochenberg, so nennet man ihn
Heut, aber in alter Sprache heißet
Er Ossa, Teutoburg ist
Daselbst auch und voll geistigen Wassers

Evil is nothing. One should
Grasp this as an eagle
His prey.
The others as well. So that they
Don't disturb the nurse
Who gives birth to the day,
When they falsely stick
To home, mocking at hardship,
And forever sit on their
Mothers' laps. For he is great
Whose wealth they inherit.
He

Above all, let the wilderness
Be spared, divinely built
According to pure law, which
God's children have,
Wandering happily
Among rocks and heather in purple bloom.
And the dark springs
Are for you, Madonna,
And your son as well as the others,
Lest as from slaves,
By force, the gods seize
What is theirs.

But at the borders, where
The Knochenberg stands, as it is now called,
But in the old tongue its name
Was Ossa, Teutoburg itself
Is there and full of spirited waters

Umher das Land, da
Die Himmlischen all
Sich Tempel

Ein Handwerksmann.

Uns aber die wir
Daß

Und zu sehr zu fürchten die Furcht nicht!
Denn du nicht, holde

            aber es giebt
Ein finster Geschlecht, das weder einen Halbgott
Gern hört, oder wenn mit Menschen ein Himmlisches oder
In Woogen erscheint, gestaltlos, oder das Angesicht
Des reinen ehrt, das nahen
Allgegenwärtigen Gottes.

Doch wenn unheilige schon
            in Menge
              und frech

Was kümmern sie dich
O Gesang den Reinen, ich zwar
Ich sterbe, doch du
Gehest andere Bahn, umsonst
Mag dich ein Neidisches hindern.

The surrounding country, where
The gods all
[Built] themselves temples.

    A craftsman.

But to us who
That

And don't fear fear too much!
Then not you, gracious one,

               but there is
A gloomy kind that doesn't like to hear
Of demigods or of the Heavenly appearing
Among men or in waves
Without shape nor honors the face of the pure,
The near and all-present God.

But when the unholy
            in crowds
              and shameless

Why do these matter to you,
O song that is pure; most surely
I die, but you
Take a different course; in vain
The envious will try to block your way.

Wenn dann in kommender Zeit
Du einem Guten begegnest
So grüß ihn, und er denkt,
Wie unsere Tage wohl
Voll Glüks, voll Leidens gewesen.
Von einem gehet zum andern

Noch Eins ist aber
Zu sagen. Denn es wäre
Mir fast zu plözlich
Das Glük gekommen,
Das Einsame, daß ich unverständig
Im Eigentum
Mich an die Schatten gewandt,
Denn weil du gabst
Den Sterblichen
Versuchend Göttergestalt,
Wofür ein Wort? so meint' ich, denn es hasset die Rede, wer
Das Lebenslicht das herzernährende sparet.
Es deuteten vor Alters
Die Himmlischen sich, von selbst, wie sie
Die Kraft der Götter hinweggenommen.

Wir aber zwingen
Dem Unglük ab und hängen die Fahnen
Dem Siegsgott, dem befreienden auf, darum auch
Hast du Räthsel gesendet. Heilig sind sie
Die Glänzenden, wenn aber alltäglich
Die Himmlischen und gemein
Das Wunder scheinen will, wenn nemlich

When you meet a good man
In times to come,
Greet him and he will think
How our days were
Full of joy and sorrow.
How one leads to the other.

There's one more thing
To say. For almost
Too quickly
Joy, lonely joy, was coming to me,
So that, failing to understand
What is mine,
I would have turned to the shadows,
For since you gave
To mortals
The tentative shape of gods,
What are words for? So then I thought, for words are hateful
To one who uses sparingly the heart-nourishing light of life.
In ancient times,
The heavenly ones interpreted themselves
How they snatched away the strength of the gods.

But we cope
With misfortune and hang flags
For the god of victory, he who sets free, and that is why
You have sent mysteries. They are holy,
The shining, but when the heavenly
Appears as an everyday thing
And the miracle seems commonplace, when indeed

Wie Raub Titanenfürsten die Gaaben
Der Mutter greifen, hilft ein Höherer ihr.

The Titan princes plunder the mother's gifts,
One who is higher comes to her assistance.

Die Titanen

Nicht ist es aber
Die Zeit. Noch sind sie
Unangebunden. Göttliches trift untheilnehmende nicht.
Dann mögen sie rechnen
Mit Delphi. Indessen, gieb in Feierstunden
Und daß ich ruhen möge, der Todten
Zu denken. Viele sind gestorben
Feldherrn in alter Zeit
Und schöne Frauen und Dichter
Und in neuer
Der Männer viel
Ich aber bin allein.

und in den Ocean schiffend
Die duftenden Inseln fragen
Wohin sie sind.

Denn manches von ihnen ist
In treuen Schriften überblieben
Und manches in Sagen der Zeit.
Viel offenbaret der Gott.
Denn lang schon wirken
Die Wolken hinab
Und es wurzelt vielesbereitend heilige Wildniß.
Heiß ist der Reichtum. Denn es fehlet
An Gesang, der löset den Geist.
Verzehren würd' er
Und wäre gegen sich selbst
Denn nimmer duldet

The Titans

It's not yet
Time. They are still
Unbound. And the indifferent don't care
About godly matters.
Let them puzzle it out
With the Oracle. Meanwhile, during the festivities,
I'll take my ease thinking of the dead.
In the old days,
Many generals died
And lovely women and poets.
Today, it's many men.
But I am alone.

      and sailing on the ocean
The sweetly scented islands
Ask where they are.

For something of them remains
In writing and in myth.
God reveals so much.
For a long time the clouds
Have influenced what's below
And the holy forest, preparing many things,
Has sent down roots.
The world's riches burn too intensely.
For we don't have the song
That will shake our spirit free.
It would consume itself,
For the heavenly fire can never

Die Gefangenschaft das himmlische Feuer.

Es erfreuet aber
Das Gastmahl oder wenn am Feste
Das Auge glänzet und von Perlen
Der Jungfrau Hals.
Auch Kriegesspiel

                    und durch die Gänge
Der Gärten schmettert
Das Gedächtniß der Schlacht und besänftiget
An schlanker Brust
Die tönenden Wehre ruhn
Von Heldenvätern den Kindern.
Mich aber umsummet
Die Bien und wo der Akersmann
Die Furchen machet singen gegen
Dem Lichte die Vögel. Manche helfen
Dem Himmel. Diese siehet
Der Dichter. Gut ist es, an andern sich
Zu halten. Denn keiner trägt das Leben allein.

Wenn aber ist entzündet
Der geschäfftige Tag
Und an der Kette, die
Den Bliz ableitet
Von der Stunde des Aufgangs
Himmlischer Thau glänzt,
Muß unter Sterblichen auch
Das Hohe sich fühlen.
Drum bauen sie Häußer
Und die Werkstatt gehet ·

Endure captivity.

Yet men enjoy
The banquet, and in celebration,
Their eyes are brightened by pearls
On a young woman's neck.
Also games of war

        and through
The garden paths
The memory of battle clatters;
The resonant weapons
Of heroic ancestors lie soothed
And still upon the breasts
Of children. But the bees hum
Around me, and where the plowman
Makes his furrows, birds
Sing against the light. Many give
Help to heaven. The poet
Sees them. It's good to rely
On others. For no one can bear his life alone.

But when the busy day
Catches fire,
And heavenly dew glistens
On the chain
Leading lightning from sunrise
To its source, even mortals
Feel its grandeur.
That's why they build houses
And the workshop is so busy
And ships sail

Und über Strömen das Schiff.
Und es bieten tauschend die Menschen
Die Händ' einander, sinnig ist es
Auf Erden und es sind nicht umsonst
Die Augen an den Boden geheftet.

Ihr fühlet aber
Auch andere Art.
Den unter dem Maaße
Des Rohen brauchet es auch
Damit das Reine sich kenne.
Wenn aber

Und in die Tiefe greifet
Daß es lebendig werde
Der Allerschütterer, meinen die
Es komme der Himmlische
Zu Todten herab und gewaltig dämmerts
Im ungebundenen Abgrund
Im allesmerkenden auf.
Nicht möcht ich aber sagen
Es werden die Himmlischen schwach
Wenn schon es aufgährt.
Wenn aber
                          und es gehet

An die Scheitel dem Vater, daß

              und der Vogel des Himmels ihm
Es anzeigt. Wunderbar
Im Zorne kommet er drauf.

Against the currents
And men exchange greetings
Holding out their hands; it's sensible
On earth, and not for nothing
Do we fix our eyes on the ground.

Yet you sense
A different way.
For proportion demands
That coarseness exist
For purity to be known.
But when

And reaches into the earth
To make it come to life,
The shaker of all things
People think the heavenly
Have come down to the dead
And the all-knowing has dawned
In a boundless emptiness.
It's not for me to say
That the gods are growing weak
Just as they come into being.
But when

                        and it goes

To the father at the summit, so that

                 and the bird of heaven
Makes it known to him. Then he appears,
Wonderful in anger.

Einst hab ich die Muse gefragt…

Einst hab ich die Muse gefragt, und sie
Antwortete mir
Am Ende wirst du es finden.
Kein Sterblicher kann es fassen.
Vom Höchsten will ich schweigen.
Verbotene Frucht, wie der Lorbeer, aber ist
Am meisten das Vaterland. Die aber kost'
Ein jeder zulezt,

Viel täuschet Anfang
Und Ende.
Das lezte aber ist
Das Himmelszeichen, das reißt
      und   Menschen
Hinweg. Wohl hat Herkules das
Gefürchtet. Aber da wir träge
Geboren sind, bedarf es des Falken, dem
Befolgt' ein Reuter, wenn
Er jaget, den Flug.

Im   wenn
Und der Fürst

      und Feuer und Rauchdampf blüht
Auf dürrem Rasen
Doch ungemischet darunter
Aus guter Brust, das Labsaal
Der Schlacht, die Stimme quillet des Fürsten.

Once I asked the muse...

Once I asked the muse, and she
Replied:
In the end you'll find it.
Those born to die can't grasp it.
About the highest mysteries, I'm speechless.
One's true native land, like the laurel,
Is forbidden fruit, the last thing
We all taste,

The beginning and ending
Deceive us far too much.
The last thing, however,
Is heaven's sign that sweeps
   and   men
Away. Even Hercules
Feared it. But since we are
Born listless, a falcon is required
And a horseman
To follow its flight.

In the   when
And the Prince

    and fire and smoke flower
On dry grass
Still unmingled with all this
The voice of the Prince, the battle's refreshment,
Wells from a good breast.

Gefäße machet ein Künstler.
Und es kauffet

       wenn es aber
Zum Urteil kommt
Und keusch hat es die Lippe
Von einem Halbgott berührt

Un schenket das Liebste
Den Unfruchtbaren
Denn nimmer, von nun an
Taugt zum Gebrauche das Heilge.

An artist makes vessels
And they are purchased

        but when
The day of judgment comes
And the lip of a demigod
Touches it like a virgin

He will never
Give away the thing he loves
To the unprolific, from that point on
The sacred is the useful.

Wenn aber die Himmlischen…

Wenn aber die Himmlischen haben
Gebaut, still ist es
Auf Erden, und wohlgestalt stehn
Die betroffenen Berge. Gezeichnet
Sind ihre Stirnen. Denn es traf
Sie, da den Donnerer hielt
Unzärtlich die gerade Tochter
Des Gottes bebender Stral
Und wohl duftet gelöscht
Von oben der Aufruhr.
Wo inne stehet, beruhiget, da
Und dort,   das Feuer.
Denn Freude schüttet
Der Donnerer aus und hätte fast
Des Himmels vergessen
Damals im Zorne, hätt ihn nicht
Das Weise gewarnet.
Jezt aber blüht es
Am armen Ort.
Und wunderbar groß will
Es stehen.
Gebirg hänget   See,
Warme   Tiefe   es kühlen aber die Lüfte
Inseln und Halbinseln,
Grotten zu beten,

Ein glanzender Schild
Und schnell, wie Rosen,

oder es schafft

But when the gods...

But when the gods are through
With creation, the earth becomes
Quiet, and the shocked mountains
Stand well-formed, their features
Firmly drawn. So it happened
That as the Thunderer argued
Sharply with his daughter,
They were struck full-force
By God's shaking light.
And a clean scent remains
In the first aftermath.
Where it inwardly resides, here
and there   calming the fire.
For the Thunderer showers
Down joy and would have
Almost forgotten the heavens
In his anger, had not
Wisdom warned him.
Now however even
Poor places flower.
And stand majestic.
Mountain overhangs   sea,
Warm   deep   but the wind cools
Islands and peninsulas,
Shrines to pray,

A shining shield,
And quick, as roses

or creates

Auch andere Art,
Es sprosset aber

                viel üppig neidiges
Unkraut, das blendet, schneller schießet
Es auf, das ungelenke, denn es scherzet
Der Schöpferische, sie aber
Verstehen es nicht. Zu zornig greifft
Es und wächst. Und dem Brande gleich,
Der Häuser verzehret, schlägt
Empor, achtlos, und schonet
Den Raum nicht, und die Pfade bedeket,
Weitgährend, ein dampfend Gewölk
                die unbeholfene Wildniß.
So will es göttlich scheinen. Aber
Furchtbar ungastlich windet
Sich durch den Garten die Irre,
Die augenlose, da den Ausgang
Mit reinen Händen kaum
Erfindet ein Mensch. Der gehet, gesandt,
Und suchet, dem Thier gleich, das
Nothwendige. Zwar mit Armen,
Der Ahnung voll, mag einer treffen
Das Ziel. Wo nemlich
Die Himmlischen eines Zaunes oder Merkmals,
Das ihren Weg
Anzeige, oder eines Bades
Bedürfen, reget es wie Feuer
In der Brust der Männer sich.

Noch aber hat andre
Bei sich der Vater.

Other means
But the sprouting of

                    many upstart
Weeds, deceptive and ungainly
As they shoot up quickly,
For the Creator makes jokes
They don't understand. They grasp and spread
In an excess of resentment. And like the fire
That burns down houses, strikes out
Indifferently, and spares no
Room, and covers all paths,
Everywhere at once, a suffocating cloud
                  an unkempt wilderness.
Seeming to be a god's. But terribly,
Inhospitably, the mad one, eyeless,
Wanders through the garden, since no man
With clean hands
Can find his way out.
Driven like an animal, he seeks
The essential. Of course,
Having use of his arms
And premonitions, a man may reach
His goal. For where
The gods have fences or markers
To show the way,
Or a pool to bathe in,
The hearts of men
Beat like fire.

But the Father has
Others by his side.

Denn über den Alpen

Weil an den Adler

Sich halten müssen, damit sie nicht

Mit eigenem Sinne zornig deuten

Die Dichter, wohnen über dem Fluge

Des Vogels, um den Thron

Des Gottes der Freude

Und deken den Abgrund

Ihm zu, die gelbem Feuer gleich, in reißender Zeit

Sind über Stirnen der Männer,

Die Prophetischen, denen möchten

Es neiden, weil die Furcht

Sie lieben, Schatten der Hölle,

Sie aber trieb,

Ein rein Schiksaal

Eröffnend   von

Der Erde heiligen Tischen

Der Reiniger Herkules,

Der bleibet immer lauter, jezt noch,

Mit dem Herrscher, und othembringend steigen

Die Dioskuren ab und auf,

An unzugänglichen Treppen, wenn von himmlischer Burg

Die Berge fernhinziehen

Bei Nacht, und hin

Die Zeiten

Pythagoras

Im Gedächtniß aber lebet Philoktetes,

For above the Alps
Poets must rely
On an eagle's flight, so their scornful
Perceptions make more than private sense.
Living above the flight
Of birds, at the throne
Of the God of Joy,
From whom they conceal
The nothingness, the prophets
Walk overhead, above the faces of men,
Like yellow fire in torn times,
Envied by those in love
With fear, shadows in Hell,

But they were driven,
A pure fate,
Opening   from
The earth's holy tables
Hercules, the cleanser, who remains
In God's eye pure to this day,
And, bearers of breath,
The Dioscuri climb up and down
Inaccessible stairs, as the mountains
Retreat at night from the
Heavenly fortress and gone now
The times
Of Pythagoras.

But Philoctetes lives in memory.

Die helfen dem Vater.
Denn ruhen mögen sie. Wenn aber
Sie reizet unnüz Treiben
Der Erd' und es nehmen
Den Himmlischen
              die Sinne, brennend kommen
Sie dann,

Die othemlosen— —

Denn es hasset
Der sinnende Gott
Unzeitiges Wachstum.

Desiring rest,
They help the Father. But when
The useless things of earth
Stir them up and the gods
Are made
                senseless, they come
Burning

Out of breath— —

For a contemplative God
Hates growth
Out of season.

Meinest du es solle gehen...

meinest du
Es solle gehen,
Wie damals? Nemlich sie wollten stiften
Ein Reich der Kunst. Dabei ward aber
Das Vaterländische von ihnen
Versäumet und erbärmlich gieng
Das Griechenland, das schönste, zu Grunde.
Wohl hat es andere
Bewandtniß jezt.
Es sollten nemlich die Frommen

und alle Tage wäre
Das Fest.
Also darf nicht
Ein ehrlich Meister

und wie mit Diamanten
In die Fenster machte, des Müßiggangs wegen
Mit meinen Fingern, hindert

so hat mir
Das Kloster etwas genüzet,

Do you think things will go…

do you think
Things will go
As before? That is, they wanted to establish
A kingdom of art. But thereby
Neglected what was native to their land
And Greece, most beautiful of all,
Went miserably into decline.
Now the state of affairs
Is completely different.
Indeed, the pious should

                    and every day would be
A festival.
                    An honored teacher
Should thus not

                    and as with diamonds
Drawn on the window by my
Indolent fingers, obscured

                    So the cloister
Was somewhat useful,

Der Adler
[Sattler Kompilation]

Mein Vater ist gewandert, auf dem Gotthard.
Da wo die Flüsse, hinab,
Wohl nach Hetruria seitwärts,
Und des geraden Weges
Auch über den Schnee,
Zum Olympos und Hämos
Wo den Schatten der Athos wirft,
Nach Höhlen in Lemos.
Anfänglich aber sind
Aus Wäldern des Indus
Die Eltern gekommen.
Der Urahn aber
Ist geflogen über der See
Scharfsinnend, und es wunderte sich
Des Königs goldnes Haupt
Ob dem Geheimniß der Wasser,
Als roth die Wolken dampften
Über dem Schiff. Die Thiere stumm
Einander schauend
Der Speise gedachten, aber
Es stehen die Berge doch still,
Wo wollen wir bleiben?

Reh.

Der Fels ist zu Waide gut,
Das Trokne zu Trank.

The Eagle

[Sattler Compilation]

My father roamed over the Gotthard,
Where the rivers plunge
Sideways toward Etruria
Then take straight paths
Over snow
To Olympus and Haimos,
Where Athos throws shadows
Toward the caves of Lemnos
Though in the beginning
My parents emerged
From the forests of Indus.
But our first ancestor
Flew over the sea,
Clear-sighted, and the king's
Golden head in awe
Of the waters' hushed secret,
As the red clouds made mist
Above the Ark. The animals stared
Dumbly at each other,
Thinking only of food,
But the mountains stand quite still.
Where will we come to rest?

Deer.

Rock goes well with pasture.
Dryness with drink.

Das Nasse aber zu Speise.
Will einer wohnen,
So sei es an Treppen,
Und wo ein Häuslein hinabhängt
Am Wasser halte dich auf.
Und was einer hat, ist
Athem zu hohlen.
Hat einer ihn nemlich hinauf
Am Tage gebracht,
Er findet im Schlaf ihn wieder.
Denn wo die Augen zugedekt,
Und gebunden die Füße sind,
Da wirst du es finden.

Drink with a meal.

If you want to live somewhere,

Make sure there are stairs.

And spend your days

In a cottage

That overhangs water.

All that you can hold

Is your own breath.

What you create by day

You find again in sleep.

When the eyes are closed

And the feet are bound in sheets,

There you will find it.

Ihr sichergebaueten Alpen…

Ihr sichergebaueten Alpen!
Die

Und ihr sanftblikenden Berge,
Wo über buschigem Abhang
Der Schwarzwald saußt,
Und Wohlgerüche die Loke
Der Tannen herabgießt,
Und der Nekar

     und die Donau!
Im Sommer liebend Fieber
Umherwehet der Garten
Und Linden des Dorfs, un wo
Die Pappelweide blühet
Und der Seidenbaum
Auf heiliger Waide,

Und

Ihr guten Städte!
Nicht ungestalt, mit dem Feinde
Gemischet unmächtig

Was
Auf einmal gehet es weg
Und siehet den Tod nicht.
Wann aber

You firmly built Alps...

You firmly built Alps!
That

And your gently glancing mountains,
Where, over the bushy slope,
The Black Forest storms
And the fir tree's needles
Pour down their full aroma
And the Neckar

      And the Danube!
In summer a loving fever
Blows all over the garden
And the lindens of the village, and where
The black poplar blooms
And the silk-tree
On a holy pasture

And

You good cities!
Not without shape, mixed up
With the enemy, powerless

What
All at once it goes away
And doesn't see death
But when

Und Stutgard, wo ich
Ein Augenbliklicher begraben
Liegen dürfte, dort,
Wo sich die Straße
Bieget, und
      um die Weinstaig,
Und der Stadt Klang wieder
Sich findet drunten auf ebenem Grün
Stilltönend unter den Apfelbäumen

Des Tübingens   wo
und Blize fallen
Am hellen Tage
Und Römisches tönend ausbeuget der Spizberg
Und Wohlgeruch

Und Tills Thal, das

And Stuttgart where
In the blink of an eye I may
Be allowed to be buried, there
Where the street
Bends, and
          Around the Weinstaig
And the city's noise finds
Itself once more on the even green
Quietly sounding under the apple trees

Of Tübingen   where
And lightning falls
On bright days
And resonant with fragrance and things Roman, the Spitzberg
Curves outward

And Thills Valley which

Das nächste Beste

[Dritte Fassung]

       offen die Fenster des Himmels
Und freigelassen der Nachtgeist
Der himmelstürmende, der hat unser Land
Beschwäzet, mit Sprachen viel, unbändigen, und
Den Schutt gewälzet
Bis diese Stunde.
Doch kommt das, was ich will,
Wenn
Drum wie die Staaren
Mit Freudengeschrei, wenn auf Gasgogne, Orten, wo viel Gärten sind,
Wenn im Olivenland, und
In liebenswürdiger Fremde,
Springbrunnen an grasbewachsnen Wegen
Die Bäum unwissend in der Wüste
Die Sonne sticht,
Und das Herz der Erde thuet
Sich auf, wo um
Den Hügel von Eichen
Aus brennendem Lande
Die Ströme und wo
Des Sonntags unter Tänzen
Gastfreundlich die Schwellen sind,
An blüthenbekränzten Straßen, stillegehend.
Sie spüren nemlich die Heimath,
Wenn grad   aus falbem Stein,
Die Wasser silbern rieseln
Und heilig Grün sich zeigt
Auf feuchter Wiese der Charente,

What is Nearest

[Third Version]

open the windows of heaven
And let the night spirit loose
The heaven-stormer, who has persuaded our land
With many unruly languages and
Has rolled his rubble
Up to this hour.
But what I want will come,
When
Therefore like the starlings
With shouts of joy, when in Gascony, places, where many gardens are,
When in olive land, and
In lovely foreign lands,
Fountains on paths overgrown with grass
The unknowing trees in the desert
Stung by the sun
And the heart of earth
Opens itself, where
Around the hill of oaks
From a burning land
The streams and where
On Sundays among dances
The thresholds are hospitable to guests
On streets strung with garlands, quietly swaying.
For indeed they sense home,
When straight   from pale yellow stone
The waters ripple silver
And holy green appears
On a damp meadow of the Charente,

Die klugen Sinne pflegend.   wenn aber

Die Luft sich bahnt,

Und ihnen machet waker

Scharfwehend die Augen der Nordost, fliegen sie auf,

Und Ek um Eke

Das Liebere gewahrend

Denn immer halten die sich genau an das Nächste,

Sehn sie die heiligen Wälder und die Flamme, blühendduftend

Des Wachstums und die Wolken des Gesanges fern und athmen Othem

Der Gesänge. Menschlich ist

Das Erkentniß. Aber die Himmlischen

Auch haben solches mit sich, und des Morgens beobachten

Die Stunden und des Abends die Vögel. Himmlischen auch

Gehöret also solches. Wolan nun. Sonst in Zeiten

Des Geheimnisses hätt ich, als von Natur, gesagt,

Sie kommen, in Deutschland. Jezt aber, weil, wie die See

Die Erd ist und die Länder, Männern gleich, die nicht

Vorüber gehen können, einander, untereinander

Sich schelten fast, so sag ich. Abendlich wohlgeschmiedet

Vom Oberlande biegt sich das Gebirg, wo auf hoher Wiese die Wälder

    sind wohl an

Der bairischen Ebne. Nemlich Gebirg

Geht weit und streket, hinter Amberg sich und

Fränkischen Hügeln. Berühmt ist dieses. Umsonst nicht hat

Seitwärts gebogen Einer von Bergen der Jugend

Das Gebirg, und gerichtet das Gebirg

Heimatlich. Wildniß nemlich sind ihm die Alpen und

Das Gebirg, das theilet die Tale und die Länge lang

Geht über die Erd. Dort aber

Gehn mags nun. Fast, unrein, hatt sehn lassen und das Eingeweid

Der Erde.   Bei Ilion aber

Tending the clever senses.　　　　　but when
The air prepares a way for itself
And the North Wind, blowing sharply,
Makes their eyes wide-awake, they fly off,
And corner to corner
Becoming aware of what is more dear,
For they are always guided by exactly what is nearest,
They see the holy forest and the flames of growth
Blossoming fragrantly and the clouds of song far away
And breathe the breath of songs. It's human
To have perceptions. But the heavenly
Also have something like that in them, and in the mornings they watch
The hours and at evening the birds. To the heavenly
This also pertains. All right then. But at those times
When I had the secret, as though from Nature, I should
Have said, "They are coming in Germany."
But now, because the earth is like the sea,
And the countries are like men,
Who cannot pass one another
But scold each other, so I say, in the well-made evening
The mountain range bends in the highlands,
Where in pastures the forests overlook
The Bavarian plain. For mountain ranges go far and stretch beyond
Amberg and the Franconian hills. These are famous. Not for nothing
Someone bent the mountain of youth sideways
And turned it to face toward home.
For the Alps are wilderness to him and
The mountain range that divides the valley and stretches full-length
Over the earth. But there

Let it run now. Nearly impure, it showed itself and the entrails
Of earth.　　　　　　　　　But near Ilion

War auch das Licht der Adler. Aber in der Mitte
Der Himmel der Gesänge. Neben aber
Am Ufer zornige Greise, der Entscheidung nemlich, die alle
Drei unser sind.

There was also the light of eagles. But in the middle
The heaven of songs. But nearby,
Angry old men on the shore of decision, all three
Of which are ours.

Tinian

Süß ists, zu irren
In heiliger Wildniß,
— — — —

Und an der Wölfin Euter, o guter Geist,
Der Wasser, die
Durchs heimatliche Land
Mir irren,
          , wilder sonst,
Und jezt gewöhnt, zu trinken, Findlingen gleich;
Des Frühlings, wenn im warmen Grunde
Des Haines wiederkehrend fremde Fittige

          ausruhend in Einsamkeit,
Und an Palmtagsstauden
Wohlduftend
Mit Sommervögeln
Zusammenkommen die Bienen,
Und deinen Alpen

Von Gott getheilet

Der Welttheil,

          zwar sie stehen
Gewapnet,

Tinian

It's sweet to get lost
In the holy wilderness,

— — — —

And drink, o kind spirit, at the wolf teats
Of the waters that wander
Through my native land
To me,

                 ,wilder once,
But now, like orphans, accustomed to the taste;
In spring, when unfamiliar wings
Return to the warmth of the woods

                 resting in solitude,
Among the willow trees
Full of fragrance
Where butterflies
Mingle with bees
And your Alps

Divided from God

The divided world,

                 indeed they stand
Armed,

Und lustzuwandeln, zeitlos

          denn es haben
Wie Wagenlauff uns falkenglänzend, oder
Dem Thierskampf gleich, als Muttermaal
Weß Geistes Kind
Die Abendländischen sein, die Himmlischen
Uns diese Zierde geordnet;

          Die Blumen giebt es,
Nicht von der Erde gezeugt, von selber
Aus lokerem Boden sprossen die,
Ein Widerstral des Tages, nicht ist
Es ziemand, diese zu pflüken,
Denn golden stehen,
Unzubereitet,
Ja schon die unbelaubten
Gedanken gleich,

And wander as they wish, timelessly

                         for the gods
Hazard us a falcon's glance, or
Like gladiators, the gods decree
These outward signs to be birthmarks
Of whose child
The West must be;

                         Some flowers
Don't grow from the earth, but sprout
In loose soil of their own will,
Counter-light of our days, nor should
One pick them,
For they stand golden,
Prepared only for what they are,
Leafless even
As thoughts,

Kolomb

[Sattler Kompilation]

Wünscht' ich der Helden einer zu seyn
Und dürfte frei, mit der Stimme des Schäfers, oder eines Hessen,
Dessen eingeborner Sprach, es bekennen
So wär' es ein Seeheld. Thätigkeit, zu gewinnen nemlich
Is das freundlichste, das
Unter allen

Heimische Wohnung und Ordnung, durchaus bündig,
Dürre Schönheit zu lernen und Gestalten
In den Sand gebrannt
Aus Nacht und Feuer, voll von Bildern, reingeschliffenes
Fernrohr, hohe Bildung, nemlich für das Leben
Den Himmel zu fragen.

Wenn du sie aber nennest
Anson und Gama, Äneas
Und Jason, Chirons
Schüler in Megaras Felsenhöhlen, und
Im zitternden Reegen der Grotte Bildete sich ein Menschenbild
Aus Eindrüken des Walds, und die Tempelherren, die gefahren
Nach Jerusalem Bouillon, Rinaldo,
Bougainville   [Entdekungsreisen
Als Versuche, den hesperischen
orbis gegen den
orbis der Alten zu bestimmen]

Gewaltig ist die Zahl
Gewaltiger aber sind sie selbst
Und machen stumm

Columbus

[Sattler Compilation]

If I wanted to be a hero
Of my own free will, with the voice of a shepherd or Hessian,
Speaking his native dialect,
I'd profess the life of a sea hero.
Because a life of action
Is best of all

Native dwelling and order, convincing throughout,
To learn barren beauty and figures
Burnt into sand
From night and fire, full of images, telescope
Polished to a trueness, utmost expertise, that is, for life
To question the sky.

But when you name them
Anson and Gama, Aeneas
And Jason, Chiron's
Student in Megara's rocky cave, and
In the shivering rain of the grotto a man's image is formed
From the forest's impressions, and knights templar who traveled
To Jerusalem Bouillon, Rinaldo,
Bougainville   [travels of discovery
seeking to distinguish the western
world from the
world of the ancients]

Their number is powerful
They are even more powerful
And strike men

die Männcr.

Dennoch

Und hin nach Genua will ich
Zu erfragen Kolombos Haus
Wo er, als wenn
Eins der Götter Eines wäre und wunderbar
Der Menschen Geschlecht,
In süßer Jugend gewohnet. Licht
Aber man kehret
Wesentlich um, wie ein
Bildermann, der stehet
Vorm Kornhaus, von Sicilien her vieleicht
Und die Bilder weiset der Länder
Der Großen auch
Und singet der Welt Pracht,

so du
Mich aber fragest

So weit das Herz
Mir reichet, wird es gehen
Nach Brauch und Kunst.

Zu Schiffe aber steigen
ils crient rapport, ils fermes maison
tu es un saisrien

Dumb.

And yet

And I will go to Genoa
To ask where Columbus lives
Where he spent
His sweet youth,
As though he were one of the gods and
The human species were wonderful. Light
But one turns
Around, like a
Picture vendor standing
In front of a corn crib, from Sicily maybe,
And shows pictures of countries
And of celebrities and
Also sings of the world's splendor,

but if

You ask me

How far my heart
Reaches, it goes
Toward custom and art.

But they embark
Il crient rapport, ils fermes maison
tu es un saisrien

Ein Murren war es, ungedultig, denn
Von wengen geringen Dingen
Verstimmt wie vom Schnee ward
Die Erde zornig und eilte, während daß sie schrien
Manna und Himmelsbrod
Mit Prophezeiungen und
Großem Geschrei, des Gebets mit Gunst,
Zum Abendessen.
Sauer wird mir dieses wenig
Geduld und Gütigkeit mein Richter und Schuzgott
Denn Menschen sind wir
Und sie glaubten, sie seien Mönche.
Und einer, als Redner
Auftrat uns als Pfarherr
Im blauen Wamms
entière personne content de son
ame difficultés connoissance
rapport tire

Doch da hinaus, damit
Vom Plaze
Wir kommen, also rief
Gewaltig richtend
Die Gesellen die Stimme des Meergotts,
Die reine, daran
Heroen erkennen, ob sie recht

It was an impatient murmur, one
Of those little things,
As when a bell one rings for supper
Is put out of tune by snow
The earth became angry and hurried,
While they shouted Manna and Heavens-bread
With prophecies and
Great cries of gracious prayer.
This upsets me, little
Patience and goodness my judge and guardian god
For we are human
And they believed they were monks.
And one, as a speaker
Appeared to us as a vicar
In a blue coat
entiere personne content de son
ame difficultes connaissance
rapport tire

But let's go,
Get moving, thus
Judging
The pure voice of the sea-god
Called the companions,
By which heroes recognize
If they've turned out

Gerathen oder nicht—

Stürzet herein, ihr Bäche
Von Leib und Gottes Gnad und Glük im seinen,
Kräfte zu begreiffen, o ihr Bilder
Der Jugend, als in Genua, damals
Der Erdkreis, griechisch, kindlich gestaltet,
Mit Gewalt under meinen Augen,
Einschläfernd, kurzgefaßtem Mohngeist gleich mir
Erschien

Das bist du ganz in deiner Schönheit apocalyptica

moments tirées hautes sommeils der Schiffer
Kolombus aber beiseit Hypostasierung des vorigen orbis
Naiveté der Wissenschaft
Und seufzeten miteinander, um die Stunde,
Nach der Hizze des Tags.
lui a les pleures

Sie sahn nun

Es waren nemlich viele,
Der schönen Inseln.

        damit
Mit Lissabon

Und Genua theilten;

Denn einsam kann
Von Himmlischen den Reichtum tragen

Right or not—

Rush in, you streams
Of love and God's favor and fortune in what's his,
To understand strengths, o images
Of youth, when Genoa was
The world, Greek, childishly shaped
And powerful under my eyes,
It lulled me to sleep, appearing to me like the spirit
of crushed poppies

That's you in your beauty apocalyptica

moments tirees hautes sommeils the sailor
Columbus alone hypostasis of previous worlds
Naiveté of science
And sighed together, at the hour,
After the heat of day.
lui a les pleures

Now they saw

The lovely isles,
For there are many.

         so that
Lisbon shared

With Genoa;

For one can't
Endure the wealth of the gods

Nicht eins; wohl nemlich mag
Den Harnisch dehnen
      ein Halbgott, dem Höchsten aber
Ist fast zu wenig
Das Wirken   wo das Tagslicht scheinet,
Und der Mond,

    Darum auch

      so

Nemlich öfters, wenn
Den Himmlischen zu einsam
Es wird, daß sie
Allein zusammenhalten

      oder die Erde; denn allzurein ist
Entweder

    Dann aber

      die Spuren der alten Zucht,

Alone; for indeed
A demigod can loosen his reigns,
                    but, to the all powerful
Such work
Is too little   where the daylight shines,
And the moon,

          Therefore also

                    so

Often when
The gods become
Too lonely, so that
Alone they hold together

                    on the earth, which is all too pure
Either

          But then

                    signs of the ancient race,

Und Mitzufühlen das Leben…

Und mitzufühlen das Leben
Der Halbgötter oder Patriarchen, sizend
Zu Gericht. Nicht aber überall ists
Ihnen gleich um diese, sondern Leben, summendheißes auch von
Schatten Echo
Als in einen Brennpunct
Versammelt. Goldne Wüste. Oder wohlunterhalten dem Feuerstahl
   des lebenswarmen
Heerds gleich schlägt dann die Nacht Funken, aus geschliffnem Gestein
Des Tages, und um die Dämmerung noch
Ein Saitenspiel tönt. Gegen das Meer zischt
Der Knall der Jagd. Die Aegypterin aber, offnen Busens sizt
Immer singend wegen Mühe gichtisch das Gelenk
Im Wald, am Feuer. Recht Gewissen bedeutend
Der Wolken und der Seen des Gestirns
Rauscht in Schottland wie an dem See
Lombardas dann ein Bach vorüber. Knaben spielen
Perlfrischen Lebens gewohnt so um Gestalten
Der Meister, oder der Leichen, oder es rauscht so um der Thürme
Kronen
Sanfter Schwalben Geschrei.

Nein wahrhaftig der Tag
Bildet keine
Menschenformen. Aber erstlich
Ein alter Gedanke, Wissenschaft
Elysium.

         und verlorne Liebe
Der Turniere   Rosse, scheu und feucht

And to experience the lives…

And to experience the lives
Of demigods or patriarchs, who sit
In judgment. But they are not equal to everything
Around them, that is, life, buzzing with heat and the shadows' echo
As if brought together
At the burning point of fire. Wastelands of gold. Or well-tended like
    the flint that ignites the life-warm
Hearth, as night strikes sparks from the smooth stone
Of day, and around dusk
A stringed instrument plays. Hunters' gunshots
Hiss toward the sea. But the Egyptian, bare-breasted,
Continues singing, in the woods, by the fire, about
Her bones aching from work. Signaling the clear conscience
Of the planet's clouds and seas
A stream rushes through Scotland, as on the lakes
Of Lombardy, and beyond into a brook. Their lives
As fresh as pearls, boys play near the shapes
Of their teachers, or of corpses, or the soft
Cries of swallows
As they circle
The crowns of towers.

No. In truth, the day
Constructs no
Human shapes. But first
An old thought, knowledge
Elysium.

         and lost love
Of contests   horses, skittish and moist

Vom Abgrund nemlich…

Vom Abgrund nemlich haben
Wir angefangen und gegangen
Dem Leuen gleich, in Zweifel und Ärgerniß,
Denn sinnlicher sind Menschen
In dem Brand
Der Wüste
Lichttrunken und der Thiergeist ruhet
Mit ihnen. Bald aber wird, wie ein Hund, umgehn
In der Hizze meine Stimme auf den Gassen der Gärten
In denen wohnen Menschen
In Frankreich
Der Schöpfer
Frankfurt aber, nach der Gestalt, die
Abdruk ist der Natur zu reden
Des Menschen nemlich, ist der Nabel
Dieser Erde, diese Zeit auch
Ist Zeit, under deutschen Schmelzes.
Ein wilder Hügel aber stehet über dem Abhang
Meiner Gärten. Kirschenbäume. Scharfer Othem aber wehet
Um die Löcher des Felses. Allda bin ich
Alles miteinander. Wunderbar
Aber über Quellen beuget schlank
Ein Nußbaum und   sich. Beere, wie Korall
Hängen an dem Strauche über Röhren von Holz,
Aus denen
Ursprünglich aus Korn, nun aber zu gestehen, bevestigter Gesang von
    Blumen als
Neue Bildung aus der Stadt, wo
Bis zu Schmerzen aber der Nase steigt
Citronengeruch auf und das Öl, aus der Provence, und es haben diese

Beginning at the Abyss...

We began of course at the abyss
And have gone forth like lions
In doubt and anger,
For men are more sensual
In the heat
Of deserts
Drunk with light, and the spirit of animals
Lies down with them. But soon, like a dog,
My voice will wander in the heat
Through the garden paths
In which people live
In France
The Creator
Frankfurt, rather, for to speak of nature
Is to take its shape, human nature, I mean,
Umbilicus of this earth, our time
Is also time, and of German making.
An overgrown hill hangs above
My gardens. Cherry trees. But a sharp breath
Blows through the holes in stone. And there I am,
All things at once. A wonderful
Nut tree bends over
The wellsprings and   itself. Berries like coral
Hang on the bush above the wooden downspout
Which they used to make of corn,
But now,
Quite frankly, it sings most forcefully of flowers
As news from town, where the smell of lemons
And oil from Provence rises almost painfully
To the nose, for which I'd like to thank

Dankbarkeit mir die Gasgognischen Lande

Gegeben. Gezähmet aber, noch zu sehen, und genährt hat mich

Die Rappierlust und des Festtags gebraten Fleisch

Der Tisch und braune Trauben, braune

       und mich leset o

Ihr Blüthen von Deutschland, o mein Herz wird

Untrügbarer Krystall an dem

Das Licht sich prüfet wenn   Deutschland

The region of Gascony. Still to be seen,
What tamed and nourished me,
A love of the skewer and holiday roast,
The table and brown grapes, so ripe
                    and gather me please o
German flowers, o my heart is turning
Into the truest crystal, in which
The light is tested when   Germany

Griechenland

[Dritte Fassung]

O ihr Stimmen des Geschiks, ihr Wege des Wanderers
Denn an der Schule Blau,
Fernher, am Tosen des Himmels
Tönt wie der Amsel Gesang
Der Wolken heitere Stimmung gut
Gestimmt vom Daseyn Gottes, dem Gewitter.
Und Rufe, wie hinausschauen, zur
Unsterblichkeit und Helden;
Viel sind Erinnerungen. Wo darauf
Tönend, wie des Kalbs Haut
Die Erde, von Verwüstungen her, Versuchungen der Heiligen
Denn anfangs bildet das Werk sich
Großen Gesezen nachgehet, die Wissenschaft
Und Zärtlichkeit und den Himmel breit lauter Hülle nachher
Erscheinend singen Gesangeswolken.
Denn fest ist der Erde
Nabel. Gefangen nemlich in Ufern von Gras sind
Die Flammen und die allgemeinen
Elemente. Lauter Besinnung aber oben lebt der Aether. Aber silbern
An reinen Tagen
Ist das Licht. Als Zeichen der Liebe
Veilchenblau die Erde.
Zu Geringem auch kann kommen
Großer Anfang.
Alltag aber wunderbar zu lieb den Menschen
Gott an hat ein Gewand.
Und Erkenntnissen verberget sich sein Angesicht
Und deket die Lüfte mit Kunst.
Und Luft und Zeit dekt

Greece

[Third Version]

Voices of fate, ways a traveler goes,
In your blue school
The blackbird's song can be heard
At a distance, amid the uproar of heaven
The cloud's good mood,
Well-tempered by God's existence, a thunder storm.
And cries out in watchfulness for
Immortality and heroes;
So many things to recall. Where
Ringing out upon it, like a drum skin,
The earth proceeds from its own ruins and temptations of the saints,
For the work takes shape from the beginning,
Follows great laws, and knowledge
And tenderness, and bright, wide heaven purely enveloped
Later clouds of song become visible.
Earth's umbilicus is firmly fixed.
Its flames and common elements
Are hidden in riverbanks of grass,
The Upper Air, pure thought, lives above.
On clear days,
The light is silver. As a sign of love,
The earth is violet-blue.
Even the humble have great beginnings.
Every day for the sake of men
God puts on marvelous clothes.
And though his face is beyond knowing,
He suffuses the air with art.
And air and time conceal
The awesome one

Den Schröklichen, daß zu sehr nicht eins
Ihn liebet mit Gebeten oder
Die Seele. Denn lange schon steht offen
Wie Blätter, zu lernen, oder Linien und Winkel
Die Natur
Und gelber die Sonnen und die Monde,
Zu Zeiten aber
Wenn ausgehn will die alte Bildung
Der Erde, bei Geschichten nemlich
Gewordnen, muthig fechtenden, wie auf Höhen führet
Die Erde Gott. Ungemessene Schritte
Begränzt er aber, aber wie Blüthen golden thun
Der Seele Kräfte dann der Seele Verwandtschaften sich zusammen,
Daß lieber auf Erden
Die Schönheit wohnt und irgend ein Geist
Gemeinschaftlicher sich zu Menschen gesellet.

Süß ists, dann unter hohen Schatten von Bäumen
Und Hügeln zu wohnen, sonnig, wo der Weg ist
Gepflastert zur Kirche. Reisenden aber, wem,
Aus Lebensliebe, messend immerhin,
Die Füße gehorchen, blühn
Schöner die Wege, wo das Land

So he won't be loved too much
With prayers or the soul.
Nature
Has remained open a long time to learning,
Like leaves, or lines and angles
And suns and moons are a deeper yellow,
But at times
The ancient knowledge of earth is in danger
Of going out amid its various histories, whether grown
Or come to pass, and boldly contending like fencers. God rules on high
And on the earth. Though his pace is unmeasured,
He limits, but the soul's energies and affections
Consort like golden flowers
So beauty is more willing
To dwell on earth, and one spirit or the other
Shows an interest in human matters.

For it's sweet to live under the high shade of trees
And hills, where the paved road is sunny
On the way to church. In their love of life, travelers
Measure with their feet how to obey Him
The length of the journey, for them, the roads
Blossom more beautifully, where the land

Griechenland

[Sattler Kompilation]

O ihr Stimmen des Geschiks, ihr Wege des Wanderers!
Denn an der Schule Blau, wo Geist von lang her toset,
Tönt wie Amsel Gesang
Der Wolken heitere Stimmung gut
Gestimmt vom Daseyn Gottes, dem Gewitter.
Und Rufe, wie hinausschauen, zur
Unsterblichkeit und Helden;
Viel sind Erinnerungen. Wo darauf
Tönend, wie des Kalbs Haut
Die Erde, von Verwüstungen her, Versuchungen der Heiligen,
Großen Gesezen nachgehet,
Denn anfangs bildet das Werk sich Wissenschaft, die Einigkeit
Und Zärtlichkeit und den Himmel breit lauter Hülle nachher
Erscheinend singen,
Sterbende nemlich müssen singen, zierend den Geist des Himmels aber
    singen daselbst
Gesangeswolken. Denn immer lebt
Die Natur. Fest aber ist der Erde
Nabel. Gefangen nemlich in Ufern von Gras sind
Die Flammen und die allgemeinen
Elemente. Lauter Besinnung aber oben lebt der Äther. Aber silbern
An reinen Tagen
Ist das Licht. Als Zeichen der Liebe
Veilchenblau die Erde. Aber wo zu sehr
Zur Ewigkeit sich das Ungebundene sehnet
Himmlisches einschläft, und die Treue Gottes,
Das Verständige fehlt.
Aber wie die Reigen
Zur Hochzeit,

Greece

[Sattler Compilation]

Voices of fate, ways a traveler goes!
In your blue school, the blackbird's song
Can be heard, where spirit of old rages,
The clouds' good mood,
Well-tempered by God's existence, a thunderstorm.
And cries out in watchfulness for
Immortality and heroes;
So many things to recall. Where
Ringing out upon it, like a drum skin,
The earth proceeds from its own ruins and temptations of the saints,
For the work takes shape from the beginning,
Follows great laws, and knowledge
And tenderness, and bright, wide heaven purely enveloped
Clouds of song become visible,
Of course mortals must sing, adorning
The spirit of heaven. For
Nature lives forever. Earth's
Umbilicus is firmly fixed.
Its flames and common elements
Are hidden in riverbanks of grass.
The Upper Air, pure thought, lives above.
On clear days, the light is silver.
As a sign of love, the earth is violet-blue.
But where the desire for eternity knows no limits,
The sacred falls asleep, and faith
In God loses its reason.
But like the round dance at a wedding,
Even the humble have great beginnings.
Every day for the sake of men

Zu Geringem auch kann kommen
Großer Anfang.
Alltag aber wunderbar zu lieb den Menschen
Gott an hat ein Gewand
Und Erkentnissen verberget sich sein Angesicht
Und deket die Lüfte mit Kunst.
Und Luft und Zeit dekt
Den Schröklichen, daß zu sehr nicht eins
Ihn liebet mit Gebeten oder
Der Seele. Denn lange schon steht offen
Wie Blätter, zu lernen, oder Linien und Winkel die Natur.
Und gelber die Sonnen und Monde,
Zu Zeiten aber
Wenn ausgehn will die alte Bildung
Der Erde, bei Geschichten nemlich
Gewordnen, muthig fechtenden, wie auf Höhen führet
Die Erde Gott. Ungemessene Schritte
Begränzt er aber, wie Blüthen golden thun
Die Kräfte sich der Seele zusammen,
Daß lieber auf Erden
Die Schönheit wohnt und irgend ein Geist
Gemeinschaftlicher sich zu Menschen gesellet.

Süß ists dann unter hohen Schatten von Bäumen
Und Hügeln zu wohnen, sonnig, wo der Weg ist
Gepflastert zur Kirche,
Und Bäume stehen schlummernd, doch
Eintreffen Schritte der Sonne,
Denn eben so, wie heißer
Brennt über der Städte Dampf
So gehet über des Reegens
Behangene   Mauren   die Sonne

God puts on marvelous clothes,
And though his face is beyond knowing,
He suffuses the air with art,
And space and time conceal
The awesome one
So he won't be loved too much
With prayers or
The soul. Nature has
Remained open a long time to learning,
Like leaves, or lines and angles.
And suns and moons are a deeper yellow,
But at times
The ancient knowledge of earth is in danger
Of going out amid its various histories, whether grown
Or come to pass, and boldly contending like fencers, as God rules on
    high
And on the earth. Though his pace is unmeasured,
He limits, but the soul's energies and affections
Consort like golden flowers,
So beauty is more willing
To dwell on earth, and one spirit or the other
Shows an interest in human matters.

For it's sweet to live under the high shade
Of trees and hills, where the paved road
Is sunny on the way to church,
And trees stand slumbering, despite
The sun's tread,
For just as it burns hotter
Above the smoke of the city
So the sun traverses the downpour
Hanged   walls   the sun

Wie Epheu nemlich hänget

Astlos der Reegen herunter. Schöner aber

Blühn Reisenden die Wege, wem

Aus Lebensliebe, messend immerhin,

Die Füße gehorchen, im Freien, wo das Land wechselt wie Korn.

Avignon waldig über den Gotthardt

Tastet das Roß, Lorbeern

Rauschen um Virgilius und daß

Die Sonne nicht

Unmänlich suchet, das Grab. Moosrosen

Wachsen

Auf den Alpen. Blumen fangen

Vor Thoren der Stadt an, auf geebneten Wegen unbegünstiget

Gleich Krystallen in der Wüste wachsend des Meeres.

Gärten wachsen um Windsor. Hoch

Ziehet, aus London,

Der Wagen des Königs.

Schöne Gärten sparen die Jahrzeit.

Am Canal. Tief aber liegt

Das ebene Weltmeer, glühend.

Like ivy, the sheet of rain hangs
Downward without branches. But the road
Beautifully blooms for travelers,
Who measure their love of life
With each footstep, where, in the open,
The landscape sways like grain.
The horse feels its way toward woody Avignon
Beyond the Gotthard, a rustle
Of laurel trees near Vergil's grave
Shades it from the unmanly sun. Moss roses
Grow
On the Alps. Flowers begin at the city gates, as untended
As crystals growing
In the wastelands of the sea.
Gardens grow around Windsor. High
Time for the King's carriage
To arrive from London.
Pretty gardens save the season.
By the canal. But the smooth ocean
Lies even and deep.

Last Poems:
1807–1843

Wenn aus der Ferne…

Wenn aus der Ferne, da wir geschieden sind,
  Ich dir noch kennbar bin, die Vergangenheit
    O du Theilhaber meiner Leiden!
      Einiges Gute bezeichnen dir kann,

So sage, wie erwartet die Freundin dich?
  In jenen Gärten, da nach entsezlicher
    Und dunkler Zeit wir uns gefunden?
      Hier an den Strömen der heilgen Urwelt.

Das muß ich sagen, einiges Gutes war
  In deinen Bliken, als in den Fernen du
    Dich einmal fröhlich umgesehen
      Immer verschlossener Mensch, mit finstrem

Aussehn. Wie flossen Stunden dahin, wie still
  War meine Seele über der Wahrheit daß
    Ich so getrennt gewesen wäre?
      Ja! ich gestand es, ich war die deine.

Wahrhafftig! wie du alles Bekannte mir
  In mein Gedächtniß bringen und schreiben willst,
    Mit Briefen, so ergeht es mir auch
      Daß ich Vergangenes alles sage.

Wars Frühling? war es Sommer? die Nachtigall
  Mit süßem Liede lebte mit Vögeln, die
    Nicht ferne waren im Gebüsche
      Und mit Gerüchen umgaben Bäum' uns.

If from the distance…

If from the distance, now that we have parted,
   I'm still familiar to you, o you
      Who shared my suffering! and the past
      Still means something good to you,

Then tell me, how does your girlfriend await you?
   In the same gardens, where after darkened
      And dreadful times we found each other
      Here by the holy streams of time before time.

This I must say, there was something good
   In your glances, when at a distance
      You happily looked around,
       A person always so detached, gloomy

In appearance. How the hours melted away,
   How calm was my soul about the truth,
      That I had been so set apart from you?
      Yes, I confessed, I was your truth.

Truly! As you wish to bring and write
   All familiar things back to my memory
      With letters, so it is with me,
      I speak of all that has passed.

Was it spring, summer? The nightingale,
   With sweet song, lived among birds
      That were not far away, in bushes,
       And the fragrance of trees was all around.

Die klaren Gänge, niedres Gesträuch und Sand
   Auf dem wir traten, machten erfreulicher
      Und lieblicher die Hyacinthe
         Oder die Tulpe, Viole, Nelke.

Um Wänd und Mauern grünte der Epheu, grünt'
   Ein seelig Dunkel hoher Alleen. Oft
      Des Abends, Morgens waren dort wir
         Redeten manches und sahn uns froh an.

In meinen Armen lebte der Jüngling auf,
   Der, noch verlassen, aus den Gefilden kam,
      Die er mir wies, mit einer Schwermuth,
         Aber die Nahmen der seltnen Orte

Und alles Schöne hatt' er behalten, das
   An seeligen Gestaden, auch mir sehr werth
      Im heimatlichen Lande blühet
         Oder verborgen, aus hoher Aussicht,

Allwo das Meer auch einer beschauen kann,
   Doch keiner seyn will. Nehme vorlieb, und denk
      An die, die noch vergnügt ist, darum,
         Weil der entzükende Tag uns anschien,

Der mit Geständniß oder der Hände Druk
   Anhub, der uns vereinet. Ach! wehe mir!
      Es waren schöne Tage. Aber
         Traurige Dämmerung folgte nachher.

The clear paths, low shrubs, and the sand
    On which we walked, made more pleasant
        By the lovely hyacinth
            Or tulip, violet, carnation.

On walls and brick houses, ivy grew green, green too
    The blissful darkness of tall avenues. Often
        In the evening, mornings, we were there,
            Spoke of many things and looked at each other gladly.

In my embrace, the young man revived
    Who, still lost, came from those fields
        He showed to me with sadness,
            But the names of those unusual places

And the lovely things he recalled, that
    On blessed shores his native country
        Blooms, also to me of great value,
            Or concealed from a distant height,

From wherever one can view the sea,
    Though none will do so. Forgive me, and think
        Of her who is still delighted because
            The enchanting day shone down on us

That started with confessions or holding hands,
    Which united us. Woe is me,
        Those were beautiful days. But
            The twilight that followed was sad.

Du seiest so allein in der schönen Welt
  Behauptest du mir immer, Geliebter! das
    Weist aber du nicht,

You are so alone in this lovely world,
   You always claim, my darling, but
      You can't really know,

Der Ruhm

Es knüpft an Gott der Wohllaut, der geleitet
Ein sehr berühmtes Ohr, denn wunderbar
Ist ein berühmtes Leben groß und klar,
Es geht der Mensch zu Fuße oder reitet.

Der Erde Freuden, Freundlichkeit und Güter,
Der Garten, Baum, der Weinberg mit dem Hüter,
Sie scheinen mir ein Wiederglanz des Himmels,
Gewähret von dem Geist den Söhnen des Gewimmels.—

Wenn Einer ist mit Gütern reich beglüket,
Wenn Obst den Garten ihm, und Gold ausschmüket
Die Wohnung und das Haus, was mag er haben
Noch mehr in dieser Welt, sein Herz zu laben?

Fame

God is linked with the perfect sound,
Attended by a very famous ear.
For a famous life is wonderful and clear.
Man goes on horse or walks upon the ground.

The joys of earth, happiness and ease,
The vineyard and its keeper, garden and trees,
They seem to me the heavenly light of clouds
Granted by the spirit to solitudes and crowds.—

When a man with goods is richly blessed,
When fruit trees grow in his garden, and dressed
In gold are his house and dwelling, what more
In the world does he need to restore him?

Das Angenehme dieser Welt…

Das Angenehme dieser Welt hab' ich genossen,
Die Jugendstunden sind, wie lang! wie lang! verflossen,
April und Mai und Julius sind ferne,
Ich bin nichts mehr, ich lebe nicht mehr gerne!

The Sweetness of this World…

I've known the sweetness of this world,
How long ago the hours of youth passed me by.
April and May and July are distant.
I'm nothing now, I live without pleasure!

FRIEDRICH HÖLDERLIN

An Zimmern (Die Linien des Lebens…)

Die Linien des Lebens sind verschieden
Wie Wege sind, und wie der Berge Gränzen.
Was hier wir sind, kann dort ein Gott ergänzen
Mit Harmonien und ewigem Lohn und Frieden.

To Zimmer

The lines of life are various as pathways
And borders weaving through mountains.
What we are here, a god makes whole there
With harmony and eternal reward and peace.

Wenn aus dem Himmel…

Wenn aus dem Himmel hellere Wonne sich
  Herabgießt, eine Freude den Menschen kommt,
    Daß sie sich wundern über manches
      Sichtbares, Höheres, Angenehmes:

Wie tönet lieblich heilger Gesang dazu!
  Wie lacht das Herz in Liedern die Wahrheit an,
    Daß Freudigkeit an einem Bildniß—
      Über dem Stege beginnen Schaafe

Den Zug, der fast in dämmernde Wälder geht.
  Die Wiesen aber, welche mit lautrem Grün
    Bedekt sind, sind wie jene Haide,
      Welche gewöhnlicher Weise nah ist

Dem dunkeln Walde. Da, auf den Wiesen auch
  Verweilen diese Schaafe. Die Gipfel, die
    Umher sind, nakte Höhen sind mit
      Eichen bedeket und seltnen Tannen.

Da, wo des Stromes regsame Wellen sind,
  Daß einer, der vorüber des Weges kommt,
    Froh hinschaut, da erhebt der Berge
      Sanfte Gestalt und der Weinberg hoch sich.

Zwar gehn die Treppen unter den Reben hoch
  Herunter, wo der Obstbaum blühend darüber steht
    Und Duft an wilden Heken weilet,
      Wo die verborgenen Veilchen sprossen;

When out of Heaven…

When out of heaven a brighter delight
    Pours down, a joy comes to men
        So that they marvel over much that is
            Visible, higher, and pleasant:

How lovely, therefore, sounds the holy song!
    How in songs the heart laughs at the truth
        That rejoices on one image—
            Over the footbridge sheep begin

A procession, that almost reaches the darkening woods.
    The meadows, however, laid out
        In perfect green, resemble that heath,
            Which, as is common, lies near

The dark wood. There, on the meadows also,
    The sheep pass their time. The naked tops
        Of hills that stand above are thinly covered
            With oaks and occasional spruces.

There, where the river is small and active,
    A man coming along that way
        Is happy to see them, there the soft
            Shape of hills and high vineyards rise.

For indeed the steps under the grapevines steeply
    Descend, where the fruit trees stand blossoming
        And the fragrance of wild hedges lingers,
            Where the hidden violets flower and spread,

Gewässer aber rieseln herab, und sanft
  Ist hörbar dort ein Rauschen den ganzen Tag;
    Die Orte aber in der Gegend
      Ruhen und schweigen den Nachmittag durch.

But waters trickle down and a soft
   Rustling can be heard all day long;
      However, the places in that region
         Rest long after noon and keep their silence.

An Zimmern
(Von einem Menschen sag ich…)

Von einem Menschen sag ich, wenn der ist gut
    Und weise, was bedarf er? Ist irgend eins
        Das einer Seele gnüget? ist ein Halm, ist
            Eine gereifteste Reb' auf Erden

Gewachsen, die ihn nähre? Der Sinn ist deß
    Also. Ein Freund ist oft die Geliebte, viel
        Die Kunst. O Theurer, dir sag ich die Wahrheit.
            Dädalus Geist und des Walds ist deiner.

To Zimmer

I say of a man, if he is good
    And wise, what more does he need? What
        Satisfies a soul? Is a stalk of corn,
            Is the earth's ripest grapevine

Grown to nourish him? The sense of it is this.
    A friend is often one's true love, and friendship an art.
        Dear friend, I'll tell you the truth. The spirit
            Of Daedalus and the forest is yours.

Das fröhliche Leben

Wenn ich auf die Wiese komme,
Wenn ich auf dem Felde jezt,
Bin ich noch der Zahme, Fromme
Wie von Dornen unverlezt.
Mein Gewand in Winden wehet,
Wie der Geist mir lustig fragt,
Worinn Inneres bestehet,
Bis Auflösung diesem tagt.

O vor diesem sanften Bilde,
Wo die grünen Bäume stehn,
Wie vor einer Schenke Schilde
Kann ich kaum vorübergehn.
Denn die Ruh an stillen Tagen
Dünkt entschieden treflich mir,
Dieses mußt du gar nicht fragen,
Wenn ich soll antworten dir.

Aber zu dem schönen Bache
Such' ich einen Lustweg wohl,
Der, als wie in dem Gemache,
Schleicht durch's Ufer wild und hohl,
Wo der Steg darüber gehet,
Geht's den schönen Wald hinauf,
Wo der Wind den Steg umwehet,
Sieht das Auge fröhlich auf.

Droben auf des Hügels Gipfel
Siz' ich manchen Nachmittag,
Wenn der Wind umsaust die Wipfel,

The Happy Life

When I approach the meadow,
Or now go to the field,
Still I am tame, even pious,
And walk through thorns unharmed.
My clothes flutter in the wind
As my mind happily asks
What lies within us, until
Its own dissolution.

Before this peaceful image,
Where the green trees stand,
As before a tavern's sign,
I can hardly just pass by,
For peace on the quiet days
Seems excellent in my view,
This you must never ask,
If you want me to answer you.

But toward the lovely brook
I search for a path so pleasant
It's like a comfortable room,
Though it follows the river, high and wild,
To where a footbridge crosses,
Ascending to lovely woods,
Where breezes surround the bridge,
And I look happily up.

Above, on the high hilltop,
I spend the occasional afternoon,
With the wind roaring in tree-tops,

Bei des Thurmes Glokenschlag,
Und Betrachtung giebt dem Herzen
Frieden, wie das Bild auch ist,
Und Beruhigung den Schmerzen,
Welche reimt Verstand und List.

Holde Landschaft! wo die Straße
Mitten durch sehr eben geht,
Wo der Mond aufsteigt, der blasse,
Wenn der Abendwind entsteht,
Wo die Natur sehr einfältig,
Wo die Berg' erhaben stehn,
Geh' ich heim zulezt, haushältig,
Dort nach goldnem Wein zu sehn.

I hear nearby the tower's clock,
And contemplation restores
The heart, as images also do,
And a soothing of one's sorrows,
Which reason rhymes with art.

Dear landscape, where streets
Run evenly through, where
The moon, that pale one, rises,
Where the evening wind is made,
Where nature is very simple,
Where the mountains loom and stand,
I go home at last, domestic,
To see the golden wine.

Der Spaziergang

Ihr Wälder schön an der Seite,
Am grünen Abhang gemahlt,
Wo ich umher mich leite,
Durch süße Ruhe bezahlt
Für jeden Stachel im Herzen,
Wenn dunkel mir ist der Sinn,
Den Kunst und Sinnen hat Schmerzen
Gekostet von Anbeginn.
Ihr lieblichen Bilder im Thale,
Zum Beispiel Gärten und Baum,
Und dann der Steg der schmale,
Der Bach zu sehen kaum,
Wie schön aus heiterer Ferne
Glänzt Einem das herrliche Bild
Der Landschaft, die ich gerne
Besuch' in Witterung mild.
Die Gottheit freundlich geleitet
Uns erstlich mit Blau,
Hernach mit Wolken bereitet,
Gebildet wölbig und grau,
Mit sengenden Blizen und Rollen
Des Donners, mit Reiz des Gefilds,
Mit Schönheit, die gequollen
Vom Quell ursprünglichen Bilds.

The Stroll

You lovely woods along the way,
Painted on a green slope,
Where I like to rest all day,
Repaid by lovely silence
For every thorn in my heart
And when my mind is clouded
By the grief that thought and art
Have cost me from the beginning,
Your lovely views of the valley,
For example, garden and tree,
And then the little bridge,
The stream that's hard to see,
How beautiful in clear distance
Those glorious pictures glimmer,
The landscape I like to visit
During mild weather.
Our friendly god strolls
With us, at first with the blue,
Thereafter preparing us clouds
In an arc of the grayest hue,
With blistering lightning and a roll
Of thunder, with charming fields,
And beauty gushing forth
From the primal image-source.

Der Kirchhof

Du stiller Ort, der grünt mit jungem Grase,
Da liegen Mann und Frau, und Kreuze stehn,
Wohin hinaus geleitet Freunde gehn,
Wo Fenster sind glänzend mit hellem Glase.

Wenn glänzt an dir des Himmels hohe Leuchte
Des Mittags, wann der Frühling dort oft weilt,
Wenn geistige Wolke dort, die graue, feuchte
Wenn sanft der Tag vorbei mit Schönheit eilt!

Wie still ist's nicht an jener grauen Mauer,
Wo drüber her ein Baum mit Früchten hängt;
Mit schwarzen thauigen, und Laub voll Trauer,
Die Früchte aber sind sehr schön gedrängt.

Dort in der Kirch' ist eine dunkle Stille
Und der Altar ist auch in dieser Nacht geringe,
Noch sind darin einige schöne Dinge,
Im Sommer aber singt auf Feldern manche Grille.

Wenn Einer dort Reden des Pfarrherrn hört,
Indeß die Schaar der Freunde steht daneben,
Die mit dem Todten sind, welch eignes Leben
Und welcher Geist, und fromm seyn ungestört.

The Churchyard

You calm place, green with new grass,
There lie man and wife, and crosses stand
Where friends go arm in arm, where
Windows gleam with bright glass.

When the holy radiance shines its light
On you at noon, when spring lingers there,
When the spiritual clouds, moist and gray,
Hurry past in beauty, in the soft night!

How quiet it is by the gray wall,
Where a tree hangs over, laden with ripeness,
With black, dewy fruit, leaves full of sadness,
But the fruit is plentiful, the tree heavy and full.

There, in the church, it's dark and quiet,
And on this night the altar is also bare,
Though pretty things still lie within it;
But in the summer, many crickets sing in the field.

When someone hears the minister talking there,
Surrounded by a group of friends who've
Come to be with the dead one, how rare
This life, what a spirit, piety never ends.

Der Frühling

Es kommt der neue Tag aus fernen Höhn herunter,
Der Morgen der erwacht ist aus den Dämmerungen,
Er lacht die Menschheit an, geschmükt und munter,
Von Freuden ist die Menschheit sant durchdrungen.

Ein neues Leben will der Zukunft sich enthüllen,
Mit Blüthen scheint, dem Zeichen froher Tage,
Das große Thal, die Erde sich zu füllen,
Entfernt dagegen ist zur Frühlingszeit die Klage.

                    Mit Unterthänigkeit
d: 3 ten März 1648.   Scardanelli.

Spring

The new day comes down from a distant height.
The morning is awakened out of the twilight.
It laughs at humanity, dressed up and bright,
And man is tenderly suffused with delight.

A new life discloses itself to the future,
It shines with blossoms, signs of happy days,
The earth seems to fill the great valley,
While in springtime sadness stays far away.

Your humble servant

March 3rd 1648.   Scardanelli.

Der Sommer

Wenn dann vorbei des Frühlings Blüthe schwindet,
So ist der Sommer da, der um das Jahr sich windet.
Und wie der Bach das Thal hinuntergleitet,
So ist der Berge Pracht darum verbreitet.
Daß sich das Feld mit Pracht am meisten zeiget,
Ist, wie der Tag, der sich zum Abend neiget;
Wie so das Jahr verweilt, so sind des Sommers Stunden
Und Bilder der Natur dem Menschen oft verschwunden.

d. 24 Mai
  1778.   Scardanelli.

Summer

When the blossoms of spring finally disappear,
Summer is here, winding itself around the year,
And as the brook glides down the valley's side,
So the mountain spreads before us in pride,
And the field appears in a greener splendor,
It's like the day when it bends to evening;
As the year lingers on, for men a summer's day
And images of nature will often fade away.

d. 24 May
  1778.   Scardanelli.

Der Herbst

Das Glänzen der Natur ist höheres Erscheinen,
Wo sich der Tag mit vielen Freuden endet,
Es ist das Jahr, das sich mit Pracht vollendet,
Wo Früchte sich mit frohem Glanz vereinen.

Das Erdenrund ist so geschmükt, und selten lärmet
Der Schall durchs offne Feld, die Sonne wärmet
Den Tag des Herbstes mild, die Felder stehen
Als eine Aussicht weit, die Lüffte wehen

Die Zweig' und Äste durch mit frohem Rauschen
Wenn schon mit Leere sich die Felder dann vertauschen,
Der ganze Sinn des hellen Bildes lebet
Als wie ein Bild, das goldne Pracht umschwebet.

d. 15 Nov.

1759.

Autumn

Nature gleams and takes on higher presence,
When the day ends amid many joys,
And so the year ends in a kind of splendor,
When the ripened fruit all shines together.

The circle of earth is thus decorated, and a sound
Is seldom heard in the open field, the mild sun
Warms the autumn day, the broad fields stand
As one panorama, and the breezes run through

Twigs and branches with a happy rustling sound,
Until the harvested fields are empty and bare;
The meaning of this image lives on as a painting,
Framed by golden splendor, hovering in the air.

Nov. 15,
1759.

Der Winter

Wenn ungesehn und nun vorüber sind die Bilder
Der Jahreszeit, so kommt des Winters Dauer,
Das Feld ist leer, die Ansicht scheinet milder,
Und Stürme wehn umher und Reegenschauer.

Als wie ein Ruhetag, so ist des Jahres Ende,
Wie einer Frage Ton, daß dieser sich vollende,
Alsdann erscheint des Frühlings neues Werden,
So glänzet die Natur mit Pracht auf Erden.

Mit Unterthänigkeit

d. 24 April   Scardanelli.
 1849

Winter

When the season's images are over and unseen,
Winter's long duration finally presses down,
The field is empty, the view seems milder,
And storms and rain showers blow all around.

And like a day of rest, so is the year's end,
Like the tone of a question searching for its answer,
But then spring's new growth appears to our eyes,
As nature shines on earth in all her splendor.

                Your humble servant

April 24,   Scardanelli.
  1849

Plans
and
Fragments

Palingenesie

[Pläne und Bruchstücke 12]

Mit der Sonne sehn' ich mich oft vom Aufgang bis zum Niedergang
den weiten Bogen schnell hineilend zu wandeln, oft, mit Gesang zu
folgen dem großen dem Vollendungsgange der alten Natur,
Und, wie der Feldherr auf dem Helme den Adler trägt in Kampf und
Triumph, so möcht ich daß mich trüge
Mächtig das Sehnen der Sterblichen.
Aber es wohnet auch ein Gott in dem Menschen das er Vergangenes
Und Zukünftiges sieht und wie vom Strom ins Gebirg hinauf an die
Quelle lustwandelt er durch Zeiten
Aus ihrer Thaten stillem Buch ist Vergangenem bekannt er durch
— —die goldenes beut

Palingenesis

[Plans and Fragments 12]

Often I desire to travel at the speed of the sun, in its wide arc,
from its rising to its setting, often in song
to follow ancient nature in its perfect course,
And, as the general wears an eagle on his helmet in war and
Triumph, so I wish that the sun would carry me,
How mighty the longing of mortals.
But a god lives in men, so they can see what has passed
And what is to come, and, as the mountain stream wanders to its
Source through time, from the silent
Book of deeds through which he knows the past
— —the sun's golden plunder

Zu Sokrates Zeiten

[Pläne und Brüchstucke 16]

Vormals richtete Gott.

Könige.

Weise.

wer richtet denn izt?

Richtet das einige
   Volk? die heilge Gemeinde?
   Nein! o nein! wer richtet denn izt?
         ein Natterngeschlecht!   feig und falsch
                  das edlere Wort nicht mehr
         Über die Lippe
O im Nahmen
                                    ruf ich

      Alter Dämon! dich herab

Oder   sende
   Einen Helden

Oder
      die Weisheit.

The Time of Socrates
[Plans and Fragments 16]

Once it was that God set things in order.

        Kings.

      Wise men.

        who judges now?

The people as a whole?
  Spiritualists and churchmen?
  No? Who then now decides?
        a bunch of vipers!   cowardly and lying
           no noble words now
      pass anyone's lips
O in the name

                I call down

     the ancient spirits

Or   send
  a hero

Or

    wisdom.

An

[Pläne und Bruchstücke 18]

Elysium

    Dort find ich ja

    Zu euch ihr Todesgötter

    Dort Diotima   Heroen.

Singen möcht ich von dir

    Aber nur Thränen.

    Und in der Nacht in der ich wandle erlöscht mir dein

        Klares Auge!

        himmlischer Geist.

To

[Plans and Fragments 18]

Elysium

   Yes there I find

   To you, you gods of death

   There Diotima   Heroes.

I'd like to sing of you

   But only tears.

   And in the night where I wander, your clear eye

     Grows dim!

          heavenly spirit.

An meine Schwester
[Pläne und Bruchstücke 19]

Übernacht' ich im Dorf

Albluft

Straße hinunter

Haus   Wiedersehn.   Sonne der Heimath

Kahnfahrt,
Freunde   Männer und Mutter.
Schlummer.

To My Sister

[Plans and Fragments 19]

I stay overnight in the village

Air of the Alb

Down the street

Home   again.   Sun of home.

Canoe ride.

Friends.   Men and mother.

Slumber.

Gestalt und Geist
[Pläne und Bruchstücke 22]

Alles is innig

    Das Scheidet

So birgt der Dichter

Verwegner! möchtest von Angesicht zu Angesicht
    Die Seele sehn
        Du gehest in Flammen unter.

Shape and Spirit
[Plans and Fragments 22]

All is inward

    That's the difference

The poet conceals

Fool! wanting to see the soul
    Face to face
        You go down in flames.

Sybille

[Pläne und Brüchstucke 23]

Der Sturm
    Aber sie schmähn
        Schütteln gewaltig den Baum doch auch die thörigen Kinder
            werfen mit Steinen

    die Äste beugt
      Und der Rabe singt
So wandert das Wetter Gottes über

    Aber du heilger Gesang.

Und suchst armer Schiffer den gewohnten

Zu den Sternen siehe.

Sibyl

[Plans and Fragments 23]

The storm
    But they hurl insults
        Forcefully shake the tree even foolish children
            throw a few stones

  the branch bends
      And the raven sings
God's weather passes over

    But you, solemn song.

And seeking the familiar the poor sailor

Looks to the stars

Der Baum

[Pläne und Bruckstücke 24]

Da ich ein Kind, zag pflanzt ich dich

Schöne Pflanze! wie sehn wir nun verändert uns
Herrlich stehest   und

wie ein Kind vor.

The Tree

[Plans and Fragments 24]

When I was a child, I planted you

    Lovely Tree! How different we seem to each other now
How splendidly you stand there   and

                like a child.

Aber die Sprache…

[Pläne und Bruchstücke 26]

Aber die Sprache—
Im Gewitter spricht der
Gott.
Öfters hab' ich die Sprache
sie sagte der Zorn sei genug und gelte für den Apollo—
Hast du Liebe genug so zürn aus Liebe nur immer,
Öfters hab ich Gesang versucht, aber sie hörten dich nicht. Denn
so wollte die heilige Natur. Du sangest du für sie in deiner Jugend
nicht singend
Du sprachst zur Gottheit,
aber diß habt ihr all vergessen, daß immer die Erstlinge Sterblichen
nicht, daß sie den Göttern gehören.
gemeiner muß alltäglicher muß
die Frucht erst werden, dann wird
sie den Sterberlichen eigen.

But Speech

[Plans and Fragments 26]

But speech—
God speaks in
Thunderstorms.
Often I've had speech
it said anger was enough and suitable for Apollo—
Do you have enough love to contain your anger also,
Often I have tried to sing, but they didn't hear you, that's
what sacred nature wanted. You sang for them in your youth
not singing
You spoke to the godhead,
but this you have all forgotten, that the first fruits belong
to the gods, not mortals.
fruit must become more common,
more everyday before it has any meaning
for those with the gift of death.

Und wenig wissen…

[Pläne und Brüchstucke 29]

Und wenig wissen, aber der Freude viel
 Ist Sterblichen gegeben,

Warum, o schöne Sonne, genügst du mir
 Du Blüthe meiner Blüthen! am Maitag nicht?
 Was weiß ich höhers denn?

O daß ich lieber wäre, wie Kinder sind!
 Daß ich, wie Nachtigallen, ein sorglos Lied
 Von meiner Wonne sänge!

And little knowledge...

[Plans and Fragments 29]

And little knowledge, but joy enough
   Is given to mortals,

Why, o lovely sun, aren't you enough,
   You blossoms of my blossoming! Not for me, in May?
     What do I know that's higher then?

O that I could be more like children!
   That I, like nightingales, could sing a song
     Of my bliss, without sorrow!

Im Walde

[Sattler Kompilation]

Du edles Wild.
Aber in Hütten wohnet der Mensch, und hüllet sich ein ins verschämte
Gewand, denn inniger ist achtsamer auch und daß er bewahre den
Geist, wie die Priesterin die himmlische Flamme, diß ist sein Verstand.
Und darum ist die Willkür ihm und höhere Macht zu fehlen und
zu vollbringen dem Götterähnlichen, der Güter Gefährlichstes, die
Sprache dem Menschen gegeben, damit er schaffend, zerstörend, und
untergehend, und wiederkehrend zur ewiglebenden, zur Meisterin und
Mutter, damit er zeuge, was er sei geerbet zu haben, gelernt von ihr, ihr
Göttlichstes, die allerhaltende Liebe.

Denn nirgend bleibt er.
Es fesselt
Kein Zeichen.
Nicht immer

Ein Gefäß ihn zu fassen.

Denn gute Dinge sind drei.

Nicht will ich
Die Bilder dir stürmen.

und das Sakrament

In the Forest

[Sattler Compilation]

You noble beasts.
But man lives in huts, dressed in shame, the more inward he
is, the more attentive also, and protects his spirit as the priestess
protects the heavenly flame, this is the limit of his understanding.
And why his willfulness and greater ability to succeed and fail
are given him, godly creature, and of these powers language
is the most dangerous, so that creating, destroying, being
annihilated, and returning to her, the mother and mistress,
bear witness to what he is, having learned from her, the most
godly, an all-preserving love.

He remains nowhere.
No sign
Binds.
Not ever

A vessel to contain him.

Good things come in threes.

I have no wish
To destroy your symbols.

and keeping the sacrament holy

Heilig behalten, das halt unsre Seele
Zusammen, die uns gönnet Gott, das Lebenslicht
Das gesellige
Bis an unser End

Ein anderes freilich ists,

            Unterschiedenes ist
    gut. Ein jeder
               und es hat
Ein jeder das Seine.

            dem dunklen Blatte,
       Und es war
Das Wachstum vernehmlich
    und   der syrische Boden,
   zerschmettert, und Flammen gleich unter den Sohlen
Es stach
Und der Ekel mich
Ankömt von wütenden Hunger
Friedrich mit der gebißnen Wange
Eisenach
Die ruhmvollen

Barbarossa
Der Conradin

Ugolino—

Holds our souls
Together, the ones that God gives us, life-light
Companion
To our end.

By all means,

              differences are
       good. Each
               and every
Has its own existence.

              the dark leaf,
        And its
Perceptible growth
       and   the Syrian soil
   crushed, and flames underfoot
Burning
And nausea
Overcoming me from desperate hunger
Friedrich with his bitten cheek
Eisenach
The famous

Barbarossa
Conradin

Ugolino—

Eugen
Himmelsleiter

Der Abschied der Zeit
und es scheiden im Frieden voneinander

So Mahomed, †Rinald,
Barbarossa, als freier Geist,

Kaiser Heinrich.
Wir bringen aber die Zeiten
untereinander
Demetrius Poliorcetes
Peter der Große
Heinrichs
Alpenübergang und daß
die Leute mit eigner Hand er gespeiset
und getränket und sein Sohn Konrad an Gift starb
Muster eines Zeitveränderers
Reformators
Conradin u.s.w.

alle, als Verhältnisse
bezeichnend.

Eugenius
Heaven's ladder

    Time's departure
        and they leave each other in peace

Thus Mohammed, †Rinaldo,
Barbarossa, as free spirit

Emperor Heinrich.
But we confuse one time
With another.
        Demetrius Poliorcetes
Peter the Great
        Heinrich's
Crossing the Alps and with
His own hands he gave the people food
and drink and his son Conrad died of poison
Perfect visionary
Reformer
Conradin, etc.

all relations
characteristic

†Höret das Horn des Wächters bei Nacht
Nach Mitternacht ists um die fünfte Stunde

Tende   Strömfeld   Simonetta.
Teufen   Amyklä   Aveiro am Flusse
Fouga   die Familie   Alencastro den
Nahmen davon   Amalasuntha Antegon
Anathem Ardinghellus Sorbonne Cölestin
und Inozentius haben die Rede unter-
brochen und sie genannt den Pflanz-
garten der Französischen Bischöffe—
Aloisia Sigea *differentia vitae*
urbanae et rusticae Thermodon
ein Fluß in Cappadocien Val-
telino Schönberg Scotus Schönberg Teneriffa

Sulaco   Venafro
                    Gegend
des Olympos.   Weißbrun in Nieder-
ungarn. Zamora   Jacca   Baccho
Imperiali.   Genua   Larissa in Syrien

† Hear the watchman's horn at night
The fifth hour after midnight

Tende   Strömfeld   Simonetta.
Teufen   Amyclae   Aveiro on the river
Vouga   the family   Alencastro its
Name therefrom   Amalasuntha   Antegon
Anathem   Ardinghellus   Sorbonne   Celestine
and Innocent interrupted the lecture
and named it the Nur-
sery of French Bishops—
Aloisia Sigea *differentia vitae*
urbanae et rusticae Thermidon
a river in Cappadocia Val-
telino Schönberg Scotus Schönberg Tenerife

Sulaco   Venafro
                 Region
of Olympus.   Weißbrun in Lower
Hungary. Zamora Jaca   Baccho
Imperiali.   Genoa   Larissa in Syria

Wenn über dem Weinberg es flammt
Und schwarz wie Kohlen
Aussiehet um die Zeit
Des Herbstes der Weinberg, weil
Die Röhren des Lebens feuriger athmen
In den Schatten des Weinstoks. Aber
Schön ists, die Seele
Zu entfalten und das kurze Leben

Und der Himmel wird wie eines Mahlers Haus
Wenn seine Gemählde sind aufgestellet.

Bei Thebe und Tiresias!
Mir will der Boden zu kahl seyn.

When the vineyard is in flames
And looks black as coal
Around the time
In autumn, because
The reeds of life breathe fire
In shadows of the vines. But
How pretty when the soul unfolds
And this brief life.

And the sky becomes a painter's house
With all his pictures on display

Near Thebes and Tiresias!
The ground too barren for me.

Ähnlich dem Manne, der Menschen frisset
Ist einer, der lebt ohne
(Liebe)

        und Schatten beschreibend hätt er
Der Augen Zorn

        Schlechthin
        diesesmal, oft aber
Geschiehet etwas um die Schläfe, nicht ist
Es zu verstehen, wenn aber eines Weges
Ein Freier herausgeht, findet
Daselbst es bereitet.

Zu Rossen, ewige Lust
Zu Leben, wir wenn Nachtigallen
Süssen Ton der Heimath oder die Schneegans
Den Ton anstimmt über
Dem Erdkreis, sehnend,

Like the man who eats men,
He who lives without
(Love)

        and describing shadows, his eyes
Would fill with anger

              Quite simply
                 this time, but often
Something happens inside one's head, impossible
To understand, but when a freeman
Goes out for a walk, he finds
the path waiting.

As for the horses, an endless desire
For life, as when nightingales
Sing their sweet-home-song or the snow goose
Sings with longing above
The circle of earth,

Streifen blauer Lilien
Kennest du   der Arbeit
Von Künstlern allein oder gleich
Dem Hirsch, der schweifet in der Hizze. Nicht
Ohn' Einschränkung.

Narcyssen Ranunklen und
Siringen aus Persien
Blumen Nelken, gezogen perlenfarb
Und schwarz und Hyacinthen,
Wie wemm es riechet, statt Musik
Des Eingangs, dort, wo böse Gedanken,
Liebende mein Sohn vergessen sollen einzugehen
Verhältnisse und diß Leben
Christophori   der Drache vergleicht der Natur
Gang und Geist und Gestalt.

Da soll er alles
Hinausführen
Außer den Langen
An eine reine Stätte
Da man die Asche
Hinschüttet, und solls
Verbrennen auf dem Holz mit Feuer.

stripes of blue lilies

Do you know   the work
Of artists alone or like
Deer roaming in the heat. Not
Without restrictions.

Narcissi, ranunculi, and
Syringas from Persia
Flowers, carnations, cultivated in pearl
And black and hyacinths,
As when instead of music heralding an entrance
There's the scent of an evil thought,
My son should forget to enter
Loving relationships and this life
Christopher's   dragon has exactly
Nature's walk and spirit and shape.

He should take
Everything
Except the long ones
To a pure place
Where someone
Scatters ashes
And burns the wood with fire.

Heidniches
Jo Bacche, daß sie lernen der Hände Geschik
Samt selbigem,
Gerächet oder vorwärts. Die Rache gehe
Nemlich zurük. Und daß uns nicht
Dieweil wir roh sind,
Mit Wasserwellen Gott
      Schlage. Nemlich
Gottlosen auch
Wir aber sind
Gemeinen gleich,
Die, gleich
Edeln Gott versuchet, ein Verbot
Ist aber, deß sich rühmen. Ein Herz sieht aber
Helden. Mein ist
Die Rede vom Vaterland. Das neide
Mir keiner. Auch so machet
Das Recht des Zimmermannes
Das Kreuz.

    Schwerdt
und heimlich Messer, wenn einer
    geschliffen
          mittelmäßig Gut,
Daß aber uns das Vaterland nicht verde
Zum kleinen Raum. Schwer ist der
Zu liegen, mit Füßen, den Händen auch.
Nur Luft.

From pagan

Io Bacche, let them learn to work with their hands

And, by the same means. Be

Forward or avenged. Vengeance,

In fact, should return to its source.

While we are raw, don't let God

Lash us with

                waves. To be sure,

We are godless,

Common folk all,

Whom God tests

Like nobility,

Yet it's forbidden

To boast about this. But the heart knows

A hero. It's for me

To speak of my fatherland. Don't

Begrudge me that. In the same way,

A carpenter makes

A cross.

      Sword

and hidden knife, when

    sharpened

                more or less well,

But don't let our native land become

Too small a place. Heavy is the

To lie at rest, feet and hands outstretched.

Only air.

FRIEDRICH HÖLDERLIN

spizbübisch schnakisch
    Lächeln, wenn dem Menschen
seine kühnsten Hofnungen
    erfüllt werden

Bauen möcht

und neu errichten
des Theseus Tempel und die Stadien
und wo Perikles gewohnet

Es fehlet aber das Geld, denn zu viel

knavish comical
    to smile, when man's
boldest hopes
    come true

I must build

and erect new
Temples of Theseus and the stadiums
and where Pericles lived

But there is no money, too much

ist ausgegeben heute. Zu Gaste nemlich hatt
ich geladen   und wir saßen beieinander

was spent today. I entertained

a guest   and we sat together

Of
Uncertain
Origin

In lieblicher Bläue

In lieblicher Bläue blühet mit dem metallenen Dache der Kirchthurm. Den umschwebet Geschrei der Schwalben, den umgiebt die rührendste Bläue. Die Sonne gehet hoch darüber und färbet das Blech, im Winde aber oben stille krähet die Fahne. Wenn einer unter der Gloke dann herabgeht, jene Treppen, ein stilles Leben ist es, weil, wenn abgesondert so sehr die Gestalt ist, die Bildsamkeit herauskommt dann des Menschen. Die Fenster, daraus die Gloken tönen, sind wie Thore an Schönheit. Nemlich, weil noch der Natur nach sind die Thore, haben diese die Ähnlichkeit von Bäumen des Walds. Reinheit aber ist auch Schönheit. Innen aus Verschiedenem entsteht ein ernster Geist. So sehr einfältig aber die Bilder, so sehr heilig sind die, daß man wirklich oft fürchtet, die zu beschreiben. Die Himmlischen aber, die immer gut sind, alles zumal, wie Reiche, haben diese, Tugend und Freude. Der Mensch darf das nachahmen. Darf, wenn lauter Mühe das Leben, ein Mensch aufschauen und sagen: so will ich auch seyn? Ja. So lange die Freundlichkeit noch am Herzen, die Reine, dauert, misset nicht unglüklich der Mensch sich mit der Gottheit. Ist unbekannt Gott? Ist er offenbar wie der Himmel? Dieses glaub' ich eher. Des Menschen Maaß ist's. Voll Verdienst, doch dichterisch, wohnet der Mensch auf dieser Erde. Doch reiner ist nicht die Schatten der Nacht mit den Sternen, wenn ich so sagen könnte, als der Mensch, der heißet ein Bild der Gottheit.

———————————

Giebt es auf Erden ein Maaß? Es giebt keines. Nemlich es hemmen den Donnergang nie die Welten des Schöpfers. Auch eine Blume ist schön, weil sie blühet unter der Sonne. Es findet das Aug' oft im Leben Wesen, die viel schöner noch zu nennen wären als die Blumen. O! ich weiß das wohl! Denn zu bluten an Gestalt und Herz, und ganz nicht mehr zu seyn, gefällt das Gott? Die Seele aber, wie ich glaube, muß rein bleiben, sonst reicht an das Mächtige auf Fittigen der Adler mit

In Lovely Blue

In lovely blue the metal roof of the church steeple blooms. Around which hover the cries of swallows, around which circles the most touching blue. High overhead, the sun tints the tin roof, but in the wind the motionless weathervane creaks. When someone descends from the belfry, the figure is so detached it's like a still life, and the sculptural shape of a man emerges from it. The windows from which the bells ring are gateways to beauty. Because gateways imitate nature, they resemble trees in the forest. Yet purity is also beauty. A solemn spirit emerges from within, out of disparate things. These images are so simple and so holy, one is afraid to describe them. But the gods, who are always good, have a wealth of virtue and joy. Which a man may imitate. From the sheer grind of his life, he may look up and ask, "Will I be like them, too?" Yes. As long as kindness remains long and pure in the heart, he can happily measure himself against the Godhead. Is God unknown? As clearly visible as the sky itself? I'd like to think so. This is man's measure. His residence on earth is well-deserved yet poetic. Yet the shadow of the starry night is no more pure, if I may say so, than man, whom they call God's image.

Is there measure on the earth? There is none. Creators and artists will never get in thunder's way. A flower is also lovely when it blossoms under the sun. The eye often finds living creatures that are prettier to name than flowers. I know this very well. To bleed in your heart and being, to completely cease being, does this please God? But the soul, I believe, must be pure for the eagle to ascend to the Almighty with

lobendem Gesange und der Stimme so vieler Vögel. Es ist die Wesenheit,
die Gestalt ist's. Du schönes Bächlein, du scheinest rührend, indem du
rollest so klar, wie das Auge der Gottheit, durch die Milchstraße. Ich
kenne dich wohl, aber Thränen quillen aus dem Auge. Ein heiteres Leben
seh' ich in den Gestalten mich umblühen der Schöpfung, weil ich es
nicht unbillig vergleiche den einsamen Tauben auf dem Kirchhof. Das
Lachen aber scheint mich zu grämen der Menschen, nemlich ich hab'
ein Herz. Möcht' ich ein Komet seyn? Ich glaube. Denn sie haben die
Schnelligkeit der Vögel; sie blühen an Feuer, und sind wie Kinder an
Reinheit. Größeres zu wünschen, kann nicht des Menschen Natur sich
vermessen. Der Tugend Heiterkeit verdient auch gelobt zu werden vom
ernsten Geiste, der zwischen den drei Säulen wehet des Gartens. Eine
schöne Jungfrau muß das Haupt umkränzen mit Myrthenblumen, weil
die einfach ist ihrem Wesen nach und ihrem Gefühl. Myrthen aber giebt
es in Griechenland.

Wenn einer in den Spiegel siehet, ein Mann, und siehet darinn sein
Bild, wie abgemahlt; es gleicht dem Manne. Augen hat des Menschen
Bild, hingegen Licht der Mond. Der König Oedipus hat ein Auge zuviel
vieleicht. Diese Leiden dieses Mannes, sie scheinen unbeschreiblich,
unausssprechlich, unausdrüklich. Wenn das Schauspiel ein solches darstellt,
kommt's daher. Wie ist mir's aber, gedenk' ich deiner jezt? Wie Bäche
reißt das Ende von Etwas mich dahin, welches sich wie Asien ausdehnet.
Näturlich dieses Leiden, das hat Oedipus. Natürlich ist's darum. Hat auch
Herkules gelitten? Wohl. Die Dioskuren in ihrer Freundschaft haben die
nicht Leiden auch getragen? Nemlich wie Herkules mit Gott zu streiten,
das ist Leiden. Und die Unsterblichkeit im Neide dieses Lebens, diese
zu theilen, ist ein Leiden auch. Doch das ist auch ein Leiden, wenn mit
Sommerfleken ist bedekt ein Mensch, mit manchen Fleken ganz überdekt
zu seyn! Das thut die schöne Sonne: nemlich die ziehet alles auf. Die
Jünglinge führt die Bahn sie mit Reizen ihrer Stralen wie mit Rosen. Die

songs of praise and the voice of so many birds. It is essence
and form. Lovely little brook, how you move me as you
roll so clearly, like the eye of God, through the Milky Way.
I know you so well, yet tears flow from my eyes. I see in
all of creation the joy of life blooming around me, which
I don't compare unjustly with the solitary doves in the
churchyard. Because I have a heart, the laughter of men
grieves me. Should I be a comet instead? I think so. Then
I'd have the speed of a bird, blossom as fire, and be innocent
as a child. To wish for more is beyond our human limit. The
cheerfulness of virtue also deserves praise from the solemn
spirit drifting among the garden's three columns. Simple
in nature and feeling, a beautiful young woman should
braid myrtle blossoms into her hair. Myrtles, however,
grow in Greece.

When a man looks into the mirror and sees his image as if
painted there; it resembles the man. Man's image has eyes
but the moon has light. King Oedipus perhaps had one eye
too many. His sufferings are indescribable, unspeakable,
inexpressible. What becomes of drama that represents such
things? What do I feel, thinking of you now? Like brooks,
I am carried away by the end of something stretching out
like Asia. Of course, Oedipus suffered the same. For a good
reason. Did Hercules suffer also? Indeed. Didn't the Dioscuri
also endure pain in their friendships? To struggle with God
like Hercules is to feel pain. To share a portion of immortality
in envy of this life is to know pain. But it's also pain when
a man is covered with summer freckles, all speckled with spots!
The pretty sun does that, drawing everything out. It leads young
men along a summer path strewn like roses with rays of sunlight.

Leiden scheinen so, die Oedipus getragen, als wie ein armer Mann klagt, daß ihm etwas fehle. Sohn Laios, armer Fremdling in Griechenland! Leben ist Tod, und Tod ist auch ein Leben.

———————————————

The sufferings of Oedipus seem the lamentations of a poor man lacking something. Son of Laios, a stranger forlorn in Greece! Life is death, and death is also a life.

—————————————————

Maxine Chernoff is the author of six books of fiction, including a *New York Times Book Review* Notable Book of 1993, *Signs of Devotion.* Both her novel, *American Heaven,* and her new and selected short stories, *Some of Her Friends that Year,* were finalists for the Bay Area Book Reviewers Award. Her books of poetry include *World* and *Evolution of the Bridge,* both from Salt Publishing in Cambridge, England, and *Among the Names* and *The Turning,* from Apogee Press. She is Chair of Creative Writing at San Francisco State University.

Paul Hoover is editor of the influential anthology *Postmodern American Poetry,* and co-editor of the literary magazine *New American Writing.* Author of eleven previous poetry collections including *Poems in Spanish* (2005), nominated for the Northern California Book Reviewers' Award, and *Edge and Fold* (2006), and Professor of Creative Writing at San Francisco State University. His prizes include the Jerome J. Shestack Award from American Poetry Review, an NEA Fellowship in poetry, and the GE Foundation Award for Younger Writers. With Nguyen Do, he has edited and translated the anthology, *Black Dog, Black Night: Contemporary Vietnamese Poetry.*

"Friedrich Hölderlin was one of the world's strangest, most rarefied poets, one we need continually to be reacquainted with. The imaginative landscape of his poetry is that of his dearly loved homeland, Germany, but it is peopled with the mythic figures, and the concepts and emotions, of classical antiquity, and his rhetoric and his formal repertoire appear to have little to do with either his own time or ours. Maxine Chernoff and Paul Hoover have taken on what seems an almost impossible task. They have made a substantial selection from this idiosyncratic, compulsively remote writer, who for much of his life was 'mad' and is often described today as a 'pure' poet, and have put his work into a language that can hold meaning and attraction for an impure age largely indifferent to the ideals Hölderlin thought and wrote by. Chernoff and Hoover, themselves poets of distinction, have brought to their versions both the instinct to make this difficult body of work transparent, and the desire to preserve its own quiddity. The resulting transcreations are a notable, rewarding, eminently readable addition to the range of Hölderlin's work in English."

—Michael Hulse